# DER NISTER'S
# SOVIET YEARS

JEWS IN EASTERN EUROPE

*Jeffrey Veidlinger*
*Mikhail Krutikov*
*Geneviève Zubrzycki*

*Editors*

# DER NISTER'S
# SOVIET YEARS

## Yiddish Writer as Witness to the People

—◆—

*Mikhail Krutikov*

INDIANA UNIVERSITY PRESS

This book is a publication of

Indiana University Press
Office of Scholarly Publishing
Herman B Wells Library 350
1320 East 10th Street
Bloomington, Indiana 47405 USA

iupress.indiana.edu

Library of Congress Cataloging-in-Publication Data

Names: Krutikov, Mikhail, author.
Title: Der Nister's Soviet years : Yiddish writer as witness to the people /
    Mikhail Krutikov.
Description: First edition. | Bloomington, Indiana : Indiana Univesity Press,
    [2019] | Series: Jews in Eastern Europe | Includes bibliographical
    references and index.
Identifiers: LCCN 2018031198 (print) | LCCN 2018033171 (ebook) | ISBN
    9780253041883 (e-book) | ISBN 9780253041869 (hardback : alk. paper) | ISBN
    9780253041876 (pbk. : alk. paper)
Subjects: LCSH: Nister, 1884-1950—Criticism and interpretation. | Yiddish
    literature—History and criticism. | Nister, 1884-1950. | Authors,
    Yiddish—Soviet Union—Biography.
Classification: LCC PJ5129.K27 (ebook) | LCC PJ5129.K27 Z78 2019 (print) |
    DDC 839/.0933—dc23
LC record available at https://lccn.loc.gov/2018031198

1 2 3 4 5  24 23 22 21 20 19

# CONTENTS

*Acknowledgments*   *vii*

Introduction: The Symbolist Years, 1907–1929   *1*

1. 1929: The Year of the Great Turn and the End of
   Symbolism   *21*

2. From Symbolism to Reality: Space, Politics, and Self in
   *Hoyptshtet*   *60*

3. The 1930s in Children's Poetry   *118*

4. The Generation of 1905   *138*

5. Text and Context of *The Family Mashber*   *159*

6. The Last Decade, 1939–1949: Revealing "The Hidden"   *216*

   Epilogue: Death of the Author and His Afterlife in
   Literary Criticism, Memoirs, and Fiction   *264*

*Bibliography*   *281*

*Index*   *293*

# ACKNOWLEDGMENTS

I BECAME INTERESTED IN DER Nister's life and work in the late 1980s, while working at the editorial office of the Moscow Yiddish journal *Sovetish heymland*. Back then, I missed several opportunities to talk to people who new Der Nister personally and could have provided invaluable information and insights—his widow, Elena Sigalovskaia, his son Yosif, the writers Shmuel Gordon and Mishe Lev, and the critic Moyshe Belenki. I could have learned much more from the poet Khaim Beider, who dedicated his life to gathering information about Soviet Yiddish writers. But I was also fortunate to be involved in the cataloguing of Der Nister's papers at the Russian State Archive of Literature and Art in 1990, where I found important previously undiscovered personal documents. About ten years later I was invited to write a new introduction for the English translation of *The Family Mashber* that was to be reissued as part of the New Yiddish Library, and although this publication has not yet materialized, it gave a new impetus to my interest in Der Nister, particularly his writings from the Soviet period. Another incentive came in the form of an invitation to lead a seminar on *The Family Mashber* at the University of Düsseldorf from my colleague Marion Aptroot. Over the past fifteen years, I have published a number of studies of Der Nister's works from the Soviet period, which I have substantially revised and expanded for this book.

During this time I have incurred many debts of gratitude to my teachers, colleagues, friends, and family. In several ways this book is a continuation of my dialogue with my mentor at the Jewish Theological Seminary, David Roskies, who encouraged me to start working on Der Nister's novel *The Family Mashber*. Another conversation partner I have had for many years is Gennady Estraikh, whose impact on this book is difficult to overestimate. I am grateful to the participants of the Mendel Friedman Conference on Yiddish Studies at Oxford—Marc Caplan, Kerstin Hoge, Roland Gruschka, Sabine Koller, Ber Kotlerman, Daniela Mantovan, Harriet Murav—as well as to the anonymous reviewer of this book's manuscript for their helpful suggestions and comments. My special thanks go to Valery Dymshits for sharing his expertise in East European Jewish culture. I would like to thank Taylor and Francis for the permission to use in chapter 6 my article "The Writer as the People's Therapist: Der Nister's Last Decade, 1939–49," published in *East European Jewish Affairs* 46 (2016), and Dr. Graham Nelson of Legenda Press for the permission to use in chapters 2, 3, and 5 my publications that previously appeared in the collections *Three Cities of Yiddish: St. Petersburg, Warsaw and Moscow*; *Children and Yiddish Literature: From Early Modernity to Post-Modernity*; and *Uncovering the Hidden: The Works and Life of Der Nister*.

My colleagues at the Frankel Center for Judaic Studies at the University of Michigan—Jeffrey Veidlinger, Shachar Pinsker, Anita Norich, Julian Levinson, Zvi Gitelman, and Deborah Dash Moore—helped me shape my ideas and offered important suggestions. I am grateful to the graduate students who read Der Nister's texts with me at our graduate seminars. I also gladly acknowledge the Faculty Summer Writing Grant from the University of Michigan, which enabled me to use a professional copyeditor. At the final stages of writing, I was fortunate to have as an editor Deirdre Casey, who helped improve my style and make my writing more clear. And it was a great pleasure to work with Dee Mortensen and Paige Rasmussen at Indiana University Press, and with Julia Turner from Amnet Systems, who made the publication process smooth and simple. My thanks to Leslie Rubin for compiling the index.

For forty years I have been supported and encouraged by my wife, Julia, to whom I owe more than I can describe.

# DER NISTER'S
# SOVIET YEARS

# INTRODUCTION

# THE SYMBOLIST YEARS, 1907–1929

AMONG THE WRITERS OF THE postclassical age in modern Yiddish literature, which begins about ten years before the passing of its three founding fathers—Yitskhok Leybush Peretz (1915), Sholem Aleichem (1916), and Sholem Yankev Abramovitsh (1917)—Der Nister (Pinhas Kaganovich or Kahanovitsh, 1884–1950) occupies a special place. His elitist and esoteric symbolist writings of the first half of his literary career, 1907–29, have been celebrated by champions of Yiddish modernism for their innovative style, uncommon imagination, and mystical profundity. Scholars and critics have analyzed his enigmatic tales for adults and children from formalist, psychoanalytical, kabbalistic, folkloric, and literary-historical perspectives. But there are still many questions around the life and work of this enigmatic author, who chose the "Hidden One" as his pen name and carefully cultivated his persona as a recluse. Perhaps one of the most intriguing is the problem of continuity and cohesiveness in Der Nister's oeuvre, which includes—along with his early symbolist tales—children's poetry, travelogues, essays, and Holocaust stories, as well as both a finished and an unfinished novel. It is commonly assumed that the year 1929, known in Soviet history as the year of the "Great Turn" or "Stalin's revolution," was also the breaking point in Der

1

Nister's literary career, when he was forced to abandon symbolism and all but disappeared from the literary stage. His comeback was painful and uneven, but within ten years, he succeeded in publishing his magisterial novel, *The Family Mashber*, which was enthusiastically received both in the Soviet Union and abroad and secured Der Nister's reputation as a leading Yiddish novelist.

Since his tragic death in the Gulag in 1950, Der Nister's symbolist works have been thoroughly studied and creatively interpreted by some of the leading scholars of Yiddish literature—Avraham Novershtern, Dov Sadan, Khone Shmeruk, and David Roskies—and two doctoral dissertations, by Delphine Bechtel and Daniela Mantovan, have dealt specifically with his pre-1929 works. Recently, after about fifteen years of relative decline in interest in Der Nister, his post-1929 writings have begun to attract fresh scholarly attention. Building on the contributions of such scholars as Sabine Boehlich, Marc Caplan, Roland Gruschka, Gennady Estraikh, Sabine Koller, Boris Kotlerman, Daniela Mantovan, and Harriet Murav, this study attempts to develop a conceptual framework for a better understanding of the prolific and diverse body of Der Nister's writings from the post-1929 period in all its complexity.

I argue that with all its shortcomings and achievements, Der Nister's oeuvre constitutes a coherent literary corpus that is exceptional in Soviet literature. As most researchers recognize, Der Nister never fully abandoned his symbolist poetics, and its elements can be traced even in his most "Soviet" works. With great effort, he managed to reinvent himself as a Soviet writer without forfeiting his creative autonomy. My interpretation seeks to underscore the distinctively synthetic nature of his work rather than stress the dichotomy between the "Jewish" and the "Soviet." Rather than trying to smuggle "Jewish" references into his presumably socialist realist texts, Der Nister sought to merge them in a new epic narrative style. These transformations of style, form, and genre took place under the distressing and painful circumstances of the Stalinist regime during the 1930s, but they also stem from Der Nister's dissatisfaction with his previous symbolist work. It was no longer possible to maintain the separation between reality and fiction that Der Nister so assiduously cultivated up to 1929. Until that year, Der Nister's fiction had been set in an imaginary space and time outside the real world. After 1929, everything he wrote—with the exception of a few poems for children—was firmly situated within real space and time in Ukraine, Russia, and Poland between the 1860s and the 1940s. He was seeking a different, more direct engagement between his imagination and reality. Reality, which previously played a subordinate role in his writing as an entry point into the world of fantasy, now became the dominant frame of reference, while fantasy was relegated to the sphere of dreams and childhood imagination. Symbolic imagery, permeated with references to Jewish religious tradition and history, continued to inform his writing, although in a more subtle and veiled fashion. Merging fantasy with reality became his way of responding to the profound sociopolitical changes of the time, but it would be an oversimplification to read his prose and poetry of the 1930s as a direct projection of that reality.

Der Nister experienced another profound shock after the German invasion of the Soviet Union, when information about Nazi atrocities in occupied Poland began to reach him in his exile in Tashkent. In response to this tragedy, he appropriated the device of historical allegory, which eventually led him to break with his "hidden" persona and dramatically reveal himself as a potential spiritual leader of the Jewish people by traveling to the Jewish Autonomous Area of Birobidzhan. The last two decades of Der Nister's career under Stalin's dictatorial regime can be interpreted, following the recurrent pattern of his tales, as an unfolding evolution from the "Hidden One" to the "Revealed One," not unlike the Hasidic paradigm of the revelatory trajectory of a tzaddik (righteous one). During his early years, Der Nister cultivated the hidden persona as a hermit, avoiding public attention and shying away from social and political activity, but his later writing is increasingly engaged with the issues and concerns of the day. During the 1940s he achieved worldwide fame, thanks to the publication of his works in Moscow and New York. He received nearly universal critical acclaim on both sides of the ideological divide, which is unique in Soviet Yiddish literature.

Any student of Der Nister can feel frustrated by the scarcity of documentation relating to his personal life. Nakhmen Mayzel, Der Nister's close associate from prerevolutionary Kiev, who later became a leading literary critic and editor and was active in promoting Soviet Yiddish literature in New York in the 1940s, reminisced about Der Nister's early years: "We, his closest friends, had never witnessed his creative 'birth pangs,' never seen him at work and never had a glimpse at his unfinished manuscript that might have revealed how he wrote and constructed a tale, how it grew out of him."[1] But despite his self-imposed isolation, Der Nister was always curious about what was going on in life and literature. In a letter to Nokhem Oyslender, he asked his friend to keep him updated on literary gossip in Odessa, complaining, "Nobody writes to me. Probably because I have asked [everyone] not to enquire about what I am doing. It's a kind of disease, but harmless and not a fake one. And I, on the contrary, like to know what all our people are doing." (Keyner shraybt mir nit. Mistam derfar, vayl ikh hob gebetn bay mir nit fregn, vos ikh tu. S'iz bay mir a krenk aza, ober a[n] umshuldike un nisht keyn blefike. Un ikh, farkert, hob dafke lib tsu visn, vos ale undzere dort tuen.)[2] Most of Der Nister's papers must have been lost during his moves, which happened under sometimes dramatic circumstances: his long journey from Ukraine to Germany via Moscow from 1920 to 1922, his return to Kharkiv in 1926, the hurried evacuation to Tashkent in 1941, and finally the move to Moscow in 1943. These relocations were followed by his arrest in 1949, when his archives were likely confiscated, as was routine in such cases. For most of his adult life, Der Nister lived in poverty and poor accommodations. His life circumstances can be reconstructed only sketchily, mostly from his letters and the memoirs of his acquaintances. Even in his personal letters to his brother Motl, which are full of bitterness and frustration, Der Nister revealed few details about his everyday life. The personality that emerges from those scarce sources appears to be intelligent, ambitious, sensitive, proud, vulnerable, fragile, agitated, and often depressed.

According to Zalman Reyzen's biographical lexicon of Yiddish authors, arguably the most authoritative reference source on Yiddish literature at the time of its publication in 1926, Pinhas Kahanovitsh was born in Berdichev in 1884 into a family whose members were learned and pious on the one side and "simple Jewish village laborers" on the other. His traditional Jewish education was strongly influenced by Hasidism. He worked as a Hebrew teacher and tutor, and for twelve years he lived under different names, likely seeking to evade the military draft, the thought of which, according to Reyzen, caused him a great deal of distress. Der Nister's first books, *Gedanken un motivn: Lider in proze* (Thoughts and motifs: Prose poems) and *Miryem: A peyresh oyfn motiv fun "Molitva devy"* (Miriam: A commentary on a motif from "Maiden's Prayer"), published in 1907, attracted attention in literary circles for their original style and the "boldness of their motifs." He contributed to Yiddish periodicals of modernist orientation, which began to appear as part of the Jewish cultural revival in Russia following the 1905 revolution and were edited by leading cultural figures such as Shmuel Niger and Y. L. Peretz. He experimented with different styles and genres, producing one book, *A tog-bikhl fun a farfirer* (A seducer's diary), in a realist style, although most of his prose and poetry was symbolist in its tenor and inspired by Jewish mysticism. The most productive period of his early career was between 1917 and 1919, when he emerged, along with David Bergelson, as "the most important Yiddish prose writer in Ukraine."[3]

Having made the decisive choice in favor of Yiddish over Hebrew[4] during his "apprenticeship" years, to use Delphine Bechtel's description of the 1907–12 period, Der Nister published three books in which he introduced some of the themes and motifs that would later become key features of his symbolist works: a spiritual quest, a wandering protagonist, and a primordial landscape, as well as particular rhythmic and syntactic patterns that make his poetic prose immediately recognizable.[5] His aesthetic taste and stylistic preferences developed under the influence of his wide reading in world literature. He drew inspiration from ancient and modern classics alike—from the *Odyssey* to *Hiawatha*. He insisted on the difference between his poetic language and "common prose" and adamantly defended his individual style against any editorial intervention. In a 1908 letter to the critic and editor Shmuel Niger, Der Nister categorically stated: "This style is myself, and I do not want and shall not 'estrange' myself from it!" (Ot der signon dos bin ikh un ikh vil nisht un vel nisht fun im zikh "opgevoynen!")[6] He felt deeply and intimately connected with Yiddish. When the prominent Russian Jewish writer S. An-sky invited the young Der Nister in 1908 to contribute to *Evreiskii mir*, at that time the most prestigious Russian Jewish journal, on the condition that Der Nister's submission must not have been published previously in Yiddish or Hebrew, Der Nister complained to Niger that he felt as if he were forced to "lead his own child to baptism" (an eygn kind tsu shmad firn). In the end, however, he accepted the condition because he desperately needed money, and this story became one of very few texts by him available in Russian during his lifetime.[7]

Comparing Der Nister's early writing with his later works, Bechtel points out their "variety in form and content": "Not only does Der Nister play with all kinds of literary forms jumping from prose to poetry, sometimes even within the same text, experimenting with poetic prose, he also selects a wide variety of topics, drawn mainly from the Jewish, but also from the Christian tradition."[8] Among his sources of inspiration and influence were Slavic and Jewish folktales; medieval Kabbalah and Hasidic tales, especially those of Rabbi Nachman of Bratslav; the nineteenth-century German Romantics, particularly their genre of Kunst-märchen; and contemporary Russian symbolists. Following their lead, he experimented with style, form, and genre. In his fiction reality merged with dreams, and familiar figures from the Hebrew Bible and the New Testament acted as symbolic characters.

Although most of his early tales take place in an abstract time and space, Der Nister already seemed to be keenly concerned with the issue of continuity between generations as crucial to the survival of Jews in the modern age. In his modernist appropriation of the Hasidic doctrine, Bechtel explains, the responsibility for maintaining this continuity lies with the generation's spiritual leader: "Should the leader forsake his mission, or arrive too early or too late, the generation is left alone and passes away without having fulfilled its purpose."[9]

Der Nister's own position in this scheme of things appears to be ambiguous. His persona was sometimes split between the powerful narrator and the weak protagonist, as in the piece "Fun Dem Nister's ksovim" (From Der Nister's writings). Bechtel identifies in this early self-representation elements of the "dithyrambic Nietzschean style of *Also sprach Zarathustra*," which, she contends, "convey the megalomania and the egocentrism which are the ultimate consequence of Der Nister's early mysticism."[10] The basic symbolic figures and configurations of Der Nister's early works undergo various transformations during his later periods, although they retain some of their essential features, such as the split of the narrative persona.

### FINDING HIS PLACE ON THE LITERARY SCENE

Not all influential critics of that time, including S. An-sky, appreciated Der Nister's literary experiments. Like other budding literati of the Kiev Group, such as the prose writer David Bergelson and the poets Osher Shvartsman and David Hofshteyn, Der Nister drew on contemporary Russian and European, particularly Scandinavian, modernism and rejected the colloquial style of Mendele Moykher Sforim and Sholem Aleichem. This aesthetic orientation contributed to his sense of loneliness. Writing to Shmuel Niger from Zhitomir in 1907, Der Nister bitterly complained that in Ukraine there was "no Yiddish word, no Yiddish interest, nothing! I read nothing in the *zhargon* [a common, somewhat derogatory Russian term for Yiddish]. I don't know what's happening in our little literary world. . . . I am reading much in Russian and German."[11] He respected the older Yiddish writers for their contribution to the creation of modern Yiddish letters but had an ambivalent attitude toward Y. L. Peretz, whom he regarded as a good writer but a superficial artist: "How beautiful is Mendele in the role of a 'grandfather' . . . and how ridiculous is Peretz's [modernist play] *The Night at the Old Market Place*! How ridiculous it is to pretend to be young at an old age." (Vi sheyn is Mendele in der role fun a 'zeydn' . . . un vi lekherlekh iz—Peretz 'Bay nakht oyfn altn mark!' Vi lekherlekh iz oyf der elter zikh 'yunglen.')[12] For Der Nister, modernist experimentation was the domain of the younger generation, while the older writers such as Peretz should have stuck to the more traditional style. Der Nister vehemently defended his elitist stance and refused to "descend from the mountain" (aropgeyn fun barg) and "come near the reader" (tsugeyn tsum lezer).[13]

The complex and ambiguous relationship with Peretz had a formative effect on the young Der Nister. Under Peretz's influence Der Nister adopted the form of the tale as a modernist, symbolist modification of the traditional folklore genre, which remained central during the first thirteen years of his career.[14] In 1909, complaining to Niger about his strained relationships with the Yiddish press in Warsaw and Vilna, Der Nister wrote that he would not even try to send his piece to Peretz, to whom "he had

never toadied" (er hot fun mir keyn khnifele nisht gehat).[15] Der
Nister later reported that he had "broken up" (ibergerisn) with
Peretz, who refused to understand his experimental work, and
yet, acquiescing, as he had done with An-sky previously, a year
later he did submit the short story "A tog-bikhl fun a farfirer"
(admittedly his most realist in style and arguably his weakest
piece) to Peretz's journal, *Yudish*. Peretz also helped Der Nister to publish his collection *Hekher fun der erd* (Higher than the
earth, 1910). Der Nister's palpable anxiety about his position vis-
à-vis the literary establishment made him apprehensive about the
opinions of others, which he tried to compensate for by assert-
ing his self-confidence: "He who believes in himself does not
need to believe even in God, let alone in Peretz." (Ver es gleybt
in zikh, darf shoyn afile in got nit gleybn. Ubifrat . . . in Peretz.)[16]
Yet many years later, in 1940, he recalled that it was under the
influence of Peretz, whom he visited in person in Warsaw, that
he turned to Yiddish folklore as well as to Hasidic and mystical literature for inspiration. After the initially cold reception,
Peretz suggested that Der Nister stay in Warsaw and take part in
translating Peretz's works into Hebrew. But true to his assumed
persona, Der Nister decided that his place was in the provinces
and returned to Zhitomir. His dislike of Warsaw as the center of
politicized and commercialized *Yiddishkayt* was matched by his
aversion to the imperial capital, which he shared with Niger: "The
main thing is: I hate Petrograd very much, with its Zionists on the
right and the *Jewish Week* [a Bundist newspaper] on the left." (Der
iker iz: kh'hob zeyer faynt Petrograd, mit di tsiyoynim rekhts,
mit der "yiddisher vokh" links.)[17] Der Nister shared this attitude
with other aspiring young writers from Kiev, such as Bergelson,
who were trying to secure their place in Jewish cultural politics
between the Hebrew-oriented Zionists and Russian-leaning
assimilationists.

Like Bergelson, Der Nister found a home for his experimental
writings in the short-lived Vilna-based journal *Di literarishe*

*monatshriftn,* which was edited by Niger, A. Vayter, and Shmaryahu Gorelik. The first (1908) issue included Der Nister's story "Poylish," which displeased the more traditionalist critic S. An-sky with its eroticism. Emerging in the aftermath of the failed 1905 revolution, this elitist publication, as Kenneth Moss explains, "scandalized the pro-Yiddish socialist and populist intelligentsia not only by its brazen demands for a separation between Yiddish culture and Jewish politics but also by its eagerness to embrace complex forms of literature manifestly inaccessible for a mass readership."[18] The link between the young Yiddish writers in Kiev and the Vilna publishers turned out to be strong. Niger also helped commission Der Nister's translations for the prestigious Kletskin press. Among the translation projects that they discussed were such diverse texts as Fyodor Dostoevsky's novels, Leo Tolstoy's *Sebastopol Tales* and *Confession,* the poetry of Rainer Maria Rilke, Selma Lagerlöf's *The Wonderful Adventures of Nils,* and the tales of Hans Christian Andersen. Moss argues that Der Nister's translations of Andersen signaled a significant turn in modern Jewish literary history because, "unlike previous translations into Hebrew and Yiddish," they "retained the Christian realia and references."[19] This innovative strategy was consistent with Der Nister's embrace of the modernist cultural trend that Moss terms the "deparochialization" of Jewish culture.

### THE RUSSIAN REVOLUTION AND ITS AFTERMATH

Whereas Der Nister's pre–World War I writings were characterized by diversity and colored by optimism, his later work became increasingly dark in mood and homogenous in style. Now concern about the fate of his generation comes to the fore: "He gives up the illusion of continuity in tradition, and examines the generation gap felt particularly strongly at his time in Jewish society, by opposing the old, lost generation with the figure of the chosen youth."[20] The catastrophic events of 1914–21—World War

I, the collapse of the Russian Empire in the revolutions, and the Russian Civil War—forced writers and artists to grapple with urgent questions that required new conceptual and aesthetic approaches. In Yiddish and Hebrew literature, this was a period of intense creative exploration, and Der Nister was one of its key figures. Acting under the auspices of the Kiev Kultur-Lige, an association with the broad and ambitious program of building a modern Yiddish culture that was supported by the newly proclaimed Ukrainian People's Republic, Der Nister was able to bring some of his ideas and dreams to fruition. His most significant contributions to the project of Jewish cultural renaissance were books for children, both originals and translations, especially the series of Andersen's tales.

Arguing against the prevailing view of Der Nister's translations of Andersen as marginal to his original symbolist prose, Kerstin Hoge suggests that these translations "can be viewed, and might have been intended, as creating a context in which to situate and lend credibility to Der Nister's symbolist prose."[21] Hoge bases her argument on her analysis of shared stylistic features between Der Nister's esoteric symbolist prose and his translations of popular children's classics. By applying his "unique stylistic signature" to his translations, Der Nister established a "literary precedent" that made his own work appear "less threatening and alien" and thus more accessible to a general audience.[22] Hoge's reading makes it possible to "view Der Nister's diverse literary works as a more coherent whole."[23] Another visual extension of Der Nister's foray into children's literature was Marc Chagall's illustration of two fairy tales, "A mayse mit a hon" (A Tale about a Rooster) and "Dos tsigele" (A Little Goat), written during World War I in the tradition of the European Kunstmärchen. Here, as Sabine Koller demonstrates, "Der Nister's text and Chagall's drawings, the rhymes and the lines, literature and art converge because of two main aesthetic features: *primitivism* and *rhythm*."[24] Chagall's avant-garde imagery echoes the characteristic features of Der

Nister's poetic style: "In his drawings for Der Nister, he expertly handles primitivist scales and Jewish overtones, with a unique visual creation."[25] This writing and translating for children enabled Der Nister to reveal the esoteric world of his imagination to a wider audience by emphasizing its nonverbal—rhythmic and visual—aspects without compromising its stylistic originality and aesthetic quality. As we shall see later on, his attempt to use a similar strategy during the 1930s was less successful. In contrast to his early books for children, which are recognized as an outstanding achievement in Yiddish modernist culture, the three lavishly illustrated books published in Kiev and Odessa in the 1930s have been largely ignored until recently. And yet, as I will argue in chapter 3, these books are important for an understanding of Der Nister's evolution as a writer.

After a nearly yearlong sojourn at the Jewish orphanage in Malakhovka near Moscow, where Der Nister worked as an educator along with Marc Chagall and other prominent cultural figures, he moved to Berlin and later to Hamburg, where he spent about four years from 1921 to 1925. While in Malakhovka, he wrote the novella "Naygayst" (New spirit), arguably the most optimistic and ambitious of his symbolist works. It appeared in the collection *Geyendik* (Walking), published in Berlin in 1923 under the imprint of the Soviet People's Commissariat for Education as part of the short-lived Soviet initiative to commission printing of educational materials in Germany. This long and convoluted narrative follows the alter ego protagonist named Pinkhes, the son of Menakhem the Priest (Der Nister's last name, Kahanovitsh, is derived from the Hebrew word *kohen*, priest), on his eastward journey to fulfill the promise of redemption that was prophesized by the Bible and Hasidic masters. This richly intertextual work has been variously interpreted by several scholars. In her comprehensive study of the novella, Sabine Boehlich describes it as Der Nister's "manifesto of symbolist poetics," which seeks to appropriate the entire Jewish mystical and prophetic tradition for modernist purposes,[26] whereas David Roskies reads it as an ecstatic messianic "manifesto" in which Der Nister attempted to "reconcile his elitism and esoteric knowledge with the demands of the collective."[27] Roskies interprets the protagonist's journey through a symbolic primordial landscape as culminating in an affirmation of the new revolutionary world, "an ecstatic vision of the rising East, and there could be no doubt whatever that this Holy East was the site of Lenin's great experiment."[28] The symbolic topos of the East as the site of new revolutionary energy was common for Russian symbolists such as Aleksandr Blok and Andrei Bely, as well as some radical Zionists such as the Austrian writer Eugen Hoeflich (Moshe Yaakov Ben-Gavriel), who championed the eclectic ideology of Pan-Asian movement. "Naygayst" was reprinted three times in Soviet publications and became a common point of reference among Soviet critics who wanted to claim Der Nister for Soviet literature.

Another central motif in this novella is the mission of a generation and the role of its spiritual leader. In an attempt to come to terms with the dispersal of Yiddish culture across Europe and the United States in the post–World War I years, Der Nister longed for a new transnational cultural community. Without spiritual leadership, he wrote from Berlin to Niger in New York; he feared that the Yiddish intelligentsia would remain rootless and would eventually "rot, one by one and collectively." He feared "a whole generation of ours will die without a final confession." As an exception among the apathetic Yiddish intelligentsia Der Nister mentioned his new friend Moyshe Lifshits, whom he recommended to Niger in a November 1922 letter as a "man who is new through and through" (a mentsh durkh un durkh a nayer) with whom "we go together" (mir geyen mit im in eynem).[29] We do not know whether Der Nister was aware of Lifshits's reputation as a Soviet agent.[30] Lifshits (who also knew Hoeflich) contributed a programmatic critical essay celebrating the new Soviet Yiddish literature in Ukraine to Geyendik. This collection, which also included poems by Der Nister's Kiev friend Leyb Kvitko, signaled the contributors' sympathy with the Soviet state and willingness to collaborate with its institutions. In 1922, Der Nister and Bergelson announced their break with the bilingual Hebrew/Yiddish magazine *Rimon/Milgroym*, dedicated to Jewish art and literature, by publishing a brief declaration in the Moscow journal *Shtrom*. Soon after, Der Nister and Kvitko moved from Berlin to Hamburg, where they found employment with the Soviet trade mission.

The reasons for Der Nister's gradual turn toward, and eventual return to, the Soviet Union were complex and remain inscrutable. Roskies wonders, "How could a writer of such notoriously difficult stories see a future for himself in a place where all bridges were uniformly horizontal" and admits that "the pivotal event of his return to the Soviet Union still eludes me."[31] Personal connections and friendships, as well as a promise of new opportunities for Yiddish culture certainly played a role. Indeed, given the increasingly difficult economic situation of the late 1920s, it is unlikely that two more collections of Der Nister's symbolist tales would have been published by commercially or ideologically motivated publishers in Germany, Poland, or the United States, but they appeared in the Soviet Union as late as 1928 and 1929. It is also possible that Der Nister envisioned the Soviet commitment to the communist ideal as a kind of "sectarian" dedication to a cause (dos sektantishe), something he found lacking in Berlin, Warsaw, and New York. In a letter to Niger written in mid-1923, he dreamed about a group of "dedicated and faithful individuals" (ibergegebene un getraye yekhidim) ready to "sacrifice themselves for the cause" without making a "compromise or peace": "If there will be no strong and mighty arm, a great and necessary unification, then—as I have said—without a final confession!"[32]

In the retrospective view of the Holocaust and the destruction of Soviet Yiddish culture in the late 1940s, this readiness to die for the cause "without a final confession" acquires a prophetic

significance. Yet it would be anachronistic to claim that Der Nister and his colleagues, lonely and frustrated in a Germany rid-
den with hyperinflation and rising nationalism, would be able to
see what Roskies describes as "the writing on the wall."[33] While
Der Nister did not share the ideological principles of Marxism-
Leninism, he could well have been, as the language of his letter
suggests, impressed by and attracted to the radical rhetoric of
communism, with its emphasis on dedication, uncompromis-
ing struggle, and unity. Indeed, as Boehlich subtly observes, Der
Nister's praise of Lifshits as a person of "great responsibility and
awareness of what he wants" (mit groys akhrayes un gevisn far
dem, vos er vil) echoes the speech with which Pinkhes addresses
his faithful followers at the end of "Naygayst": "East! East! Your
day rises soon and it will find us on the mountains, and your light
will find us in great responsibility: we know what we want and
what we kneel here for." (Mizrekh! Mizrekh! Dayn tog geyt bald
oyf un af di berg er gefint undz, un likht dayn undz zen vet in
groysn akhrayes: mir veysn vos viln, un nokh vos mir do knien.)[34]

## RETURN TO UKRAINE

David Roskies identifies the "fault line" in Der Nister's career
with his break with *Milgroym* in 1922 and links this political
shift with the turn in the conceptual orientation of Der Nister's
tales. From "elitist and supremely optimistic," they increasingly
become "allusive, using satire to conceal and reveal their critical
perspective."[35] At this stage, Der Nister introduces elements of
realism, making his stories "begin with a real and recognizable
setting before moving off into the upper reaches of the imagination."[36] Thus, there are several distinct trends that mark this
turn. Story settings acquire realistic elements, and the mystical
narrative perspective changes. The motif of the restoration of
harmony in the world (corresponding to the kabbalistic concept
of *tikkun*, Hebrew for "improvement" or "restoration") gives way

to disintegration (the kabbalistic concept of *shevirah*, Hebrew for "breaking") brought about by the forces of evil. Characters acquire psychological depth and become more controversial, and the overall atmosphere turns darker. These trends begin to emerge in the tales that comprise the first two-volume edition of *Gedakht* (Imagined, Berlin, 1922–23), which Delphine Bechtel hails as the "apogee of Der Nister's allegorical symbolism," and become dominant in the two Soviet collections: *Fun mayne giter* (From my estates, 1928) and the second, revised edition of *Gedakht* (Kharkiv, 1929).[37] The tales written after Der Nister's return to the Soviet Union in 1925 "correspond to the disintegration of Der Nister's allegorical-symbolist system."[38] Using structuralist textual analysis, Bechtel seeks to "reconstruct the psychological and moral code from the oppositions in the text,"[39] antinomies such as truth and falsehood, beauty and ugliness, faith and doubt. Der Nister, she argues, "is not directly interested in propagating traditional Jewish ethics, he creates a new set of values for the Jewish individual in modern times, but he uses the traditional frame of values because of its dualistic structure."[40] In contrast to Bechtel, Roskies reads these tales as an expression of Der Nister's spiritual anguish over the existential condition of his generation and his own "dream of redemption through art" in an increasingly repressive world dominated by authoritarian ideologies, for which he used an idiosyncratic mystical symbolist idiom: "Der Nister donned the cloak of Jewish mystic, high priest, or prophet, the better to explore the universal reaches of creation, revelation, and redemption."[41]

### STRUCTURE OF THIS BOOK

While accepting both Bechtel's and Roskies's approaches as insightful and productive, I will try to demonstrate that Der Nister's position in Soviet literature before and after his return to the Soviet Union was not as precarious or marginal as has often been assumed. To understand his somewhat unique position, we need to carefully examine the critical reception of Der Nister's work by Soviet critics during the 1920s. Chapter 1 starts by analyzing the lively critical discourse surrounding Der Nister's work in the Soviet Union during the 1920s and then moves to the controversy over his last two collections of symbolist tales in 1928 and 1929. A close analysis of Der Nister's situation in the context of Soviet, and particularly Ukrainian, literary politics at that crucial moment offers fresh perspective in revisiting his last and perhaps most uncanny symbolist tale, "Under a Fence," which marks the ultimate disintegration of his imaginary universe. Chapter 2 focuses on the 1934 travelogue *Hoyptshtet* (Capitals), which represents Der Nister's first attempt to reinvent himself as a Soviet realist writer after a period of forced silence. This peculiar fusion of formulaic Soviet propaganda with bizarre phantasmagorical fantasies conveys Der Nister's impressions of his new home city of Kharkiv, then the capital of Soviet Ukraine, as well of his visits to Leningrad and Moscow in 1931–32. This text fits into the experimental trend in Soviet literature at the turn of the 1930s, when some of the former symbolist writers, such as Andrei Bely, tried to find a place in the increasingly rigid socialist realist framework. Chapter 3 looks into Der Nister's artistically problematic attempt to write children's poetry in the Soviet style, which is contrasted with the resounding success of his friend Leyb Kvitko, who managed to reinvent himself as a children's poet after a similar critical attack in 1929. During the 1930s, Der Nister published three lavishly illustrated collections of children's poems, marked by occasionally repulsive cruelty to animals and dark pessimism. My reading of these poems is informed by the current research in Russia on the phenomenon of Stalinist literature for children. Chapter 4 examines Der Nister's unfinished draft *Fun finftn yor* (From the year 1905) as an attempt to produce a novel about the 1905 Russian Revolution in compliance with the tenets of socialist realism. This abandoned novel can be regarded as part of Der

Nister's larger project of writing a literary history of his own generation. It is precisely the roughness of the draft that helps us better understand the challenges that Der Nister faced on his way to becoming a realist writer. My analysis highlights specific aspects of Der Nister's treatment of the revolutionary theme that deviate from the normative Stalinist historical account of the Russian Revolution and places his work into the broader comparative context of Russian and Yiddish prose at that time.

Chapter 5 presents a reconstruction of Der Nister's work on *The Family Mashber* during 1934 and 1947. It draws on archival material and offers an interpretation of the novel in the context of Soviet historical fiction and scholarship of that time. After his failure to secure a niche position in Soviet literature as a travel writer or a children's poet and to produce a "revolutionary" novel conforming to the rules of socialist realism, Der Nister finally succeeded by mastering the historical novel genre in the late 1930s. At that time the historical novel had come to occupy an important if peripheral position in the genre hierarchy of socialist realism. Situating the novel's action in mid-nineteenth-century Berdichev enabled Der Nister to revisit his ethical and aesthetical concerns of the 1920s and to produce a multilayered epic narrative that could appeal differently to audiences inside and outside the Soviet Union. Chapter 6 moves to Der Nister's Holocaust stories of 1942–46, which represent the final stage in his lifelong effort to restore the broken continuity of the imaginary Jewish historical narrative. The mission that Der Nister conceived for himself as a writer—to be a spiritual leader of his generation—reached its culmination in his trip with a transport of Jewish settlers from Ukraine to Birobidzhan in 1947. This journey can be seen as Der Nister's attempt to enact his symbolist dream: overcoming the catastrophic disruptions of Jewish history by bringing the immemorial wandering of the Jews to an end and willfully initiating a new national revival in the Soviet Far East. Tragically, this desperate gesture was destined to end in the complete destruction of Yiddish culture on Stalin's orders in 1948–49 and Der Nister's death in a prison hospital as a result of a botched surgery. The epilogue will discuss Der Nister's legacy in Soviet Yiddish literature and his impact on two generations of Soviet Yiddish writers, as well as his reception outside the Soviet Union.

### NOTES

1. N. Mayzel, "Der Nister—mentsh un kinstler," 14.

2. RGALI, f. 3121, op. 1, d. 39 (letter to Oyslender, no date [likely around 1927]), l. 3.

3. Reyzen, *Leksikon*, vol. 2, col. 580.

4. On Der Nister's Hebrew poetry, see Finkin, "Der Nister's Hebrew Nosegay."

5. Bechtel, *Der Nister's Work*, 4.

6. Novershtern, "Igrotav shel Der Nister el Shmuel Niger," 175.

7. Ibid., 179.

8. Bechtel, *Der Nister's Work*, 49.

9. Ibid., 95.

10. Ibid., 75.

11. Novershtern, "Igrotav shel Der Nister el Shmuel Niger," 170.

12. Ibid., 180.

13. Ibid.

14. Bechtel describes Der Nister as "perhaps the most faithful heir of Peretz" in Yiddish literature (Bechtel, *Der Nister's Work*, 34).

15. Novershtern, "Igrotav shel Der Nister el Shmuel Niger," 179.

16. Ibid., 181.

17. Ibid., 200.

18. Moss, *Jewish Renaissance in the Russian Revolution*, 157.

19. Ibid., 205. More on this journal and the controversies it produced in Moss, "Jewish Culture between Renaissance and Decadence."

20. Bechtel, *Der Nister's Work*, 97.

21. Hoge, "Andersen's *Mayselekh* and Der Nister's Symbolist Agenda," 45.

22. Ibid., 51.

23. Ibid.

24. Koller, "*A mayse mit a hon. Dos tsigele.* Marc Chagall illustrating Der Nister," 67.

25. Ibid., 68.

26. Boehlich, *"Nay-gayst,"* 158.

27. Roskies, *Bridge of Longing,* 218.

28. Ibid., 194.

29. Novershtern, "Igrotav shel Der Nister el Shmuel Niger," 202.

30. More on Lifshits and his environment in Vienna and Berlin in Krutikov, *From Kabbalah to Class Struggle,* 60, 107–8. It is worth noting that Lifshits, unlike Kvitko and Der Nister, never went to the Soviet Union and immigrated to Palestine instead.

31. Roskies, *Bridge of Longing,* 217.

32. Novershtern, "Igrotav shel Der Nister el Shmuel Niger," 205. This letter is the last one in Niger's archive.

33. Roskies, *Bridge of Longing,* 217.

34. Boehlich, *"Nay-gayst,"* 145.

35. Roskies, *Bridge of Longing,* 211.

36. Ibid.

37. Bechtel, *Der Nister's Work,* 105.

38. Ibid., 106.

39. Ibid., 143.

40. Ibid., 132.

41. Roskies, *Bridge of Longing,* 195.

# ONE

—꙰—

# 1929

## *The Year of the Great Turn and the End of Symbolism*

### DER NISTER AND SOVIET CRITICISM BEFORE 1929

After his return to Ukraine from Germany in 1926, Der Nister settled in Kiev but soon moved to Kharkiv, which served as the capital of Soviet Ukraine from 1919 to 1934. In this new burgeoning center of Ukrainian and Yiddish literary life, Der Nister joined the literary association Boy (Construction), a group of Yiddish "fellow travelers" who did not share the radical aesthetics of proletarian writers. They declared their literary credo in a manifesto that appeared in the Kharkiv-based journal *Di royte velt* (The red world), the best Soviet Yiddish literary periodical of that time: "The evolution of literary form should now lead to clarity and simplicity, so that literature, without diminishing its value, should become the property of the common people."[1] The significant words in this statement are *evolution* and *value,* which are meant to safeguard the autonomy of literary creativity. Of course, *clarity* and *simplicity* were not qualities easily associated with Der Nister's style, but the evolutionary approach to literary development allowed some temporary freedom from these prescriptions. As Gennady Estraikh explains, members of this "elitist" group "were fully loyal to communism, but at the same time they continued the tradition of the Kultur-Lige and aimed at further developing the tradition of sophisticated national-revolutionary literature rather than proletarian mass-literature."[2] Until 1929, Boy largely controlled *Di royte velt*, whereas the group's opponents in Ukraine clustered around the Yiddish Bureau of VUSPP (All-Ukrainian Association of Proletarian Writers), whose official organ was *Prolit* (Proletarian literature).[3] More aggressive adversaries of the Ukrainian "fellow travelers," such as Khatskl Dunets and Yashe Bronshteyn, belonged to the Belorussian Association of Proletarian Writers in Minsk.

During the 1920s, Der Nister enjoyed a generally positive reception by Soviet critics, particularly among those also from Kiev, such as Nokhum Oyslender, Yekhezkl Dobrushin, and Moyshe Litvakov, who dominated the critical discourse in early Soviet Yiddish literature both intellectually and politically. They appreciated Der Nister's experimental style and his innovative use of the symbolic imagery of traditional Jewish culture for the representation of revolutionary upheaval. They expressed some reservations about the abundance of mystical and religious references, but they believed that this problem could be resolved in the future, when Soviet Yiddish culture developed a new, secular, and socialist metaphorical vocabulary and symbolic repertoire of its own. In 1924 Oyslender positively contrasted Der Nister's prerevolutionary symbolist style with the "naïve dreams" of the Jewish artistic renaissance of the early twentieth century, referring to the concept promoted by the Vilna publication *Literarishe monatshriftn*. He argued that Der Nister's dramatic imagery of "chaotic disorder" reflected the young writer's "organic distrust of artistry" and therefore could not be "measured by aesthetic criteria."[4]

At that early stage of Der Nister's literary career, Oyslender explained, Der Nister attempted to depict the world at the prehistoric threshold of its creation. Although Der Nister's imagination was influenced by kabbalistic mysticism, he invented a new symbolic language suitable for representing the revolution as a new story of creation out of chaotic raw matter. And in that "language of chaos" one could already discern certain social and national themes. In his interpretation of Der Nister's prerevolutionary symbolist period, Oyslender echoed ideas of Andrei Bely, a prominent Russian symbolist writer and theorist. For Bely, symbolism was an aesthetic response to deep existential crisis. In "Symbolism," an essay first published in 1909 in the liberal newspaper *Kievskaia mysl'* (Kiev thought), which could have been familiar both to Oyslender and Der Nister, Bely wrote: "It [contemporary art] is animated by the awareness of some uncrossable divide between us and the recent age; it is a symbol of the crisis of worldviews; this crisis is deep; and we have a vague premonition that we are standing on the border of two great periods in the development of humanity."[5] As opposed to the more traditional mode of artistic creativity as representation of reality through symbolic forms, a symbolist artist "does not want to see the surrounding world because in his soul sings the voice of the eternal; but this voice is wordless, it is the chaos of the soul," Bely wrote a year earlier in another essay with the same title.[6] Nine years later, responding to the 1917 revolution, Bely developed this idea in more concrete terms: "A revolutionary epoch is preceded by the vague envisaging of future forms of the post-revolutionary reality . . . in a fantastic mist of the arts; there, in the unclear utterings of a tale, we are presented with a nebulous future true reality [*byl'*]."[7] Adjusting Bely's ideas to the Soviet age, Oyslender seeks to present Der Nister as a revolutionary symbolist, whose artistic intuition enabled him to discern the traces of the new creation emerging from what Bely termed the "native" (*rodimyi*) chaos of his creative imagination. For the prerevolutionary age during which Der Nister began his creative experimentation, his vision of the coming revolution as a cosmic cataclysm was a progressive step compared to the "silent negation" of the revolution by other writers of that time. Although Oyslender did not name those writers, his most likely target was David Bergelson. In a programmatic essay titled "Literatur un gezelshaftlekhkayt" (Literature and society, 1919), Bergelson argued that political upheavals could only be represented artistically in literary prose at a certain remove in time.[8]

Using the terminology of the contemporaneous theories of Russian formalism, Oyslender described Der Nister's literary method as "planting social and historical motifs into the cosmic fabula." Thus, history merged with myth in the symbolic narrative of the revolution, which was projected onto the story of creation. Yet before the revolution, Yiddish literature was not yet ready for that innovative "cosmic fabula," and no one could appreciate Der Nister's "active ethicism" as a response to the actual concerns of that time. To provide this mythological narrative with a spatial trajectory, Der Nister introduced the "wanderer" figure who traversed the primordial cosmic landscape as the newly created cosmos was entering the age of history. It was the recurrent motif of the wanderer legend that marked Der Nister's historical optimism, which distinguished him from his pessimistic colleagues, Oyslender argued. Der Nister's wanderer was a new symbolic figure signifying "the departure point of a new tradition in modern Yiddish literature."[9] He was neither a familiar maskilic hero seeking to redeem his backward Jewish community through enlightenment, nor a mystic in search of divine revelation. This figure was a worldly character who searched for a purpose within the confines of human settlement at the time when unformed raw matter was being shaped by human civilization. Der Nister's early wanderer figure was not a psychological character. He emerged out of a multitude of inanimate objects and living creatures that personified different human qualities, whereas his sole function was to bear a moral message.

On the critical side, Oyslender remarked that the rigid wanderer construction made Der Nister's stories static and formulaic. Even more problematic, in Oyslender's opinion, was the figure's limited ability to represent adequately the scope of the revolution.

Even in "Naygayst," his most radical tale, Der Nister treated the revolution in the old-fashioned terms of "wandering prophesy" as an abstract call for the awakening of raw matter, which diminished the significance of the historical transformation produced by the revolution. Oyslender concluded his analysis on a hopeful note that Der Nister would eventually rise to the challenge of the new revolutionary epoch and discover new artistic means for its adequate representation. This optimism was based on the analysis of Der Nister's style, which Oyslender believed to be "earthy." Even the most fantastic images were remarkably concrete in their details, firmly grounded in the earthly landscape as if they possessed a solid weight. Der Nister's artistic discipline exercised control over his fantasy, and did not let it fly away into exotic realms. His depictions of imaginary events grew out of the elemental core of each phenomenon, embedding his symbolism in the concrete dimensions of time and space. At the level of syntax, the mark of Der Nister's original style was a long spiral sentence structure, which absorbed individual details and nuances and compressed them into a compact and coherent image.

Among the admirers of Der Nister's art were not only "fellow travelers" like Oyslender but also leading communist functionaries, such as Shakhne Epshteyn, the editor of *Di royte velt*, and Moyshe Litvakov, the editor of the Moscow newspaper *Der emes* (The truth), the Yiddish equivalent of the Russian *Pravda*.[10] Whereas Oyslender's analysis focused on the structural and stylistic features of Der Nister's tales, Litvakov was interested in situating Der Nister in the broader context of Yiddish literary history. In 1926 he described Der Nister as "one of the deepest phenomena in our literature," serving as an important link between the prerevolutionary past and the Soviet present. Litvakov further elaborated: "He has come from the depths of popular Hasidism, and he draws his literary and artistic nourishment from Peretz. The origins of his art are buried in the remote age of Rabbi Nahman of Bratslav."[11] Litvakov was in agreement with Oyslender regarding the significance of the wanderer motif and mystical imagery, but he also pointed to its folkloric roots: "He is searching, Der Nister—he is searching for the secret of the world, of the human world order, of the individualized meaning of the people, of his own artistic 'self.' He is an indefatigable 'wanderer' from his own works, and on his way he generously disburses tales and parables, legends and riddles full of fantastic characters from Hasidic folklore.... This is an original, thoroughly Jewish poet who searches for a way to artistic universalism."[12] Litvakov also emphasized the secular aspect of Der Nister's quest for the divine. Both Oyslender and Litvakov agreed that the Jewish cultural heritage need not be discarded. It could be thoroughly cleansed of the vestiges of religious mysticism, and the resulting material would then be recycled to construct a new secular and communist Yiddish culture. Like Oyslender, Litvakov also concluded his assessment of Der Nister's work on a hopeful note: "We follow him arduously, hoping with fast-beating heart that any moment the *nister* [hidden one] can become a *nigle* [revealed one], that he will reveal to us the hidden secret of ideas and the social meaning of the Hasidic element, that we will be dazzled by the sun-beams of Hasidic-*folkstimlekhn* [in the folk spirit] universalism."[13] Litvakov referred here to a Hasidic concept, according to which the genuine tzaddik was to remain hidden from the world during the first part of his mission, which he spent wandering in search of a spiritual calling. Only after that could he reveal himself through miracles and establish his presence in the community.

Perhaps the latest Soviet endorsement of Der Nister's symbolism came from Isaac Nusinov, at that time a respected Soviet Marxist scholar of European, Russian, and Yiddish literature who held professorial positions at several Moscow universities. In his foreword to the 1929 edition of *Gedakht* (Imagined), Nusinov conceded that Der Nister's writing remained "a problem in the history of Yiddish literature," because his commitment to symbolism constricted his ideological and artistic horizons.[14]

Nusinov further differentiated between two kinds of symbolism in the history of world literature, a "reactionary" and a "revolutionary" one, and warned that some writers who began as progressive symbolists later transformed into reactionary ones.[15] Moreover, even a progressive symbolist writer of the past had his limitations because he belonged to a social group that had no "concrete ways for solving social conflicts," which drove the writer away from concrete social reality into the realm of "symbolic abstraction."[16]

Surveying Der Nister's evolution as a writer up to 1929, Nusinov recognized him as a central figure of the post-1905 generation. The revolutionary experience of 1905 inspired his creativity, but the defeat of the revolution pushed him away from "social activity" into "reclusive concealment" (*nezirishe farborgnkeyt*) from reality. Der Nister withdrew from all political and ideological activity, whether socialist or nationalist, and sought refuge in "national folksiness" (*folkstimlekhkeyt*), which he tried to elevate in his writing into an "eternal and all-human category."[17] This search led him away from his direct predecessor, Y. L. Peretz, and toward the folkloric tradition of the Hasidic storyteller Rabbi Nahman of Bratslav. Nusinov regarded this turn from modernism to Hasidic folklore positively, because it steered Der Nister clear of Peretz's nationalist ideology. Der Nister's creative embrace of Rabbi Nahman's legacy allowed him to "clear his tales of any external mark of time and place, of any national or historical characterization." As an artist, Der Nister was preoccupied not with national issues but with the individual's quest for a purpose, which he depicted through symbolic imagery.[18]

As Nusinov explained, this was an artistic response of a thoughtful writer before the October Revolution. Powerless to change society, he turned toward "extra-historical abstraction," for which he developed a specific symbolist style and form.[19] Der Nister drew his imagery from religious mystical literature, but he was not a religious mystic himself. He used this imagery merely as his "verbal material," which was "organic" for someone whose childhood was steeped in the religious legacy of medieval Judaism. Nusinov's final verdict was ideologically calibrated: "Der Nister is not, and never will be, able to fully attain realistic creativity due to his artistic nature. His way of comprehending our reality remains that of symbolic exegesis, of interpretation through symbolic images. It is Nister's responsibility to put this interpretation to the service of this revolutionary 'New Spirit' [referring to 'Naygayst']. And this is a legitimate demand from our readership."[20] Today, Nusinov's introduction may appear blunt in its critical dogmatism, but at that time it served a special function, which in Soviet literary jargon was termed "locomotive." Its purpose was to justify the publication of a problematic text by highlighting its ideological "flaws" while at the same time mitigating their harmfulness through ideological acrobatics as a way of anticipating and preempting future critical attacks. It is also important to keep in mind that all three leading Soviet Yiddish critics of the 1920s and 1930s, Oyslender, Litvakov, and Nusinov, were Der Nister's close associates from Kiev. Their consistent support reflected both their shared aesthetic values and a sense of group loyalty.

### THE SYMBOLIST EPILOGUE

Safeguarded by Nusinov's critical introduction, the revised 1929 edition of *Gedakht* was the last collection of Der Nister's symbolist works. In retrospect we can assume that its intended audience was a particular segment of Soviet Yiddish readers who were familiar with Der Nister's early works and could appreciate the novelty of his most recent tales. By the late 1920s, this elitist segment of the Yiddish readership was diminishing: according to the statistics of library lending in 1930, Der Nister's works were in particularly low demand compared both to the older classics and to contemporary writers.[21]

*Gedakht* opens with "A Tale of a Hermit and a Kid" (A mayse mit a noged un mit a tsigele) originally published in 1913 under the title "A mayse" (A tale). The story is framed as a leisurely conversation among three bored demons on a frosty and moonlit winter night. The demons capture a young goat that belongs to a witch and ask the witch to tell them a story in exchange for releasing her kid. The hero of the witch's story is a hermit who lives in a cave in a faraway forest, where "he became wild and overgrown, and looked like a wild animal with a human face," so that even when he encountered a wolf or a bear, the animal would step aside with "animalistic awe" (khaye-opshay).[22] The hermit receives an order from a man with "mute and commanding eyes" (shtume un bafoylndike oygn) to follow him. After a long journey through the woods, they meet a dwarf who tries to confuse the hermit with an absurd conversation. This is the first of many obstacles that the hermit must overcome on his mission to find the "kernel" with the "truth" in an imaginary universe controlled by evil forces guarding the deeply hidden kernel. To prevent the hermit from finding the kernel, these evil forces attempt to distract him with worldly pleasures, such as a beautiful palace, and discourage him by attempting to convince him of the futility of his quest. On his way, the hermit meets a dwarf who tells him: "Little man, heaven is made up" (dem himl, mentshele, hot men oysgetrakht), and there is "nothing to search for, don't go, don't search."[23] The hermit learns that there are many wanderers in pursuit of the same goal, each one with "his shape and form . . . and each one has his manner, his world and his grain" (tsil iz dokh eyner, nor geyers farsheydn, gefint men—in geshtalt un in form . . . un yeder zayn shteyger, zayn velt un zayn kern).[24] Eventually the hermit is directed to a witch who lives in a cave in a field. It was her kid that was captured by the demons. The hermit reaches the demons as they are listening to the witch telling them that very story. They run in terror, the witch flies to the moon on her broom, and the hermit finds the kernel of truth at the same spot where the story began.

As David Roskies succinctly describes this peculiar compositional loop, "The quest comes back to consume the literary
frame."[25] In his reading of the tale, "The central action consists
of inaction; the scene of greatest struggle is within an empty
space . . . the truth lies buried in the ground; it directs the seeker
within himself and to the power of the imaginative realm."[26]
Although Roskies reads this story from a different, indeed opposite, mythopoetic perspective than the Marxist Nusinov does,
both interpretations agree on one point. They view the hermit
figure as a symbolic representation of a frustrated intellectual
who shuts himself off from the world and seeks truth in passive
solitude. Explaining Der Nister's aspiration as a writer, Roskies
remarks: "The goal of Der Nister's description is to create something that is noticeably an artifice, but so perfect that it reflects,
in a way, all levels of reality and no level in particular."[27] In this
early tale, Der Nister has already introduced a formal structure
that cuts across levels of fictional reality. Instead of using the
traditional framing scheme of a "story within a story," with fixed
boundaries separating core stories from their external frames,
Der Nister dissolves these boundaries by making the characters
from the inner stories penetrate into the outer realms in a radical narrative gesture that would become the mark of his modernist style.

This violation of narrative boundaries may seem to contradict
the common perception of Der Nister as an escapist who believed
that truth resides outside mundane reality. In the end, the hermit turns from a fictional character in the witch's story—a mere
figment of her imagination—into a "real" figure by entering the
world of the demons, chasing them away, and finding the kernel.
On the last stretch of his journey, the hermit switches roles with
the kid. Now the kid becomes the leader, and the hermit follows
him in his final approach to the kernel. The tale's message appears
to be that a genuine quest has the strength to breach the border between imagination and reality and influence events in the

here and now. Moreover, the notion that everything is fantasy ("Heaven is made up," the dwarf tells the hermit, trying to dissuade him from persisting in his quest) is clearly associated with the forces of evil, which try to prevent the hermit from finding the kernel of truth. This interpretation casts doubt on Roskies's conclusion concerning the circular structure of Der Nister's stories, which, in his reading, "suggests that whatever life's ultimate goal, it can be found only within the closed circle of the human mind, within the purview of *Gedakht*."[28] Rather than employing a circular structure, Der Nister uses a spiral scheme here, which for Andrei Bely represented a future synthesis between the linear evolutionary structure and the "dogmatic" circular one: "The truth of *spiral* connects *circle* and *line*. The combination of the three movements is in the ability to direct all the ways of moving one's thoughts."[29] Indeed, in his early symbolist tales, Der Nister already begins to pave the way to his later realist style by deliberately breaching the divide between reality and the autonomous realm of the imagination. While his imagination remained largely confined to the circular structure, reality applied a constant pressure to push forward. His transition to realism after 1929 can thus be seen not as a forced renunciation of symbolism but as the next rung in the spiral of stylistic experimentation, however difficult this process must have been in the Soviet context of the 1930s.

"A mayse" was Der Nister's first text written in the genre that Delphine Bechtel describes as "allegorical symbolist tale, which he used exclusively and developed to the point of mastery until 1929."[30] It also introduced the peculiar variation of the "box structure" as a key feature of that type of tale. Der Nister's symbolist tales "usually begin with a 'frame story' (sometimes two), which encircles one or more 'told stories,' and in the end the 'frame story' and the 'told story' merge and the reader realizes that they are actually part of the same complex."[31] Chronologically, Bechtel divides this corpus into two parts, before and after Der Nister's return to the Soviet Union in 1926. The later tales become

problematic and ambiguous in their meaning, and their characters acquire psychological complexity and depth as Der Nister
"increasingly relocates the conflict within the hero."[32] At the stylistic level, this complexity and ambiguity appear in the tension
between the allegorical and the symbolic modes of narration.
Whereas the allegorical message is transmitted through clear-cut
dichotomies of good versus evil, truth versus lie, solitude versus
civilization, and movement versus stasis, in the symbolic mode
these oppositions become opaque: "the real goal is unknown,"
and "crucial things are ineffable by their essence, and thus only
conveyable through the suggestive power of the symbol.... Only
the symbol can conceal and reveal simultaneously, keeping its
dense expressive power."[33]

The symbolic mode gradually overtakes the allegory, and the
plot lines become confusing and their meaning opaque. The early
optimistic belief in *tikkun* (restoration of the original order) in
"A mayse," in which all obstacles have been overcome, the kernel
of truth found, and the demons expelled, becomes ever more
problematic as the reader progresses through the more complex,
ambiguous, and darker later tales of *Gedakht*. Bechtel describes
the post-1926 period as the "collapse of storytelling."[34] Eventually
the quest motif disappears altogether, and the obstacles that the
first-person protagonist faces lose their meaning and purpose.[35]
The settings become more realistic and more similar to the modern urban environment with all its ambiguities and contradictions: the loss of individuality in mass culture, the collapse of
moral values, and the rise of totalitarian mass mentality.

All these trends reach a climax in "Unter a ployt (reviu)"
(Under a fence: A review), the concluding tale of the collection,
which also appeared in the July 1929 issue of *Di royte velt* and
marked, in David Shneer's words, the "high point" of the journal's "openness."[36] This tale effectively closes the corpus of Der
Nister's symbolist writings. The first-person protagonist of the
story, a former hermit scholar, has abandoned his vocation due to

lack of disciples and has become a circus acrobat. The dangerous horseback act that he has to perform with Lili (a name evoking Lilith, the mythological female demon responsible for seducing Adam), a sadistic dominatrix in a lilac tricot, also includes his beloved daughter. His worst fear comes to pass as his daughter falls off the horse and suffers a severe head injury. This incident triggers a series of nightmarish visions that play themselves out in the deranged scholar's mind. In one vision, he conducts a trial at the circus of his former teacher and colleagues and sentences them all to death. In another vision, the situation is reversed. The protagonist stands accused by his teacher of abandoning his vocation and pursuing worthless goals. This time, it is he who receives a death sentence and is burned to ashes. Miraculously, he survives the execution and pronounces his last verdict: "I spoke from the ashes and said: 'Stand up, my teacher and students. I deserved what was done to me. I brought you to shame, and you turned me to ash, and we're even, all equally brought to nothing. There won't be any grief in the circus. What kind of circus person was I really?'"[37] The story ends with the narrator waking up in his bed with a hangover.

This macabre and enigmatic tale has received a number of insightful interpretations by scholars. Roskies suggests that "Under a Fence" is to be read "perhaps even as a response to 'New Spirit,'" which was reprinted a year earlier in the collection *Fun mayne giter* (From my estates, 225), and describes the story as "the most modern, the most overtly psychological, and the most openly derivative of European literary sources" of Der Nister's tales.[38] Roskies reads it both as a premonition of the coming Stalinist terror, "the forced confession of the many writers—Jews and gentiles—who would soon perish without a trace"[39] and as a "universal parable on the fate and function of art in the modern world,"[40] a parable of an artist torn between two worlds that are symbolically represented by the circus and the monastic tower. When applied more broadly to the modern Jewish condition, this tale can also be read as a critical "statement on assimilation to European society."[41] According to Chone Shmeruk, Der Nister's tale is "nothing less than a grotesque portrayal of a Soviet writer's struggles and hardships."[42] In his detailed analysis of the tale, Shmeruk contends: "Der Nister had in advance put on trial the possible or already achieved transformation of a symbolist writer working under Soviet conditions. The feeling of guilt seems to dominate and accompany this transformation."[43] Concluding his study, Shmeruk admits: "The interpretation of 'Under a Fence' attempted in this paper may leave open other alternatives. Our concentration on specific incidents and on a schematic interpretation of the review may have distorted other possibilities and occasionally overshadowed some other meanings of the story."[44]

The motif of trial and execution as public spectacle, which resonates so powerfully with contemporary readers as a sort of foreshadowing of the Stalinist show trials, may have been inspired by the ideas of the prominent Russian avant-garde theater director and theorist Nikolai Evreinov. On October 18, 1918, in Kiev Evreinov gave a public lecture provocatively titled "Theater and Scaffold: On the Origins of Theater as a Public Institution" (Teatr i eshafot. K voprosu o proiskhozhdenii teatra kak publichnogo instituta). He argued that the origins of modern theater lie in the spectacle of public execution, which in turn is rooted in the ancient sacral ritual of human and animal sacrifice. And although Christianity tried to suppress pagan rituals, it could not leave people without public performance because "public theater is the greatest need of any developed nation."[45] The "Christian" theater had the same foundation as the pagan one: a public execution, now in the symbolic form of crucifixion. Evreinov emphasized that the reason for that public execution was a crime—though in Christianity it was sins of others, not those of Jesus: "The Crucified is the original hero of the medieval public theater."[46]

In Russia, the first play, performed in 1672, was based on the biblical story of Esther, which culminated in the public execution of Haman and his sons. Medieval audiences enjoyed these performances so much that the church had to come up with new spectacles, presenting the torture of sinners in the hell: "The Hell as a grandiose scaffold, fraught with elaborate torments, attracted all minds and hearts of the Middle Ages."[47] Presenting his argument from a different perspective, Evreinov claimed that cruelty to toys and animals is inherent in the child's psychology. When peasant children grow up without the moralistic influence of modern education, their cruel games develop into "a scaffold ferment" for the public performance. After an excursus into the ethnography of performance among different peoples, Evreinov concluded: "Wherever we turn in search of the origin of theater—to history, child psychology or ethnography—everywhere we stumble upon some open or hidden marks of the scaffold, where the executor and the victim (human or animal) are the first, at the dawn of the art of drama, to define, through their acting, the attractive power of this institution that is new to the crowd—an institution that is to become theater only in the future."[48] Evreinov's lecture, a concoction of popular ideas borrowed from Nietzsche and Russian decadence, made a powerful impression on the Kiev audience; one of the Jewish reporters compared it to a "monologue of a Sadist."[49] I have no hard evidence that Der Nister attended this lecture, but it is likely that he was familiar with its ideas. As we shall see, the motif of trial, repentance, and execution as public spectacle reemerges in Der Nister's writings in different genres, such as reportage, children's poetry and realist prose during the 1930s. But its first appearance occurs in "Under a Fence."

Other meanings of "Under a Fence" are explored by Marc Caplan. In contrast to Roskies's and Shmeruk's readings of the story as an allegorical critique of the rise of Stalinist totalitarianism, Caplan provocatively removes the story from the Soviet context and reads it as a reflection of "the author's experiences in Germany during the 1920s." He interprets the story in biographical terms as a juxtaposition of "the motif of a student leaving his academy [in this case, yeshiva] with the conventional European narrative of the journey from the provinces to the metropolis."[50] Caplan traces its Yiddish roots to the popular motif of the "fallen yeshiva student," which acquires a new, universal significance in the context of the modernist metropolitan culture of Weimar Berlin. He also compares "Under a Fence" with the film *Der blaue Engel* (The blue angel, 1930), arguing that both works draw upon Heinrich Mann's 1905 novel *Professor Unrat* by focusing "on the powerlessness, the impotence, and the humiliation of the scholastic ideal."[51] This leads Caplan to conclude that "Under a Fence" is "of a piece" with Der Nister's translations from world literature: "combining a romantic belief in the ability of storytelling to remake the world with the modernist's resignation to the fact that all stories have already been told."[52] In other words, the protagonist's vision of destruction reflects the modernist interpretation of the collapse of world culture. Thus, "Under a Fence" can be understood as the simultaneous fulfillment and failure of the Yiddishist project of "deparochialization," taking Jewish culture out of narrowly defined national concerns. By focusing on the relationships among the characters and tracing their roots in the European and Jewish cultural traditions, Caplan's interpretation deemphasizes the central motif of trial, accusation, and denunciation, which will become prominent in Der Nister's later works.

One can argue, however, that at this critical moment in his life and career, Der Nister opposed the idea of deriving a "meaning" from a work of literature. "Under a Fence" offers a remarkable clue in this regard, as if its author had already anticipated—and dismissed—an allegorical reading of the kind discussed above. Not unlike some of the later interpreters, one of the protagonist's former students is eager to draw a clear conclusion from his teacher's confusing tale: "What do you mean, sir? Why are you saying all this? Surely you must have something in mind?" To which the teacher replies: "But I had nothing else in mind, nothing else in the world. The only thing in my heart was the memory of how I had been insulted."[53] It is the memory of a raw emotion rather than an intellectual or ethical concern that lies at the core of the tale. The protagonist's rejection of interpretation supports Bechtel's thesis concerning the "collapse of allegorical symbolism" in Der Nister's later tales. These tales, she argues, are no longer organized "around a central ideational referent, neither God, nor truth, nor any set of traditional values."[54] She compares Der Nister's later tales to Kafka, with both authors expressing an "irreducible opposition between a distinctively allegorical system and the obscurity of the message, between the tendency to allegorize the world and the inability to find a meaning for the allegory."[55]

One of Der Nister's sources of inspiration and influence was the nineteenth-century German Romantic writer E. T. A. Hoffmann.[56] Building on this connection, Shmeruk suggests that by naming the protagonist's teacher Merardus after the first-person narrator of Hoffmann's novel *The Devil's Elixirs*, Der Nister may have been alluding to the early Soviet literary group the Serapion Brethren (named after Hoffmann's literary circle in Berlin and the title of another of his works).[57] Indeed, one can find structural and thematic parallels between Der Nister's tales and the short story "Rodina" (The homeland, 1922) by Lev Lunts, one of the founders of the Serapion Brethren. It was published in *Evreiskii almanakh* (The Jewish almanac, 1923) and could have been known to Der Nister, although there is no evidence to suggest that the two writers knew each other. It is even less likely that Lunts read Der Nister's writing, because he grew up in an assimilated Jewish family in St. Petersburg and likely did not read Yiddish. Around the same time as Der Nister, Lunts moved to Germany, where he lived in 1923–24 and died in Hamburg at the age of twenty-three. "Rodina" is set in Petrograd on an unusually hot summer evening. Two friends—the first-person narrator and his fellow "Serapion brother" Veniamin Kaverin (who would later become a prominent Soviet writer), to whom the story is dedicated—are talking about their Jewishness over glasses of home brew. Either in reality or in a drunken dream (it is not clear which), they end up in the synagogue, where they enter through a little door an alternative reality.

Behind this door, postrevolutionary Petrograd has been transformed into ancient Babylon, and Lev turns into Yehudah, an assimilated Babylonian Jew who attempts to make a dangerous escape through the desert to Jerusalem. In the desert he encounters his old friend Benyomin (a reincarnation of Kaverin), who left Babylon earlier and has become a Jewish zealot. Instead of greeting the exhausted refugee, Benyomin orders one of his Judean warriors to kill Yehudah because "he betrayed his people and shaved off his beard."[58] Yehudah falls down, and the Judeans throw stones at him. As the narrator recovers from his nightmare, he finds himself back in Petrograd in front of a shop window. He is looking at "a small bald man, with a narrow forehead and sly wet eyes, dirty and nasty. That's me. I recognized myself. And I realized: all that was beautiful and ancient—the high forehead and the excited eyes—it all had been left over there, on the road that runs through Circesium and Riblah to Jerusalem."[59] There are a number of parallels between "Rodina" and "Under a Fence": both have a box structure of a story within a story, which eventually turns out to be a product of the first-person narrator's intoxicated fantasy. The narrator's recovery from his dream is triggered by his violent death as the result of a punishment meted out by someone formerly close to him, his friend or teacher. But unlike Der Nister's Yiddish tales, Lunts's Russian story has content and a message that are explicitly Jewish. During his drunken visionary journey to his imaginary ancient homeland, Lunts's protagonist discovers his Jewish identity as an ancient legacy that he has betrayed by assimilating into the cosmopolitan culture of ancient Babylon and contemporary Petrograd. The allegorical meaning of "Rodina" seems straightforward, if not free from irony. Assimilation leads to physical and moral degradation, as is testified by the pathetic image of the modern Jew in the shop window, and eventually is to be punished by death.

In 1929, the young writer named Shmuel Godiner, who was mentioned by Moyshe Litvakov as one of Der Nister's followers, published a collection of stories that was written between 1923 and 1929. As the title, *Figurn afn rand* (Figures on the edge), suggests, the heroes of the stories are marginal characters unable to find their place in mainstream Soviet society. They range from a Lubavitcher Hasid from Shklov selling cigarettes in Moscow to former revolutionary heroes unable to transition into mundane routines. Among the latter is the protagonist of the story "Toyt-urteyl" (Death sentence), a former Red Army commander named Tits, who is standing trial for the embezzlement of trade-union funds and a murder. Unsure whether a death sentence would be justifiable for a revolutionary hero, the judge, a young woman named Marta, has decided to pay him a visit in prison for an informal chat. Their encounter develops into an erotic attraction, and they share, apparently in Yiddish, memories of moments in their lives when they experienced violence and expressed protest. The next morning Marta receives a phone call from a regional Communist Party official urging her to dispose of Tits as quickly as possible and to get on with the next case. To answer the phone call, Marta must put her naked foot on a bearskin on the floor, a gesture that brings to mind the dominatrix heroine of Leopold von Sacher-Masoch's *Venus in Fur*. During the conversation, Marta's attempt to present a legal argument is cut short: "You know very well what kind of law rules among revolutionaries and Communists."[60] A similar view is shared by Tits's brother, a revolutionary sailor, who believes that a Communist should not be treated as an ordinary horse thief. It would be better for his heroic brother to be "dispatched in a comradely manner" than to suffer the humiliation of cleaning prison latrines like an ordinary criminal.[61]

The theme of the new, revolutionary justice that follows its own logic counter to conventional legal norms was central to

Soviet literature of the 1920s. One of the best-known examples is the novel *Razgrom* (The rout, 1927) by Aleksandr Fadeev, a burgeoning proletarian writer who would go on to have a successful bureaucratic career in the Union of Soviet Writers. The novel's main character, the Red Army commander Levinson (incidentally, Jewish), confronts the moral dilemma of taking away a Korean family's only pig in order to feed his soldiers. It is clear that the family will not survive the winter without that pig, but it is equally clear that Levinson's soldiers need food. In the end, the lives of the Korean peasants is sacrificed for the cause of the revolution. The issue of revolutionary justice is explored in a more complex way in David Bergelson's novel *Midas-hadin* (Measure of judgment), which was published in book form simultaneously in Vilna and Kiev in 1929, the same year as *Gedakht* and *Figurn afn Rand*. Reflecting on the Judaic connotations of the concept of *din* in Bergelson's title, Sasha Senderovich and Harriet Murav identify two aspects: "On the one hand, harsh and unrelenting, *din* is associated with evil, the demonic realm, and the conditions of exile. On the other hand, din, in the sense of order, limit, and containment, prevents the force of God's creative power from overwhelming creation—it is a necessary force, so long as it is balanced by mercy."[62] The condition of revolution creates a situation in which *din* rules unrestrained, creating "a world of nightmarish, unrelenting punishment."[63] What makes Der Nister and his followers different from many artists' postrevolutionary treatments of this issue is the narrative perspective. Like Franz Kafka in *The Trial*, Der Nister and Godiner take on the position of the accused rather than the accuser and present the events from his point of view. Yet they do not fully exonerate the victim, nor do they reject the validity of the new justice. Instead, they focus on the traumatic effects of this experience on both sides of the divide, showing how blurred the boundary can be between the accuser and the accused, whose roles can be swapped more easily than others might think.

In the late 1920s, Der Nister was engaged in an elaborate and hazardous artistic exploration of the increasingly ambiguous conditions of that time, which defied any straightforward representation by means of parable or allegory. He constructed a grotesque situation that prefigured, in a symbolic form, the real-life scandal that the publication of "Under a Fence" would immediately trigger. The writer was subject to public criticism and forced to confess the sins he had committed by writing and publishing his tale. Der Nister's provocative move in publishing the tale exposes the cruelty of the Soviet system of ideological control and simultaneously affirms the power of the artistic imagination to influence reality. Der Nister uses the structural device of breaching the divide through different layers of narrative, which he had introduced in his early stories, and in "Under a Fence," it reaches its perfection. Here he creates an opening between the imaginary narrative space of the tale and the actual space of Soviet reality. As we shall examine further, "Under a Fence" can be seen as a kind of symbolic "fence" in Der Nister's literary evolution. It separates his symbolist and his realist periods, closing the earlier modernist project of "deparochialization" and opening the new project of preservation of the Jewish historical and cultural legacy in Soviet culture. Although conservative in its aspiration, this new project would be more daring, demanding, and ultimately dangerous. Entering the "circus" of Soviet literary politics, Der Nister will have to perform a variety of acrobatic tricks until he finds new stylistic forms that will be both adequate for his purposes and acceptable by Soviet standards. The experience of persecution and trial becomes transposed from the realm of dark fantasy into the reality of everyday life. These motifs become prominent in Der Nister's writing during the 1930s, reemerging in different forms in his travelogues, novel, Holocaust tales, and even children's poetry. The trauma of 1929 will remain a powerful impetus and a rich source of inspiration for the rest of his life, until his last trial and death in prison.

## THE SCANDAL OF "NISTERISM"

For some writers, such as the prominent novelist Israel Joshua Singer, Der Nister personified the pretense and arrogance of the Kiev style in literature and life. Reminiscing about the Kiev literary circle, which he got to know during World War I, Singer singled out Der Nister in 1942 in the New York newspaper *Forverts*: "The place of honor was occupied by Der Nister, a writer of pretentious tales about demons, ghosts, daredevils and hobgoblins. [Yekhezkel] Dobrushin, the 'theoretician' of the group, announced openly during one meeting that, had the writers of the whole world been given a chance to read Der Nister's work, they would have broken their pens."[64] Much more significant than the disapproval of the "bourgeois" American writer was the aggressive ideological offensive undertaken in 1929–31 by leading Yiddish critics from Minsk who represented the radical "proletarian" wing of Soviet Yiddish literature. They occupied key positions in BelAPP, the sister organization of the Russian Association of Proletarian Writers (RAPP) in Belarus. Founded in 1925, RAPP was just one among many writers' associations. It had a large membership and was ideologically rigid, and its members aspired to control Soviet literature in its entirety. Sensing the political turn in 1929, its leaders took it upon themselves to assert the hegemony of "proletarian realism" over all of Soviet literature.[65]

During the 1920s, critical debate in Soviet literature revolved around the issue of individual creative freedom versus collective commitment in the new revolutionary culture. One position, represented by the Pereval (Pass) group, perceived the revolution as a "new Renaissance"; the Russian literary historian Galina Belaia explains: "In their eyes the revolution had to become an intense spiritual movement that would take over 'the entire social life and the entire inner world of man.'"[66] Their Proletkult opponents denied the primary role of individual creativity, promoted collectivist art, and regarded writing as a professional craft that could be practiced as mass production. Aleksandr Voronskii, one of Pereval's leading theorists, argued in 1923 that the new revolutionary style, which he termed "neorealism," would emerge out of a synthesis of realism, Romanticism, and symbolism.[67] Thus, Voronskii explained, "In neorealism, the symbol is provided with realist character, while realism becomes symbolic and romantic."[68] Another issue dividing Pereval from the proletarian writers was their attitude toward the prerevolutionary cultural legacy. While the theorists of Pereval believed that it could and should be utilized for the construction of a new Soviet culture, their "proletarian" opponents flatly rejected its value. Voronskii's position was shared by those Yiddish critics who saw the potential for new synthetic art in Der Nister's writing, whereas the "proletarian" critics identified Der Nister's style with the class enemy. Thus, despite his reclusive character, Der Nister found himself in the vortex of a cultural war, which reached its climax by 1930.

The critical debates of the late 1920s had wide-ranging practical repercussions. As Evgeny Dobrenko explains: "It was the age during which all cultural institutions were bureaucratized once and for all and the main parameters of Stalinist culture formed, from the cult of the leader to the production novel. It was the age of the final onslaught on the traditional culture of the intelligentsia."[69] Relying on the support of the Communist Party, RAPP organized a series of high-profile critical campaigns to show its strength against prominent writers who belonged to the previously tolerated category of "fellow travelers." Voronskii had already been removed from a high-level editorial position in 1927, and next it was the turn of high-profile writers such as Andrei Platonov, Evgenii Zamiatin, and Boris Pilniak, who tried to combine their commitment to the October Revolution and the Soviet state with modernist experimentation in form and style. Critics of RAPP demanded that literary works be straightforward and accessible to an average reader with a basic Soviet education. In addition, these RAPP campaigns "initiated a de facto ban on the publication of the works of Russian émigré writers in the USSR and Soviet writers abroad."[70]

This ban had a particularly strong effect on Yiddish literature. Whereas the majority of Russian émigré writers were hostile to the Soviet regime, many Yiddish writers abroad, particularly in the United States, left Russia before the October Revolution because of oppression and discrimination by the tsarist regime. They were generally, although not unreservedly, sympathetic to the Soviet Union, which they regarded as friendly to Jews and supportive of Yiddish culture. Quite a few of them visited the Soviet Union in the 1920s and wrote positive reports in the American Yiddish press. Some American Yiddish writers maintained close personal connections with their Soviet colleagues, particularly with the Kiev Group. But in 1929 the relationship between the Soviet Yiddish writers and their colleagues abroad was negatively affected by the outbreak of violence between Jews and Arabs in Palestine. The Soviet Union took the Arab side, which forced a number of prominent American Yiddish writers to break with the communist newspaper *Morgn frayhayt* and eventually to change their attitude toward the Soviet Union.[71] Among the first victims of the new campaign against publications abroad was the young writer Shmuel Gordon, at that time a student in the Yiddish department of Moscow State Pedagogical Institute, who published his poems in the Warsaw weekly *Literarishe bleter* (which was regarded as progressive and was edited by Nakhman Mayzel, a former leading member of the Kiev Group). The critical assault on the hapless Gordon was followed by attacks on literary heavyweights such as Peretz Markish, David Hofshtein, and Leyb Kvitko, all of whom were associated with the Kiev Group.

In the autumn of 1929, Khatskl Dunets, a leading Belorussian proletarian critic and cultural functionary, published a critical survey titled "On the Literary Front: Notes to the Annual Literary Balance Sheet" in the Minsk journal *Shtern*. Using ideologically charged language with hints of political denunciation,

Dunets calibrated the gravity of particular authors' transgressions. He described the three-thousand-copy print run of Der Nister's *Fun mayne giter* as a "reactionary act verging on sabotage," especially compared to the smaller print runs of books by such bona fide proletarian poets as Izi Kharik and Aron Kushnirov. (Dunets ignored the fact that poetry usually had smaller print runs than prose.)[72] In the politically charged atmosphere of that time, a public accusation of "sabotage" (*shederay* in Yiddish, *vreditel'stvo* in Russian) was a signal that could be followed by the arrest and imprisonment of the accused person. It is significant therefore that Dunets directed his accusation not against Der Nister himself but against his publisher and stopped on the verge of making a direct accusation. The editors of *Di royte velt*, who had regularly published Der Nister's symbolist stories since 1926, came to his defense.[73] They chose to respond to the criticism of the Ukrainian Yiddish critic Avrom Vevyorke, a less influential figure than Dunets, who also tried to present "Nisterism" as a politically dangerous trend in Soviet Yiddish literature. The editors' response was carefully articulated: "The editorial board of *Di royte velt* is not a great admirer of Der Nister's symbolism, allegorism and abstractionism. We by no means consider it positive that Der Nister is separated from our reality and is an artist, so to say, outside time and space. But Der Nister is a great master of language, he is a writer of great creativity and imagination [*fantazye, bilderishkayt*]. This is his value, and this makes him interesting, perhaps not for the broad masses but for a chosen few [*yekhidey-sgule*] who should learn from him. Shall we publish him or not?"[74] Answering this rhetorical question affirmatively, the editors of *Di royte velt* reminded their opponents that Soviet literature had a number of original writers with deep roots in the prerevolutionary period. Those writers were now searching for new ways of writing to better depict the new Soviet reality. It was a difficult process, but one they felt should be supported by publications—provided there was enough paper for them.

After all, the works of the prominent Russian symbolist Andrei Bely were published in the Soviet Union! The editors of *Di royte velt* attempted to defuse the accusation against Der Nister as the ringleader of a dangerous literary group by presenting him as a harmless, marginal individual:

> Nisterism is not an ideal, not a school, it is not even a trend in our Soviet Yiddish literature; and one cannot disregard and ignore Der Nister, a living writer who tries to liberate himself from Nisterism. Whether he will succeed—this is a different question. . . . But it would be bad politics to push him away, especially in such a journal as *Di royte velt,* which does not represent any particular group or trend but is the organ of the entirety of Soviet Yiddish literature. Of course, Der Nister's most recent work, "Under a Fence," published in the 7th issue, requires an interpretation, but the tendency is clear: rejection of idealism and transition to materialism.[75]

But this line of defense, typical for "fellow travelers," had no ideological purchase in 1929. In 1928 and 1929, Der Nister was fortunate to publish two collections of his symbolist tales that were written between 1913 and 1929. By the end of 1929, such publications would not be possible, even in *Di royte velt.* For a few years, he survived by translating a wide range of literary works, among them Lev Tolstoy, Soviet Ukrainian writer Ivan (Izrail) Kulik, Russian modernist Boris Pilniak, and French novelists Emile Zola and Victor Hugo.[76]

Yet the attack on Der Nister was mild compared to the more aggressive campaign against his friend Leyb Kvitko, by that time a prominent literary figure and one of the editors of *Di royte velt.*[77] Whereas Der Nister was chastised for his "reactionary" style, Kvitko was accused of the graver political crime of "peddling counter-revolutionary propaganda." His ideological failings were exacerbated by his ad hominem attack on Moyshe Litvakov, the powerful editor of the central Soviet Yiddish newspaper *Der emes.* In a sarcastic satirical poem (*sharzh*), Kvitko created a crude caricature of Litvakov as *shtink-foygl Moyli* (stink-bird Moy[she]

Li[tvakov]), which fouls everything that is good in Yiddish culture. The fact that such a poem could be published at all and even included in Kvitko's first major collection, *Gerangl* (Struggle), provides us with a fascinating glimpse into the intrigues of the Soviet Yiddish literary establishment. Gennady Estraikh interprets this publication as an indication of an attempted plot by the Kharkiv writers to remove Litvakov from his position.[78] Defending himself, Kvitko published a brief "Clarification" (Derkelrung), in which he argued that it is "not permissible that those who feel themselves insulted by the epigrams should use the interests of the proletarian revolution and proletarian culture as a cover for their wounded pride."[79] Its publication shows that the editors of *Di royte velt* initially misjudged the gravity of the situation.

In his survey, Dunets compared Kvitko's case with the highly resonant cases of Evgenii Zamiatin and Boris Pilniak in Russian literature, both of whom lost their positions in the Soviet literary establishment due to the publication of their works abroad. Although Kvitko, unlike Markish or Gordon, did not commit this kind of transgression, Dunets argued that his poem was a grave subversive act of counterrevolutionary propaganda. The exposure of Kvitko's work was important because it helped mobilize "public opinion" (*gezelshaftlekhkayt*) in Soviet Yiddish literature.[80] As a key figure in the Minsk group of proletarian critics and therefore hostile to the modernist trends emanating from Ukraine, Dunets was no friend of Litvakov, but he seized the opportunity to defend a fellow communist by dealing a blow to the rival Ukrainian fellow travelers. Showing solidarity with one of its members, the editorial board of *Di royte velt* retorted that Kvitko's misdemeanor was not as grave as Pilniak's and Zamiatin's "counter-revolutionary" crimes.[81] However, the last word belonged not to Yiddish literati but to the Communist Party. The discussion ended with the official declaration by the Communist Party's Central Control Commission, which ruled that Kvitko's poem was not merely an expression of his own arrogance regarding proletarian writers but a clear "attack of class enemy forces on the Jewish working masses."[82] Kvitko was removed from the editorial board of *Di royte velt*, and Henekh Kazakev-ich was fired from the position of editor in chief of Tsentrfarlag, which had published Kvitko's book.

The militant champions of Yiddish proletarian literature in Minsk such as Dunets, Ber Orshanski, and Yashe Bronshteyn were influential members of BelAPP. Unlike Kiev, Minsk had no prerevolutionary modernist tradition to build upon, and its Yid-dish cultural establishment strived to create a new, proletarian literature from scratch. During the tsarist period, Minsk had a significant, predominantly Jewish and Yiddish-speaking, work-ing class with strong socialist organizations. This legacy served as a fertile ground for the invention and promotion of a new, strictly proletarian Soviet culture. In addition, as Elissa Bemporad has demonstrated, Yiddish cultural activity in Soviet Belarus had a strong regional bias: "Much more than its Ukrainian counter-part, Belorussian regional identity had to be constructed by scholars, instilled in the intelligentsia, and then disseminated en masse."[83] Like their Russian senior colleagues, the activists of BelAPP interpreted the political turn of 1929 as an opportun-ity to take ideological control over Soviet Yiddish literature. An attack on Der Nister was a step in advancing their agenda. In the first 1930 issue of *Shtern*, Dunets, at that time a deputy minister of education in Belarus, published an essay sarcastically titled "On a Worn-Out 'Uniform' without a 'General.'" Responding to the Ukrainian critics' defense of Der Nister as a master of literary style, he flatly denied any artistic value to Der Nister's works. Arguing also against Litvakov, Dunets decried Der Nis-ter's language as obsolete, stagnant, and lacking in the function of social communication. Dunets dismissed Der Nister's ideas as mere "symbolist idealistic epigonery," rooted in the false idea of a separation between spirit and matter and based on a belief that redemption would reconcile all social contradictions and would make peace between predators and their victims. In conclusion, Dunets dismissed Der Nister as an anachronism in Soviet literature who had no place in the contemporary age: "His eyes are obscured and his ears are stopped," and his tales are a "panopticon of cripples and demons."[84]

In 1930, adjusting to the change in the ideological climate, Litvakov tried to modify his positive evaluation of symbolism: "Proletarian art ... can undergo transformation according to its own ways and needs, therefore it can also use Symbolic methods of collecting, applying, and organizing lexical material, and, as a result, enriching the intellectual and ideological vocabulary of the language." Litvakov further clarified his position on Der Nister: "By rejecting in Der Nister Der Nister's ideology, I maintain that from the point of view of word-fabric (verter-geveb) and of striving for artistic generalization, Der Nister represents a higher stage than Sholem Aleichem."[85] Litvakov responded to Dunets's criticism in Di royte velt with a half-hearted repentance. In a short piece titled "The Nister Problem," Litvakov admitted that he was not able to resolve the complicated issue of distinguishing between recognizing Der Nister's talent and his contribution to "literary technology," on the one hand, and the harmful effect of symbolism as a style that was irreconcilable with proletarian realism, on the other. Litvakov went on to say that, in trying to protect Der Nister, he had exaggerated the link between Der Nister's creative method and the ideology of Jewish folk masses, leading him to defend "Nisterism." Yet Litvakov tacitly disagreed with Dunets and continued to insist that Der Nister had had a positive effect on Soviet Yiddish literature, in particular on the younger generation of writers like Shmuel Godiner.[86] Meir Wiener, another leading Marxist critic at that time based in Kiev, who became friends with Der Nister in Berlin, took up a similar line of defense. According to a press report from a meeting of the Kiev District Committee of the Communist Party, Wiener tried to suggest a compromise. On the one hand, he believed that "it is not right for Nister to mentor a literary group. True, he has influence because he is a strong artist and many young people learn from him." On the other hand, Wiener readily conceded that "recently Nister has tried to distance himself from his traditions, and this is a fact that must be welcomed."[87]

Der Nister and his colleagues in Kharkiv and Kiev inhabited a multilingual and multiethnic cultural space in Ukraine. Some Ukrainian writers, such as Pavlo Tychyna, spoke Yiddish, whereas some Jews, such as Ivan (Izrail) Kulyk occupied prominent positions in the Ukrainian literary establishment. Kulyk and Tychyna translated Kvitko's poetry into Ukrainian, while Der Nister translated Kulyk's novel *What Had Happened to Vasyl Rolenko*, about the life of a Ukrainian immigrant in the United States, into Yiddish.[88] Mayhill Fowler metaphorically describes the situation in Kharkiv's literary and artistic circles as a "literary fair," borrowing the image from the title of the Ukrainian literary magazine *Literaturnyi iarmarok*: "The literary fair was emerging from the multi-ethnic southwest provinces, they had all grown up in multi-ethnic spaces and institutions, whether the village, the city, or the imperial or Red Army."[89] This colorful modernist publication appeared in Kharkiv for one year only, in 1929, and was edited by a leading figure of the Ukrainian cultural revival, Mykola Khvyl'ovyi. The magazine *Literaturnyi iarmarok* (Literary fair) published Ukrainian translations of Der Nister's and Kvitko's works, which indicates that Ukrainian colleagues held some interest in the work of Yiddish modernists.[90] Besides an active literary scene, Kharkiv had a lively theater culture. In 1929, Les Kurbas, the leading Ukrainian director, staged "the first-ever Ukrainian-language review show." The show, *Hello from Radiowave 477!*, was performed in the "premier theatre of the republic, and it starred and referenced the premier cultural elites, the literary fair."[91] Inspired by Kurbas's trips to Berlin in 1927 and 1928, this performance was the result of his desire to bring small forms and cabaret style to the Ukrainian stage. But Der Nister's taste in theater was more conservative; he favored a more traditional, psychological style. The Ukrainian writer Yuri Smolych, who befriended Der Nister in Kharkiv in the early 1930s, recalls in his memoir having "sharp disputes" about contemporary theater: "I lumped together the 'psychological theater' with the 'literary theater' as inefficient and amorphous, while Nister was inclined to label excessive theatrical expressiveness as 'farce' (*balagan*)."[92] It is possible that Der Nister's imagination transformed his dislike of the cabaret style of Kurbas's short-lived theatrical experiments into the macabre carnivalesque of "Under a Fence"—a connection that may be alluded to by the tale's subtitle, "Review."

Smolych regarded Der Nister, who was about twenty years his senior, as a "patriarch" who began his literary career in the age of the founding fathers of Yiddish literature—Sholem Aleichem and Mendele Moykher Sforim—before the October Revolution. Neither Smolych nor Der Nister had read each other's works, but a possible "psychological reason" for their closeness, Smolych recollects, was the fact that both were subject to criticism by the proletarian writers' organizations.[93] Smolych included theses recollections in the chapter of his memoirs written in 1968, when he was already a highly respected senior figure in Soviet Ukrainian literature, though it remained unpublished until 1990. The broader agenda of Smolych's voluminous memoirs was to recover the memory of the Ukrainian cultural revival of the late 1920s and early 1930s, which was brutally suppressed by Stalin's regime. He portrayed the Jewish intelligentsia in Ukraine as supporters of the Ukrainian cause. As opposed to the Russian intelligentsia, "Jews easily switched to the Ukrainian language, used it in their daily interactions, and sent their children not to Russian but to Ukrainian schools."[94] For their part, Ukrainians welcomed Jews: "One couldn't even speak of a possibility of antisemitism among the Ukrainian intelligentsia. We lived in perfect harmony [*dusha v dushu*]."[95] However, as recent research has demonstrated, the relationship between Jewish and Ukrainian intelligentsia was not

so idyllic, and some Ukrainian modernists did harbor some antisemitic feelings. The union between Jewish and Ukrainian intelligentsia was largely a strategic one, a means of defense against
Russian cultural domination. The first conversation between the
two writers was sparked by Smolych's innocent question about
Zionism, which figured prominently among Der Nister's ideological "sins." Smolych's vivid depiction of that moment offers a
rare glimpse into the reality of literary life in Kharkiv:

> Nister was sitting on a little bench in the courtyard of the Blakitny
> Literary Club[96]—it was spring, bright greenery all around, the sky
> was clear and high, and Nister was enjoying the first warm rays of the
> May sun. Far away, people played volleyball . . . Nearby were stand-
> ing groups of writers, who had come out for a smoke. Perhaps there
> was a meeting or a discussion there, and they were having a break.
> Apparently, this meeting had something to do with Nister. Other-
> wise, why would I have turned to him with this question: "Pinkhus
> Mendelevich," I said, "I am, of course, familiar with the political
> assessment of Zionism, but I haven't formed my own opinion yet,
> so please, tell me . . ."
>
> I wasn't able to finish my question. Quiet and gentle . . . always
> polite and amiable, Nister suddenly flushed with anger. He even hit
> the bench with the fist and furiously turned at me: "All this is insinu-
> ations, all this is slander," he nearly yelled, "never, and nowhere in
> my works or in any conversations, did I say anything good about
> Zionism! I reject it, I consider it nonsense, do you understand?"[97]

When Der Nister calmed down and realized that Smolych did
not intend to provoke him, he explained in detail the reasons for
his aversion to Zionism. Smolych admits that he does not recall
exactly what Der Nister told him but remembers that he ironically described the Zionist program as a plan to create "a state
under the aegis of the Brodskys and the Ryabushinskys with a
government of Hasidic *tzaddikim*," which would be subordinated
to the political interests of the great powers. (While the Brodskys
were indeed one of the wealthiest Jewish families in the Russian
Empire, the Ryabushinskys were not Jewish but belonged to the

Old Believer branch of Orthodox Christianity; it seems unlikely that Der Nister would have mentioned them together in this context.) Zionism, Der Nister concluded, according to Smolych's imprecise memory, was a "new modification of the pogrom of the Jewish poor by Jewish hands."[98] It is possible, given Der Nister's prerevolutionary views, that he sincerely disliked Zionism, especially in its political form. But it is also possible that Smolych exaggerated Der Nister's anti-Zionist feelings in order to conform Der Nister's image to the official Soviet position, which firmly and unequivocally condemned Zionism as a nearly fascist form of bourgeois nationalism. Smolych was likely more accurate in depicting Der Nister's nervous reaction to his question, which reflects Der Nister's sense of anxiety and vulnerability at that time. According to Smolych, Der Nister was also skeptical of the Soviet project of turning Jews into farmers and resettling them first in Crimea and later in Birobidzhan. He believed that the "exterritoriality of the Jewish nation has become a historical fact" and that Jewish national identity should be preserved through language, education, and culture. "The perspectives were guaranteed" by the Soviet government, which also secured the political equality of Jews among other nations of the Soviet Union.[99]

### THE DECLINE OF PROLETARIAN HEGEMONY

The ascendency of RAPP lasted until 1932, when another sudden shift in party policy altered the disposition of forces in Soviet literature yet again. In April 1932 the party unexpectedly dissolved RAPP, and its leadership was severely reprimanded for their "deviations" and excessive criticism. This maneuver cleared the way for a new era: "After 1932 and the elimination of RAPP as an intermediary, the entire cultural landscape was finally made level, institutionally, ideologically, and aesthetically: the era of the Union of Soviet Writers and socialist realism had come."[100] Responding to the change, the Ukrainian Yiddish literati at once seized the initiative. A special "plenary session" was convened at the Kiev Institute for Jewish Proletarian Culture immediately following the party's resolution concerning the elimination of RAPP.[101] One of the participants was the prominent Marxist literary scholar Max Erik, who had emigrated from Poland to the Soviet Union in 1928; he initially settled in Minsk but, apparently unable to get on with his new "proletarian" colleagues, moved to Kiev in 1931. He criticized Bronshteyn for his crude dismissal of symbolism and for the general lack of a "dialectical" approach to literature. Dismissing Bronshteyn's dichotomy between the progressive proletarian and the reactionary bourgeois styles, Erik introduced an intermediate, mixed "petty-bourgeois" element, which made room for a selective integration of nonproletarian writers like Bergelson and Der Nister.[102] Without mentioning Isaac Nusinov by name, Erik reiterated Nusinov's concept of "petty-bourgeois" style, which served as a coded word for modernism, as a necessary transitional stage from the old to the new literature. Following this development, in the summer of the same year, *Di royte velt* published Der Nister's travel essay on Moscow under the rubric Shtet un derfer (Cities and villages).[103]

The turbulent period of conflicts and power struggles in Soviet literary politics came to an end in 1934 with the creation of the Union of Soviet Writers, which effectively put literature under the direct control of the Communist Party. As part of "multinational Soviet literature," Yiddish literature received a new historical narrative from a Marxist-Leninist perspective. The critic and literary historian Israel Serebriani began his career as a poet in prerevolutionary Kiev and later moved to Minsk, where he earned a candidate of science (PhD equivalent) degree in Yiddish literature at the Belorussian Academy of Sciences. He dedicated his research, as the title of his essay stated, to the "Problem of the So-Called Kiev Period in Yiddish Poetry after the October Revolution." He described the literary situation in Kiev at the beginning of the Soviet period as a "complex political-literary and cultural mesh [*iberflekht*]," in which "national-democratic" and "proletarian" trends were closely intertwined. Presaging the view of contemporary scholars such as Moss and Estraikh, Serebriani emphasized the close connection between the Kiev "Yiddishist" trend and the Vilna publication *Literarishe monatshriftn,* which promoted the elitist concept of the Jewish national "renaissance" by means of new literary creativity.[104]

Serebriani further argued that the authors and editors of the Kiev almanac *Eygns* (1918) "inherited" the prerevolutionary Yiddishist notion of elitist modernism as a new form of Jewish national secular art. Some traces of that ideology could be discerned later, "even on the pages of the communist Yiddish press."[105] As evidence, Serebriani used the 1921 publication of fragments of Der Nister's "In shlikhes fun naygayst" (On the mission of the new spirit, an earlier version of "Naygayst") in the Kiev newspaper *Komunistishe fon* (Communist banner), which the editors introduced as "a kind of communist vision."[106] It was the residue of "national-democratic" ideology and aesthetics in Soviet literature that concerned Serebriani most. Perusing the communist press of the early 1920s, when Kiev was already firmly under Bolshevik control, he came across a report of Nusinov's talk at a Kiev press club. At that time Nusinov acted as the representative of the Soviet authorities in charge of the Bolshevization of the Kultur-Lige in Kiev. In his talk Nusinov presented Kiev as a center of Yiddish literature "by and for the intelligentsia," contrasting it to Warsaw as the hub of mass literature. It was in Kiev, Nusinov argued, that modernist trends had emerged in Yiddish literature, and they were to be evaluated by "universal," rather than "Jewish," criteria. The works of such Kiev authors as Bergelson, Der Nister, and others justly belonged to modern world literature, while they were also of "deep national-historical significance."[107]

By revisiting Nusinov's 1920 views from the rigid ideological perspective of the 1930s, Serebriani tried to expose him as a "bourgeois nationalist." But this belated attempt by a Minsk critic to denounce his Kiev colleague was not successful. By 1934, Nusinov had become one of the leading Marxist authorities on literature, as is testified by his study of Rosa Luxemburg's views on literature, published in the same collection as Serebriani's study. Nusinov held a number of professorial positions in Moscow and was an editor of the prestigious *Literary Encyclopedia*. He clearly occupied a much higher place in the Soviet academic and literary hierarchy than Serebriani, a freshly minted provincial PhD. Serebriani's attempt to undermine Nusinov's authority by digging up his old ideological "errors" may indicate that the rivalry between Minsk and Kiev had not faded, even as Yiddish literature was consolidated under the auspices of the Union of Soviet Writers. But now the authority of Minsk was restricted to the territory of Belarus, whereas the members of the Kiev group, such as Nusinov and (until 1937) Litvakov, occupied dominant positions in Moscow, the new center of Soviet Yiddish literature. Although Der Nister was stuck in Kharkiv, which lost its status as the capital of Ukraine to Kiev in 1934, he could still count on the support of his powerful friends in Moscow.

## NOTES

1. [Untitled], *Di royte velt*, nos. 5–6 (1927): 140.

2. Estraikh, "Der Nister's 'Hamburg Score,'" 13. On the dissolution of Boy in 1930, see Krutikov, *From Kabbalah to Class Struggle*, 163–64.

3. For more detail on Yiddish literary politics in 1927–29, see Shneer, *Yiddish and the Creation of Soviet Jewish Culture*, 170–73.

4. Oyslender, *Veg-ayn-veg-oys*, 40.

5. Andrei Bely, "Simvolizm," 255.

6. Ibid., 337.

7. Bely, "Revolutisa i kultura," 301.

8. An English translation of this essay by Joseph Sherman titled "Belles-lettres and the Social Order" was published in Sherman and Estraikh, *David Bergelson: From Modernism to Socialist Realism*, 337–46.

9. Oyslender, *Veg-ayn-veg-oys*, 40.

10. Estraikh, "Der Nister's 'Hamburg Score,'" 14.

11. Litvakov, *In umru*, pt. 2, 69.

12. Ibid., 70.

13. Ibid.

14. Der Nister, *Gedakht*, i.

15. Ibid., vi.

16. Ibid.

17. Ibid., xii.

18. Ibid., xiii–xiv.

19. Ibid., xiv–xv.

20. Ibid., xvi.

21. According to the statistics of library lending, Leyb Brovarnik, "Vos hot men geleyent in Kiever Vintshevski-bibliotek in 1930 yor," *Di royte velt* 1 (1931), 220–21, cited in Estraikh, "Der Nister's 'Hamburg Score,'" 14.

22. Der Nister, *Gedakht*, 8.

23. Ibid., 18.

24. Ibid., 25.

25. Roskies, *Bridge of Longing*, 198.

26. Ibid., 198–99.

27. Ibid., 206.

28. Ibid., 199.

29. Bely, "Krizis kul'tury," 286.

30. Bechtel, *Der Nister's Work*, 105.

31. Ibid., 119.

32. Ibid., 142.

33. Ibid., 195.

34. Ibid., 253.

35. Ibid., 215.

36. "Unter a ployt (reviu)," *Di royte velt*, no. 7 (July 1929): 8–34; Shneer, *Yiddish and the Creation of Soviet Yiddish Culture*, 172. The story was translated by Seymour Levitan as "Under a Fence: A Review," in *Ashes Out of Hope*, ed. Greenberg and Howe.

37. Der Nister, "Under a Fence: A Review," 217.

38. Roskies, *Bridge of Longing*, 225.

39. Ibid.

40. Ibid., 229.

41. Ibid.

42. Shmeruk, "Yiddish Literature in the USSR," 254.

43. Shmeruk, "Der Nister's 'Under a Fence,'" 281.

44. Ibid., 284.

45. Ivanov, "'Milyi lektor', on zhe—'sovremennyi markiz de Sad,'" 24.

46. Ibid., 25–26.

47. Ibid., 28.

48. Ibid., 37.

49. Ibid., 17.

50. Caplan, "Hermit and the Circus," 174.

51. Ibid., 186.

52. Ibid., 193.

53. Der Nister, "Under a Fence: A Review," 197.

54. Bechtel, *Der Nister's Work,* 264.

55. Ibid., 265.

56. This connection was first mentioned by Shmeruk and discussed in more detail in Bechtel, *Der Nister's Work,* 261–62.

57. Shmeruk, "Der Nister's 'Under a Fence,'" 280.

58. Lunts, "Rodina," in *Literaturnoe nasledie,* 257. My translation.

59. Ibid., 258.

60. Godiner, *Figurn afn rand,* 80.

61. Ibid., 90.

62. Senderovich and Murav, "David Bergelson's *Judgment,*" xxvi.

63. Ibid., xxvii.

64. Israel Joshua Singer, "A briv fun Amerike," *Forverts,* June 7, 1942. Cited in Estraikh, *In Harness,* 32.

65. On the significance of this year in Jewish history in general and in Soviet Yiddish culture in particular, see Diner and Estraikh, *1929: A Year in Jewish History.*

66. Belaia, *Don Kikhoty 20kh godov,* 7.

67. Ibid., 37.

68. Ibid.

69. Dobrenko and Tikhanov, *History of Russian Literary Theory and Criticism,* 44.

70. Ibid., 46.

71. This conflict is described in detail in Estraikh, *In Harness,* 128–34.

72. Dunets, "Oyfn literarishn front," 72.

73. "A mayse mit a grinem man" appeared in *Di royte velt* in 1926; "Tsigayner" in 1927; and "Unter a ployt" in 1929.

74. *Di royte velt* 9 (1929): 189.

75. Ibid., 190.

76. For more details about the critical campaign against Der Nister, see Shmeruk, "Der Nister's 'Under a Fence,'" 266–69.

77. "The Kvitko Affair" is analyzed in detail in Shneer, *Yiddish and the Creation of Soviet Jewish Culture,* 173–76.

78. Estraikh, *Evreiskaia literaturnaia zhizn' Moskvy*, 145–49.

79. Leyb Kvitko, "Derklerung," 195.

80. Dunets, "Oyfn literarishn front," 70.

81. *Di royte velt* 10 (1929): 147.

82. *Di royte velt* 11–12 (1929): 224.

83. Bemporad, "'What Should We Collect?,'" 87.

84. Dunets, "Vegn opegebliakevetn mundir," 141.

85. Quoted in Estraikh, *In Harness*, 130–31.

86. Litvakov, *Af tsvey frontn*, 171.

87. "Partey-baratung baym kiever kreyz-partkom," 87. More on Wiener and Der Nister in 1929 in Krutikov, *From Kabbalah to Class Struggle*, 155–58.

88. More on the interactions between prominent figures in Ukrainian and Yiddish literature in that period in Estraikh, "Yiddish Kultur-Lige," 210–12.

89. Fowler, *Beau Monde*, 85.

90. Der Nister, "Sp'ianilo," ("Shiker," first published in 1926 and included in *Fun mayne giter*, 1928.) To my knowledge, this is the only translation of Der Nister's symbolist tales in the Soviet Union.

91. Fowler, *Beau Monde*, 101.

92. Smolych, "Z 'zapysiv na skhyli viku,'" 171.

93. Ibid., 161.

94. Ibid., 160.

95. Ibid., 162.

96. Opened in 1925, this club was located in the city center and served as "a locus of elite sociability" (Fowler, *Beau Monde*, 74).

97. Smolych, "Z 'zapysiv na skhyli viku,'" 162.

98. Ibid., 164.

99. Ibid., 169.

100. Dobrenko and Tihanov, *History of Russian Literary Theory and Criticism*, 52.

101. For a detailed analysis of this session, see Krutikov, "Learning Stalin's Yiddish."

102. Ibid., 23. On Bronshteyn's reaction to the dissolution of RAPP, see Krutikov and Selemenev, "Yasha Bronshteyn and His Struggle for Control over Soviet Yiddish Literature."

103. Der Nister, "Moskve."

104. Serebriani, "Tsu der problem fun azoygerufenem 'kiever period,'" 154–55.

105. Ibid., 155.

106. Ibid., 166.

107. Ibid., 156.

# TWO

# FROM SYMBOLISM TO REALITY

*Space, Politics, and Self in* Hoyptshtet

THE FIRST BOOK DER NISTER published after the 1929 deba-
cle was the collection *Hoyptshtet* (Capitals). It exemplifies his
departure from the enigmatic and esoteric symbolist style of the
1920s and signals a turn to mainstream Soviet socialist realism.
Its four chapters, written between 1931 and 1933 and published
during those years in Kharkiv's *Di royte velt* and *Shtern*, report
on the progress of Soviet construction projects in five different
locations. Three of the chapters, in keeping with the title, convey
the author's impressions of three capital cities: Kharkiv as the
new capital of Soviet Ukraine, Moscow as the new capital of the
Soviet Union, and Leningrad as the former capital of imperial
Russia. The fourth chapter consists of reportages from a Jewish
agricultural colony in Crimea and the Dunayevtsy shtetl in Podo-
lia, a historic area in southwestern Ukraine. Der Nister spent the
early 1930s trying to find a place in the new centralized structure
of Soviet literature, which took its definitive form with the establishment of the Union of Soviet Writers in 1934. And even though,
as Chone Shmeruk notes, *Hoyptshtet* "did not evoke enthusiasm
among Soviet critics," the fact that the book was published was a
sign of success and recognition.[1]

Unabashedly enthusiastic about the Soviet present and communist future and scathingly critical of the tsarist past, this series

of reportages also offers remarkable intellectual reflections on the sociohistorical role of art and the artist, which is helpful in understanding Der Nister's mind-set during this period. His desire to adjust to the new rules and norms of socialist realism is obvious. Perhaps somewhat less obvious is his elaborate attempt to expand these norms by incorporating elements of fantasy and symbolism into the realist master narrative. Sabine Koller aptly describes his method: "He creates a documentary narrative and carnivalizes it at the same time. He appropriates the officially approved genre using creative devices that were officially stigmatized."[2] As Yuri Smolych recalls, transition to the realistic genre of reportage was not easy for Der Nister, "who had lived his whole previous life in the light of fairy tale, fantasy, and symbolism. But Nister wrote reportages [narysy] not because this genre was in the greatest demand in those years. . . . No, this wasn't what prompted Nister to radically change his literary taste. He delved into the genre of reportage because he was seeking a radical break from his [previous] style as well as his worldview." Der Nister tried to catch up with Soviet literature by mastering the style of "factual literature" (literatura fakta), which was prominent in the 1920s. In hindsight, Smolych interprets this effort as a conscious attempt to "pave the way to realism, which was recognized . . . as the sole true and right style. . . . But his dream was about a novel, a realist novel."[3] Der Nister's situation was not unique in Soviet literature at that time, and it was even more common in Soviet Ukrainian literature. As the literary historian Myroslav Shkandrij points out, "The post-1928 period demanded a fundamental reinterpretation of the nature and function of literature and art." In practice, this meant the rejection of the "autotelic view" that "was accepted by Ukrainian Modernists and Symbolists, for whom literature dealt with symbolic facts, mythical and metaphorical frameworks that rearranged patterns of experience and revealed the world by transcending reality." Instead, "The counterposition that became hegemonic in the thirties stressed the primacy of social function: literature and arts were to serve the party's educational and agitational tasks."[4]

Like his Ukrainian colleagues, Der Nister faced another challenge, which Shkandrij describes as "national difference." Whereas the period of the 1920s in Ukraine can be characterized as "a struggle between Russian centralizing and hegemonic views, on the one hand, and demands for autonomy among national republics, on the other,"[5] the end of the decade saw a radical turn toward administrative centralization and Russian cultural hegemony in Ukraine. The new policy was imposed through public debates with predetermined outcomes, the closing of literary organizations and journals, and, most dramatically, show trials of the Ukrainian intelligentsia. "The most famous of these trials, which took place in 1930, was a kangaroo court staged in a public theatre in Kharkiv. Forty-five Ukrainian academics were accused of belonging to an underground counter-revolutionary organization. . . . The charges were entirely trumped-up and the forced confessions served as pretexts for massive waves of arrests."[6] This trial marked the beginning of Stalinist anti-Ukrainian policy, which culminated in the mass famine of 1932–33. In comparison, the situation of the Yiddish intelligentsia was more secure, but given Der Nister's sensitivity and the intensity of the critical campaign of 1929, he could not have felt particularly safe. As I shall try to demonstrate, the anxiety and fear that he experienced during the early 1930s left discernible traces in his writing of that time.

The result of Der Nister's wrestling with realism may not have been as accomplished artistically as his earlier and later works, but *Hoyptshtet* occupies an important place in the transition from the symbolist tales to Der Nister's magnum opus, the novel *The Family Mashber* (*Di mishpokhe Mashber*, 1939–47). Here, for the first time, Der Nister breaks with the abstract symbolist mode of representation and sets his narrative in real, contemporary Soviet urban and rural settings. No less significant is his engagement with architecture as a meeting site between symbols and reality, both contemporary and historical. Koller describes this collection as a "laboratory between facts and fiction in a transitional period of a symbolist author trying to become a socialist one."[7] It is precisely its experimental character, its stylistic imperfections, and its narrative inconsistencies that reveal Der Nister's painful adjustment to the new reality of Joseph Stalin's dictatorship in Ukraine.

### ALONE IN KHARKIV

Based on what is known about Der Nister after his return to the Soviet Union in 1926, there is little evidence to suggest that he strongly opposed Soviet ideology and practice. He cultivated his enigmatic persona but also resented his marginal position in Soviet literature, which became especially painful after 1934, when the capital of Soviet Ukraine was moved from Kharkiv to Kiev and he found himself stuck in a provincial backwater while most of his more successful colleagues and associates moved to the new capital. But the migration to Kiev had a positive outcome for Der Nister. He was able to move into one of the vacated apartments in the newly built writers' housing cooperative Slovo (Word), where he became neighbors with Yuri Smolych.[8] Smolych recalls:

> I got to love that wonderful old man. One cannot be alone, one needs some soul mate. At that time I felt very lonely, my closest friends had moved to Kiev, and some of them were no longer [Smolych hints at arrests of the Ukrainian intelligentsia during the purges a year or two earlier]. In Nister I found a receptive heart and felt a possibility of a new friendship. . . . We talked a lot about our past—and perhaps it's in conversations about the past, the time of youth and childhood, that friendship and affection begin between people.[9]

Sometime in 1934 Der Nister decided to write a letter to his younger brother Motl, apparently after a long period of silence. Motl, or Max Kaganovitch (1891–1978), as he became known, had briefly studied sculpture in Moscow before immigrating to Berlin in 1920 (where the brothers could have still been in touch). According to his obituaries, he settled in Paris in 1924, where he socialized with Chaim Soutine, Tsuguharu Foujita, and the artistic community at La Ruche. He opened a gallery at Boulevard Raspail around 1930, edited artistic publications, organized exhibitions, consulted wealthy American and Swiss collectors, and eventually moved to Switzerland. In 1973 he donated paintings from his collection by Van Gogh, Monet, Renoir, Pissarro, Cezanne, Gauguin, Vlaminck, and Derain to what would become the Musée d'Orsay, where they are now displayed in a room named after him. Max Kaganovitch also donated paintings to museums in Israel, Switzerland, and Moscow, and his donation to the Pushkin Museum of Fine Arts bought an apartment for Der Nister's widow in Moscow (according to an unverified rumor that I heard in Moscow in the late 1980s). But, as his obituary in the Paris Yiddish newspaper *Naye prese* noted, he had no interest in Jewish life.[10]

Der Nister's letter starts somewhat grudgingly: "Dear Motl, I do not want to apologize for not writing to you all this time.... I would not write to you even now, if it were not for an important issue that forces me to turn to you. It's about myself." (Tayerer Motl, ikh vil zikh nit farentfern far dir, far vos ikh shrayb dir nit di gantse tsayt, vayl ikh kon zikh nit farentfern ... ikh volt oykh itst nit geshribn, ven nit eyne a vikhtike zakh, vos tsvingt mikh tsu dir zikh vendn. S'handlt zikh vegn mir.) Der Nister further explained his predicament: the publishing houses where he could obtain occasional jobs were moving to Kiev. But for him, "Moving to Kiev is out of question because to get an apartment there at this moment is impossible" (forn keyn Kiev iz ummeglekh, vayl a dire dort tsu krign inem itstikn moment iz oysgeshlosn), due to the shortage and high cost of housing. Being away from the new center of publishing meant that he would not get "technical" jobs, which usually went to local residents. He had no other option but to appeal, however reluctantly, to his brother for help. Der Nister further elaborated on his situation in Soviet literature:

> And if you ask: why have I been doing only technical jobs and not writing my own original works? I will answer that what I have written until now is very much unsellable, it's very stale merchandise. There is no place for symbolism in the Soviet Union. And I, as you know, have for all these years been a symbolist. To switch from symbolism to realism for someone like me, who has worked so hard to perfect his method and style of writing, is very difficult. This is not a question of technique—for this, one has to be born anew, one has to turn his soul inside out.
>
> (Az du vest fregn: far vos hob ikh zikh farnumen nor mit tekhnisher arbet un nisht mit shraybn eygene, originele zakhn?—Vel ikh dir entfern, az dos, vos ikh hob geshribn biz aher, iz bay undz itst shtark opgefregt, s'iz zeyer a geshlogn artikl. Simbolizm hot in ratnfarband keyn ort nit. Un ikh, vi dir iz bavust, bin fun ale yorn a simbolist— ibergeyn fun simbolizm tsu realizm iz far a mentshn, vi ikh, velkher hot a sakh gehorevet af tsu farfolkumen zayn metod un oyfn fun shtaybn—zeyer shver. Dos iz nisht keyn frage fun tekhnik, do muz men vi af s'nay geboyrn vern, do muz men iberkern di neshome af di andere zayt.) [11]

As we shall see in chapter 5, at that time Der Nister had already started working on *The Family Mashber*, which began to appear serially in 1935.

## A TRADE LIKE ANY OTHER

The genre of *fartseykhenung*—a literal translation of the Russian term *ocherk*, a form popular in nineteenth- and twentieth-century Russian literature—is a hybrid of the essay and reportage. It is based on the personal impressions of the author, often inspired by a visit somewhere interesting, and often complemented by a certain amount of research or investigation. In Yiddish literature this genre was inaugurated by I. L. Peretz in his *Bilder fun der provintsrayze* (Impressions from a journey to the provinces, 1891), a series of highly subjective sketches from his visit to the Lublin region of Poland as a member of a statistical expedition. The genre of travelogue had become especially popular in Yiddish literature with the development of the Yiddish press during the interwar period, when many prominent writers set off to explore new developments in the Soviet Union, Poland, and Palestine. No less important was the *ocherk* genre in Soviet literature, particularly among socially engaged writers who were sent to various locations to report on the achievements of the new socialist society.[12] The *ocherk* was perceived as a hybrid genre particularly suited to the age of rapid socialist construction. Sergei Tretyakov, one of the champions of factuality in Soviet literature, wrote: "The *ocherk* emerges and stands at the intersection of artistic literature and newspaper journalism. . . . From artistic literature it takes visuality, imagery, plot construction, and from the newspaper—actuality, topicality, concreteness."[13] Tracing the evolution of the *ocherk* genre in Soviet literature, Tretyakov notes further that its flourishing coincides with the first five-year plan, from 1928 to 1932, the same period when Der Nister was trying to catch up with the rapid transformations in Soviet literature.[14] In Ukraine, this was also a period of "stormy development" of the genre of travel reportage, which initiated, as Mykola Waskiw has put it, the "process of self-discovery" in Ukrainian literature. Soviet Ukrainian writers actively engaged in travel writing, feeling the need to "fill out gaps" in the literary representation of their own country and the rest of the world.[15]

Like in other travelogues of that time, we should be careful to distinguish the first-person narrative voice in Der Nister's reportages from the real author, who continues to hide under the newly invented persona of a "Soviet" narrator. An important feature of Der Nister's new style is the reference to other writers and their works, which reveal his sources of artistic inspiration and trace the process of his creative thinking at that critical time. Apart from the last chapter, which is only tangentially related to the main theme of the book, *Hoyptshtet* has few Jewish characters or references. Instead, it is replete with references to Russian and world literature and history—from Fyodor Dostoevsky to Henrich Heine, and from Peter the Great to Vladimir Lenin—which gesture toward the new scope of Der Nister's cultural horizons. His trips to Leningrad and Moscow—evidently sponsored by *Di royte velt,* where his reportages first appeared in 1932–33—signal the adoption of Russian cultural hegemony and the reorientation of the Ukrainian Yiddish elite toward Russia as the custodian of the progressive cultural legacy of all of humanity. This move also helped separate Yiddish from ideologically toxic Ukrainian culture and avoid accusations by association. It also shows that the Ukrainian Yiddish intelligentsia were more politically savvy than their Belarusian colleagues, many of whom fell victim to the purges of 1935–37, accused of Belarusian "bourgeois nationalism." It was more than ten years later that the Yiddish elite from Ukraine suffered a similar fate, during Stalin's last round of persecutions in 1948–53.

Der Nister comes closest to Peretz in his reportage "Eyns a shtetl" (One of the shtetls), which concludes the last chapter of *Hoyptshtet* but was written before the first chapters. Its subject, the transformation of the traditional Jewish shtetl into a Soviet industrial town, is the most "Jewish" piece in the collection. Dated 1931, it exemplifies Der Nister's effort to master the art of a realistic depiction of contemporary Soviet life while still remaining within the geographical borders of Ukraine and the thematic scope of the shtetl-oriented Yiddish literary tradition. Together with a group of reporters from the Kharkiv Yiddish daily *Shtern,* he visited the town of Dunayevtsy, located near the pre-1939 Soviet border with Poland and Romania. Their mission was both to describe the life of a typical Soviet Ukrainian shtetl and to collect statistical data about its residents. At first glance, the shtetl appears to be a modern town, and Der Nister describes it as "even somewhat similar to a big city." One can no longer find here the picturesque "little Chagallesque houses (*hayzelekh-shagal*), with one window higher, the other one lower, like squinting eyes on a face,"[16] which were a signature feature of the traditional shtetl. But the visitor soon discovers that the shtetl consists of two different quarters. The municipal offices and the cloth factory are located in the modern, upper part, while the lower part, populated by impoverished artisans and petty traders, has a desolate look, reminding the narrator of medieval ghettos. Here, streets are narrow, crooked, and incredibly dirty: garbage and excrement is dumped into the streets from the densely built houses, which lack sanitary facilities. The streets are abandoned save for a dogcatcher, accompanied by three boys who are helping him catch strays.

The narrator's visit to collect statistical data from a Jewish family in the lower part of town recalls a similar situation in Peretz's *Bilder*. The house, with a dirty earthen floor and leaking roof, looks as if "the entire year it was a rainy and muddy Hoshano-Rabo day [an autumn Jewish festival]." Inside are half-naked, barefoot children who survive on bread and water. Their "half-idiot" father Beni gets regular beatings from his sister, and their mother's eyes are half closed from trachoma. Before the revolution, Beni was a water carrier who could occasionally afford better food for his children. Now, as a menial worker at the cloth factory, he is worse off economically, although more enthusiastic about his work as part of the factory collective. His worn-out wife describes their miserable living conditions in detail, and then her mother-in-law joins in, complaining that she can barely afford bread by selling matches, candies, and buttons at the dying market. Yet, the narrator assures the reader, even in this kind of family, among the lowest of the low, one can sense the awakening of a new consciousness and a desire for change in the conditions of life.[17] He detects signs of this awakening in the people's critical attitude toward the authorities, who are not doing enough to provide for the town's needs. To illustrate how the new Soviet consciousness has already penetrated the lowest strata of shtetl society, Der Nister returns at the end of his reportage to the figure of the dogcatcher. In the old days, the narrator tells the reader, this was one of the most despised occupations among Jews, but now it has become a respected trade like any other. The shtetl dogcatcher purchased a license from the town council and has a contract with the leather factory, which pays him for the hides according to their size and quality.

It is difficult for us to understand how these naturalistic, often repulsive portrayals of raw reality were perceived by Der Nister's contemporary readers and what they say of his "real" attitude toward Soviet policy. The crudely realistic details, such as the habit of throwing excrement under a neighbor's door or the practice of confiscating soiled women's underwear and selling them in the cooperative shop in lieu of unpaid taxes have a more striking effect on the reader than formulaic declarations of the success of Soviet policy that are not supported by any factual evidence. The narrator explains that the goal of his visit was to learn what was happening to the neglected, old-time, petty-bourgeois Jewish types, for whom the Soviet regime "had already said Kaddish," and who had been "chewed and spit out" by Soviet literature.[18] Similarly, the modern urban writer Peretz set off in 1890 from Warsaw "to see what's going on in the shtetls."[19] Indeed, the figure of the old market woman eking out a meager living by selling bric-a-brac and the depiction of shtetl Jews in the main square gaping at the urban visitors who have come to collect statistics have close parallels in Peretz's travelogue.

Is Der Nister practicing some kind of subversive writing between the lines by hinting that he, like Peretz, is skeptical about the effect of modernity on Jewish life? Is he using repulsive naturalistic details as an artistic device to subvert official Soviet rhetoric and expose its shallowness? Analyzing the similar transformation of Ukrainian modernists "who had been educated on revolt and iconoclasm" into "conforming political instruments" during the late 1920s and early 1930s, Shkandrij emphasizes the tension between "overt" forms of propaganda and "covert," subconscious, or spontaneous artistic responses to reality. He lists a number of prominent works of Ukrainian literature and art "with ambiguous and subversive messages," and Der Nister's reportage from Dunayevtsy can be placed within this category.[20] To keep the broader context in mind, we should remember that one year after Der Nister's visit, Dunayevtsy, like the rest of Soviet Ukraine, was decimated by the Holodomor, a famine engineered by the Soviet regime and aimed predominantly at the Ukrainian peasantry. Compared to those horrors, the misery in the Jewish shtetl appears mild, but Der Nister, like other Soviet Yiddish writers, seems to have completely ignored this tragedy in his reportages. Thus, even if he attempted to be subversive and critical of the regime's policies, his audacity had clear limits. He could be critical of local authorities but would not touch the policies and practices of the Communist Party. To better understand the complexity of Der Nister's writing, we should perhaps avoid reading it through clear-cut ideological binaries and assume that he, like some of the Russian modernists of that time, such as Andrei Platonov or Isaac Babel, was excited by the grandiosity of the Soviet utopian project but also terrified by the destructive effects of its implementation. Der Nister's attempts to master the realist style reveal the inner struggle and anxiety occasioned by trying to identify with both the victim and the executioner.

## CRIMEA: BUILDING UTOPIA IN THE STEPPE

Beginning in the early nineteenth century, the Russian government tried, without much success, to make Jews "productive" by settling them in the newly annexed territories of what is today southern Ukraine. During the 1920s and early 1930s, the Soviet government pursued a similar policy, only with more vigor and efficiency. A number of public organizations and government agencies, with substantial material support from foreign sponsors, encouraged Jews to migrate from the decaying shtetls of Belarus and Ukraine to designated rural areas, first in the steppes of the Crimean Peninsula, and later in the Birobidzhan area in the Far East. The collectivization policy, which was violently enforced from 1929 on, had a somewhat-less-violent impact on Jewish farmers in Crimea, where Jewish colonies received support from the United States and enjoyed some degree of autonomy. As Jonathan Dekel-Chen notes in his study of Jewish agricultural colonization in the Soviet Union, "While collectivization yielded gradual political penetration, it certainly did not establish control over daily routines in the colonies."[21]

As part of his reeducation as a realist writer, in 1931 Der Nister joined a group of journalists on a tour of some of the newly created Jewish collective farms in Crimea, at that time an autonomous republic within the Russian Soviet Federative Socialist Republic, to report on their successes. In *Hoyptshtet* these reportages form the two first sections of the last chapter, preceding "Eyns a shtetl." The first section, "Shnit" (Harvest), is an upbeat depiction of the joint effort of local farmers and city dwellers sent to assist with the harvest. Der Nister's representation is based on a stark contrast between the progressive city and the backward countryside. He enthusiastically reports how "urban culture begins to conquer the steppe" as a result of the new Soviet policy of industrialization and collectivization.[22] On the way to the Jewish settlement, he observes a newly organized Tatar collective farm, which he contrasts to the "dark nest" of a traditional village, where the figure of a Tatar woman carrying a child reminds him of the biblical story of Hagar and Ishmael. This peculiar association is potentially ambiguous, as it not only indicates the backwardness of the Crimean "natives" but also may hint at their expulsion by the (Jewish) newcomers, just as Hagar was expelled by Abraham at Sarah's request. After the Tatar communist leadership was

removed in Crimea in 1927–28, the new Russified leadership of
Crimea "conformed entirely to directives from Moscow, and the
peninsula was among the nation's leaders in the proportional rates
of dekulakization and collectivization."[23] Yet it remains unclear,
as in so many other instances, whether Der Nister's ambiguity is
deliberate.

The narrator assures his reader that local peasants will eventually have to "give up their backwardness and stubbornness
because . . . a new wind blows from the steppe" (veln muzn fun
zeyer opgeshtanenkayt un akshones nokhgebn, vayl . . . a nayer
vint kumt funem step).[24] As we shall see, the cliché of the "new
wind from the steppe" will evolve in Der Nister's narrative into a
symbolic image of grand proportions, evoking his darkest symbolist fantasies of the 1920s. Der Nister portrays the Jewish farmers as former urban dwellers who have a hard time adjusting to
the new rural conditions. But their experience of collective labor
on the land has not only deeply transformed their personalities
but also their language. The first-person singular pronouns I and
my were gradually giving way to the plural forms we and our.[25]
Upon his arrival at the Jewish agricultural colony, the narrator
meets a team of students from the Moscow Yiddish Theater Company who have come to help with the harvest. During the day the
young actors work in the fields, and at night they perform for the
farmers in a large cow barn. Looking at their joyful enthusiasm,
the narrator imagines a "stranger" (fremder) who would not be
able to grasp the relationship between the city and the village
represented by the actors in the cow barn. The imaginary stranger
would wonder what theater has to do with the harvest, or "the
great culture with the peasant" (groys-kultur mit poyer). This
figure of an imaginary stranger brings to mind the formalist concept of "defamiliarization" (ostranenie), which was introduced by
Viktor Shklovsky in his seminal 1917 essay "Art as Technique"
and of which Der Nister may have been aware. For Shklovsky,
defamiliarization was an essential feature of poetic language that

differentiated it from ordinary speech. In Der Nister's writing, a reference to the imaginary stranger can signal a switch from the "ordinary" realist mode of narration to fantasy. This figure will later reappear in *The Family Mashber* as an artistic device that enables the author to justify the split between two narrative voices, a *bona fide* socialist realist and a "defamiliarized" symbolist "stranger."

The visiting Yiddish theater company helps the collective farmers to adjust to their new situation by bringing "a greeting from the city, a reminder of culture, a relief and a reward for the sense of estrangement and separation."[26] The night performance by the Moscow company merges theater with reality. The actors draw inspiration from laboring with the farmers in the fields. On the makeshift barn stage, they present to their audience not only the positive but also the negative aspects of the collectivization process. They vividly impersonate loafers, saboteurs, and class enemy agents, as well as conscientious laborers and communist functionaries who unmask and fight the enemy. This staged performance of the class struggle prompts the audience to start a self-purging process among themselves. Following the play, the difference between the stage and the stalls disappears as the viewers begin arguing and accusing each other.[27] Remarkably, as the narrator points out, after a sleepless night spent watching the play and performing the purge, the next day the farmers of that village are the first to come out to the fields and work with greater alacrity than the others. The ritual of mutual accusation and persecution, first observed on stage and later performed by the audience, appears to have a mobilizing and exhilarating effect on the farmers' collective. It was precisely this bringing together of performers and spectators in an act of social unification that was promoted by the theorists of "factual literature." Tretyakov proposed that "genuine 'art for all'" should not aim to turn its audience into spectators but rather empower them to acquire the "skills of building and organizing raw material which have been a particular property of the specialists in the arts."[28] He identified two "commanding heights" of contemporary Soviet dramaturgy: "authenticity of representation and topical social relevance."[29]

Collectivization was a prominent theme in the Soviet literature and art of that time. In Ukraine, the main event in the theater season of 1929–30 was the production of *Dictatorship*, a play by Ivan Mykytenko, an ambitious former medical student who personally participated in collectivization and the "liquidation of the kulaks as a class," to use the official Soviet formula of the time. The performance of *Dictatorship* in Kiev involved the active participation of the audience. According to some reports, "Apparently, actors tossed 'Get the Grain' signs out into the audience as a way of involving them in grain collections and underscoring the contemporary relevance of the play."[30] In Kharkiv, the production of *Dictatorship* by Les Kurbas created a scandal because of its use of avant-garde effects: "Kurbas reduced the power of Mykytenko's writing, and increased the power of theatrical image.... It was no longer the text on the scene with the kulaks, but rather the image of the kulaks towering over their property that reached the audience." However, as Mayhill Fowler suggests, Kurbas's innovations did not subvert the message of the play and turn a "pro-collectivization drama" into an "anti-collectivization drama."[31] Der Nister's description of the play staged in the Crimea colony resembles the drama "Der step brent" (The Steppe Is on Fire) by the Ukrainian Yiddish writer Avorm Vevyorke. It was indeed staged by Efraim Loyter, the director of the Kharkiv Jewish theater who was also the director of the actors' school at the Moscow State Yiddish Theater (GOSET), around 1930. Judging by Der Nister's depiction of the night performance at the collective farm, Yiddish actors also used elements of avant-garde theater to convey the cruel political message in the most vivid and dramatic form. Today, this episode appears terrifying, but it reveals an important and often neglected aspect of totalitarian regimes, namely, the use of terror to consolidate the masses and stimulate their enthusiasm for work.

The optimistic mood changes in the second section of the chapter, "A nakht mit a tog" (A night with a day). After the night performance, the next morning the narrator with a group of journalists meets some elderly Jews who do not fit into the cheerful picture. A lonely bookkeeper in the dairy barn, happy to have someone to talk to, tells him the sad story of his ruined life. Formerly a happy and well-off family man, he lost everything during the civil war pogroms by Ukrainian nationalist gangs. Now he lives and works in the barn, together with the cows. To the question of whether he still prays, he responds with a smile: "No, I've got even with the Lord of the Universe. He owes me nothing, I owe him nothing."[32] Unable to find a place for his guests to sleep in the barn full of swarms of stinging flies, he directs them to the nearby school building, which turns out to be infested with fleas. Eventually the narrator and his colleagues find refuge in the school director's office and sleep through the morning. In the meantime, the weather changes dramatically, and a strong wind from the steppe brings scorching heat and dust, which covers the village and makes it look like the grave of a settlement that once stood in its place.[33] Der Nister's striking description of the dust storm evokes imagery from his symbolist tales, in which the hero suddenly finds himself in a surreal landscape as part of the spiritual test, whereby he has to undergo a painful bodily transformation. The sinister Dustman figure appeared in Der Nister's last symbolist tale, "Under a Fence" (Unter a ployt), as an agent of evil who convinces the hermit protagonist to burn down a monastery, lures him into the circus, and stages a mock trial for his former fellow hermits at which, as Roskies puts it, "to the hysterical delight of the crowd," the hermit "outdoes the rest in ridicule."[34] This association may be of limited purchase as a potential value judgment of the Soviet policy of collectivization, but it helps us understand the internal workings of Der Nister's creative imagination as he transitioned from symbolism to realism.

Unable to keep his eyes open because of the terrible heat (another folkloric symbolist motif indicating the character's failure to stand the test), the narrator envisions people wrapped in furs on a sleigh, desperately lashing a horse that refuses to move, "and the people in the sleigh don't look like people anymore, but like inflated humped bundles covered with snow" (di mentshn in shlitn zeen shoyn vi keyn mentshn nit oys, nor vi farshneyte un farblozene klumkes ayngehorbete).[35] His confusion is so deep that when he hears people remark that the temperature is close to seventy degrees, he is unable to understand whether it is below or above zero. Farmers returning from the fields have deformed faces as if lashed by the "heat whip" (hits-baytsh).[36] Although this symbolist imagery and the physically impossible figure of 70 degrees Celsius may suggest that the narrator's experience is a fantasy, the ending of the story is completely mundane.

One of the farmers who comes back from the fields turns out to be the narrator's former neighbor from K. (Kiev), Shneyer, who once had a shop at the busy corner of Gershuni Street (named after of the famous Jewish leader of the socialist-revolutionary terrorist organization, the street was renamed in 1937) and Great Zhitomirskaya Street. This address can offer us a clue to Der Nister's location in Kiev after his return from Berlin. In 1926, when the Soviet state was bringing the New Economic Policy to a close by drastically increasing the taxation of private enterprises, Shneyer realized that his business had no future. At first he did not want to give up, imagining himself a modern Jacob wrestling with the angel of the Soviet regime, but, unlike his biblical counterpart, he was defeated. He underwent a profound ideological transformation and became a respected member of the collective farm. Referring to a popular Soviet allegory of that time, the narrator associates the heat wave with the "fire of the revolution," which burnt off bourgeois dross and forged new "human metal"[37] out of the old petty bourgeois material. However, the narrator manages to sleep through the heat storm and thus avoids the painful remolding experience himself. The story ends on an ironic note with a touch of obscenity. The narrator is told, the collective farm's bull had once stopped doing his job impregnating cows. When the veterinarian who was called did not show up, Shneyer crawled under the bull, identified the problem, and "greased and healed the member" (im geshmirt un dem eyver oysgeheylt).[38] Again, as on previous occasions, the reader is left with ambiguity. Does this "low" ending subvert the heroic story of transforming a "parasite" into a "productive element of socialist society"? What are we to make of the somewhat jarring transitions between symbolism, naturalism, and social realism? Is this an indication of Der Nister's difficulties in mastering a new way of writing, or, as some contemporary scholars suggest, are we to look for deeper, encoded, subversive meanings aimed at the attentive insider reader versed in Der Nister's enigmatic style?

## FROM COUNTRYSIDE TO METROPOLIS: KHARKIV, A CAPITAL *EX NIHILO*

With Der Nister's focus moving from shtetls and villages to big cities, Jewish themes and characters fade into the narrative periphery. Der Nister sees the city as a stage where the major historical forces of progress and decline face off, keenly observing the material reflections of historical development on the urban space. Rapidly developing Kharkiv offered him a good vantage point for seeing the future through the lens of the newly constructed space. In 1919, Kharkiv became the first capital of the Ukrainian Soviet Republic, rather than Kiev, then still the capital of the independent Ukrainian People's Republic. Situated in the eastern part of Ukraine, closer to the borders of the Russian Federation and farther from the border with Poland than Kiev, Kharkiv was also regarded as less nationalist and more proletarian. Although it was located outside the Jewish Pale of Settlement before 1917, it had a significant and relatively prosperous Jewish population and boasted one of the largest synagogues in the Russian Empire, built in the eclectic modernist style by the St. Petersburg architect Yakov Gevirts in 1913; in 1923 it was closed and converted into a Jewish workers club. When Der Nister moved to Kharkiv after his return from Berlin and a brief sojourn in Kiev, he, like many other newcomers, found himself in a situation described by Olga Bertelsen in her study of the writer's housing cooperative Slovo, where Der Nister would eventually move: "The competition for working and living space in Kharkiv was fierce in the 1920s. In 1927, the population in Kharkiv increased from 155,000 to 409,000 people. According to the calculations of Kharkiv statisticians, the average living space was 5.7 square meters per person, which constituted approximately two-thirds of the space needed to be considered sanitary. Most people shared communal flats that were wildly overpopulated. Sheds, summer houses, cellars, and attics were inhabited by several families each."[39] The immense scope and breathtaking speed of the city's transformation make Der Nister's narrator dizzy:

> And in my head there is a disordered hodgepodge of different images from different ages, and analogies and comparisons between then and now suggest themselves, and the times of Catherine II come to my mind, and right next to them the Tractor Factory for instance, and I want to compare them but there is no comparison.
>
> (Un in kop mishn zikh mir in umordenung farsheydene bilder fun farsheydene epokhes, un analogies betn zikh un farglaykhungen fun amol mitn haynt, un s'kumt mir Ekaterine der tsveyters tsaytn afn zinen, un bald take—trakterboy, lemoshl, un ikh vil farglaykhn un s'iz fort keyn farglaykh nit.)[40]

Kharkiv's prerevolutionary past was utterly unremarkable. Der Nister ridicules the inability of the tsarist government and local administration, from the time of Catherine II on, to turn it into a city of any significance. But out of what Der Nister calls "garbage" (*mist*), the Soviet regime is able to build a truly modern, future-oriented capital for the new Soviet Ukraine after the defeat of its enemies in a bloody civil war.[41]

Der Nister describes the miraculous emergence of the metropolis as a new creation conjured ex nihilo by fiat of the Communist Party, paraphrasing the kabbalistic concept *yesh me-ayin*: "how from nothing becomes something" (vi fun a nisht vert a yesh).[42] Construction is going on around the clock under electric lights, which invert the laws of nature by turning night into day. The magnetic power of the new city pulls in people from surrounding areas, "so that entire provincial shtetlekh have moved here, and the provinces have built their colonies here" (un azoy hobn gantse provints-shtetlekh aher ibergevandert, un azoy hobn provintsn gantse do kolonies gebildet).[43] The architectural centerpiece of the futuristic city is the grandiose complex of Gosprom buildings situated around the large main square.

This most ambitious and original project of Soviet constructivism, at that time the tallest building in the Soviet Union and one of the tallest in Europe, served as the seat of the Soviet government of Ukraine and was inaugurated on the eleventh anniversary of the October Revolution in 1928. The narrator especially appreciates the novelty of the constructivist style: "It is good that the buildings that now make you especially happy are the kind without past and without tradition." (Gut, vos dafke azoyne binyonim on nekhtn un on traditsyes makhn dikh itst freyen.)[44] Another structure on the same square, the still-unfinished building of the Central Committee of the Communist Party of Ukraine, appears to him as a giant musical instrument containing "rare melodies" within its walls (di muzik un zeltene melodies in zayne vent bahaltn), which is another variation on the theme of architecture as a repository of the future.

The imposing vision of Kharkiv's new central square reminds the narrator of the party purges. As in "Shnit," the Kharkiv purges are portrayed as a staged public show. But this time they appear more like a festive ritual than an improvised trial, a ritualized public confession by party members before large, enthusiastic crowds. Notwithstanding some minor obligatory criticism, the purge ritual is described as a celebration of the heroism of venerable communists. A remarkable episode occurs when a man with a scar on his forehead appears onstage, and the audience enthusiastically greets him, yelling *zhid*. At first, this sounds like a derogatory word meaning "Jew" that was banned from Soviet discourse. But it turns out that during the civil war this man was captured with other Red Army soldiers by Simon Petlyura's Ukrainian nationalist army. When the Jews were ordered to step aside from the others, he, although not a Jew, joined his Jewish comrades. The enraged captors cut the word *zhid* on his forehead, and since that time it had been his honorary nom de guerre. This episode may have had some basis in reality, but it also alludes to the well-known story "Der tseylem" (The cross) by the American Yiddish writer Lamed Shapiro, in which the Jewish protagonist bore on his forehead the sign of the cross that was cut by the pogromists.[45] In both cases, the symbolic word-scar on the character's face has a transforming impact on his personality. It makes Der Nister's Zhid a more loyal communist, while Shapiro's hero becomes determined to seek vengeance against antisemites.

Der Nister allegorically likens the massive construction sites of socialist industry to new altars or temples where the future is being forged. The use of religious symbolism allows him to highlight the contrast between the past and the present. Under Catherine's rule, construction was done by slaves for their masters, akin to the pagan fetish worship of wood and stone in ancient Egypt. By contrast, the narrator sees communist construction as a religious ritual of "self-worship by the masses, who have lived up to new needs and requirements of their own" (zelbstfarerung fun groyse masn, vos zaynen tsu eygene groyse naye foderungen un baderfenishn dervaksn).[46] That ambiguous combination of self-worship and self-sacrifice produced new creations with new names, such as TsK (Central Committee) or Traktorboy (Tractor Factory).[47] Hinting at the kabbalistic belief in the mystical power of permutations of letters, Der Nister adds that these newly invented abbreviations instilled unease in the enemies of the Communist Party, while providing solace to its friends. And to safeguard himself from suspicions of smuggling symbolism in through the back door, Der Nister indicates that the narrator is not quite sober while indulging in this religious symbolism. The motif of drinking was common in Der Nister's symbolist tales, such as "Shiker" (The drunk) in which, as Delphine Bechtel argues, alcohol "is both an instrument of degradation and a means of elevation."[48] As we shall see, in the apparently realistic portrayal in "Kharkiv," Der Nister uses the device of an intoxicated narrator as license for a fantastic vision that includes a very literal elevation.

After having a few drinks to celebrate the fourteenth anniversary of the October Revolution (that is, November 7, 1931), the narrator strikes up a conversation with a policeman guarding the empty new square, telling him about a peculiar surreal vision he had one night. He describes seeing the giant Gosprom complex, with the participants of the purges standing on its roofs, slowly rise like a dirigible, float over the peacefully sleeping fields, woods, and villages of Ukraine, and alight next to St. Sophia's Cathedral in Kiev's central square. As a welcoming gesture, St. Sophia's Cathedral offers its domes to the guests for them to play with. The passengers, Zhid among them, take out straws and begin to blow soap bubbles, which grow into the domes of the cathedral. Each one of those bubble domes contains a clergyman of a certain rank. When one of the guests coughs, the bubbles begin to burst one after the other, together with the clerics that they contain, metaphorically reenacting the collapse of the old regime.[49] To console Kiev for the loss of its beautiful golden domes, the guests advise her to look forward, not backward. In a fairy-tale gesture, they cast a fishing net into the Dnieper River three times. The first two catches dredge up scraps from the ancient, medieval, and more recent prerevolutionary past, while the third one lands a "golden fish of the future with plenty of promise" (a tsukunft-fishele, a fil-tsuzogndiks). In the name of Kiev, St. Sophia's Cathedral thanks the guests for remembering their older relative, and the entire Gosprom crew sets off again, in order to be back in Kharkiv in time for the diligent office workers arriving at work in the morning.[50] The fantastic adventure ends mundanely enough exactly where it started: "Here we are, Comrade policeman, and you are again at your post, and I am still a little . . . haven't quite sobered up." (Un ot zaynen mir gekumen, khaver militsioner, un du bist oyf dayn post vider, un ikh nokh alts abisl . . . nokh nisht ingantsn oysgenikhtert.)[51]

This odd vision, the narrator explains (apparently sober), should not seem so strange, because now, when radio and airplanes are familiar to every village boy, "No novelty is a novelty anymore." (Itst zaynen keyne khidushim keyn khidushim.) Therefore, he wonders, "Can such a gigantic construction, an entire street of buildings, with twelve- and fourteen-floor buildings connected through corridors that look like long train cars, also float in the air?" (Kon shoyn oykh aza makhine, a gantser gasn-binyen, mit moyern, mit tsvelf- un fertsn- shtokike korpusn, mit koridorn, vos zeen oys vi lange tsug-vagones, velkhe fareynikn a korpus mit a korpus, inderluftn flien?)[52] The association between drunkenness and flying was not uncommon for Der Nister's symbolist writing. In "Shiker" (The drunk), the drunken protagonist split into two doubles, one of whom, called Gilgl (reincarnation of soul), at some point appears to swing between the sky and the earth on a giant swing. In "Kharkiv" this surrealist vision is embedded in an apparently realist narrative of a reportage.

The imaginary meeting between the two signature buildings of the new and the old capital—the Gosprom building and St. Sophia's Cathedral—symbolically represent an encounter between the future and the past. The bizarre visit by air of the Gosprom building to the cathedral and the ritualistic exchange of presents can be regarded as a parody of the Christian pilgrimage ritual. Kiev, as Taras Koznarsky explains, "in some years

attracted as many as a hundred thousand visitors . . . all eager
to see holy churches and relics and acquire blessings and abso-
lutions from sins, as well as souvenirs." Pilgrims approaching
the city envisioned it as "standing as if in the air or in the sky,"
and this experience of Kiev, "repeated and amplified by others,
became the key element of perception of the city and the most
reproductive textual model, generating future encounters, dis-
coveries, and expectations."[53] Der Nister's exuberant fantasy adds
to this imagery the magic fish motif from Alexander Pushkin's
"Tale of the Fisherman and the Fish," merging both with the
avant-garde project of flying cities envisioned by the early Soviet
architects and artists of the suprematist school, such as Lazar
Khidekel and Nikolai Ladovskii. Ladovskii's disciple, Georgii
Krutikov, presented a design for a flying city as his diploma project at the Higher Institute of Technical Art (VKhUTEIN) in
1928, which caused a stir among his examiners.

Kiev—which became the capital of Soviet Ukraine in 1934,
regaining its historic status—reemerges in the 1936 reportage
"Me tantst oyf di gasn" (Dancing in the streets) in the Kharkiv
Yiddish newspaper *Shtern*. Der Nister depicts the public celebration of the fifteenth anniversary of the liberation from Polish
occupation and the final establishment of the Soviet regime in
1920. The city has changed beyond recognition: "It looks as if
someone has infused something under its skin, nudging it out
of its previous state and making it pulsate much faster." (S'zet
oys vi emetser volt ir arunter gelozt unter der hoyt epes azoyns,
vos hot zi a rir geton fun ir fryerdikn tsushtand un zi gemakht
pulsirn fil hastiker.) At the same time, people's movement is
well-ordered and self-regulated: "They already know when and
where to cross the street, and when and for whom to wait. The
crowd regulates its own traffic, waiting for no one, neither for the
policeman's warning nor for someone's instructions." (Men veyst
shoyn, vu un ven di gasn ibertsugeyn, ven un vemen ibertsuvartn.
Der oylem regulirt shoyn aleyn zayn farker, nisht vartndik

oyf keynem, nisht oyf vorenungen fun militsionern, nisht oyf keynems onvayzung.) It appears from this description that the ordinary residents of the city have already internalized the new rules and follow them with joy and enthusiasm. Kiev streets have changed their names and appearances. Streetcar tracks have been removed from Kiev's main thoroughfare, Khreshchatyk, which between 1923 and 1937 was called Vorovsky Street after the Soviet diplomat assassinated in Switzerland in 1923, and "the street has gained both in length and in width, in its perspective and its broadness" (di gas hot gevunen i in der leng, i in der breyt, in ir perspective, vi in ir rakhves), so that all streets stream into it like rivers from the hills, unlike streets in any other city. The public celebration carries from early morning till late into the night.[54]

As he watches people dance in the streets, the narrator recalls the years he spent abroad:

> I have never seen such joy among the masses. After the war [World War I] all joy completely vanished. Their dances were the dances of the dead. In our country, people dance not to forget themselves but, on the contrary, to recall the memories of the years of struggle and suffering.
>
> (Keyn mol nit gezen aza freyd bay masn. Nokh der milkhome iz di freyd in gantsn oysgerunen. Zeyere tents—meysim-tents. Bay undz tantst men nit kdey zikh tsu fargesn, nor farkert, kdey zikh tsu dermonen un aroysrufn in zikorn di kamf- un layd-yorn.)

The spectacle of street dancing reminds the narrator of the time he spent in Kiev during the difficult years of the revolution and the civil war, when the city was plundered by various armies and gangs, and Khreshchatyk was "half-dead." One image from that time has stuck in his memory: "A fiddler, half-madman half-beggar, preoccupied with his 'playing' and not expecting any alms, but captivated by his 'art,' starts singing and dancing with fervor. . . . Inspired and entranced by himself, by his own immersion, and by his ability to extract such terribly wondrous sounds from his fiddle." (A halb-duler halb-betler, farnumen mit zayn 'shpiln,' nit gevart oyf nedoves, nor di 'kunst' hot im farkhapt, ongehoybn tsu zingen, untergetantst mit bren. . . . Farkhapt, bagaystert fun zikh aleyn, fun zayn eygener fartifkayt un fun aroyshern fun zayn fidl azoyne beyzvunder.) The narrator was attracted to this strange figure who managed to forget himself amid the surrounding misery, and the two impressions, the "madman on the sidewalk" and the "air of robbery" (royb-luft) of that day, complemented each other perfectly, like two expressions of the same insanity (umzinikeyt). Now the same spot is occupied by a band of jolly young musicians who have no recollection of that time. They are celebrating a different occasion, the relocation of the capital to Kiev and the restoration of the city's "material and spiritual abundance" (materialer un gaystiker shefe).[55]

Soviet people appear in this description as a self-disciplined, happy, and amnesiac collective devoid of any sense of individuality and privacy. Ironically, in this jubilant celebration of the anniversary of the city's liberation, the narrator, presumably a visitor from Kharkiv, is the only one who actually remembers the past, which for him is associated with the memory of the lonely deranged fiddler. While the narrator admires the rejuvenated Soviet city, he remains mentally attached to his past experiences of surviving the war and exile. In his description, the complete absorption of the individual self into the new Soviet collectivity sharply contrasts with the equally complete loneliness and self-absorption of the street player. The symbolism of this image is accentuated by its likeness to the iconic fiddler figure in Marc Chagall's painting The Fiddler, a hint that probably would not escape the attention of those readers who, like Der Nister, still remembered the pre-Soviet period (the possibility of that association is supported by Der Nister's reference to Chagall in the depiction of Dunayevtsy discussed above). It is worth noting, however, that the Jewishness of the fiddler is not mentioned; indeed, the word Jew does not appear in the entire reportage.

As Der Nister remarks in a footnote, "Kharkiv" was written in 1931–32, before the capital was moved to Kiev. In retrospect, his enthusiasm regarding Kharkiv's constructivist utopia appears misplaced, especially considering his bitter complaints to his brother concerning the provincial atmosphere in Kharkiv after 1934. Even less appropriate for 1934 was his enthusiasm for the new Soviet Ukrainian culture, which by that time had already been crushed by Stalin, who had most of its leading figures arrested and executed a few years later. But perhaps most inexplicable is the enthusiastic representation of purges as a ritual of collective purification and renewal, which appears in a number of Der Nister's works during the 1930s.[56] The uncanny mutation of the torturous and alienating experience of the hermit's trial in "Under a Fence" into a joyous perfromance of collective affirmation of communist commitment brings to mind an association with Nikolai Evreinov's extravagant concept of the origins of modern theater from "scaffold," the spectacle of public execution, which could have influenced Der Nister, as discussed in the introduction. But it is puzzling from a contemporary perspective and raises difficult questions. Was Der Nister's upbeat enthusiasm a form of sarcasm, perhaps a way of secretly communicating with likeminded readers over the heads of ideological censorship? Or did he genuinely commit to the communist ideal and socialist-realist aesthetics as a result of some sort of self-purging? Or perhaps his response was some bizarre combination of both possibilities. Leaving the moral problem aside, it seems that Der Nister was fascinated by the aesthetic aspect of the public exposure, trial, and execution. He would depict these acts even in his poetry for children, as we shall see in the next chapter.

This dilemma has not only moral, aesthetic and psychological dimensions but also a spatial one in the realm of Der Nister's imagination, which can be helpful in understanding the complexity of his worldview after 1929. The new Soviet metropolis of Kharkiv is radically different from the urban settings in the late symbolist tales that Der Nister wrote after his return to the Soviet Union. There, as Bechtel notes, "Modernity revolves around the urban world, which strangely coexists with the marvelous world of the tale," and "the hero is often confronted with the masses that populate the modern city."[57] The symbolist city appeared as a monstrous apocalyptic space dominated by uncontrollable crowds: "There is an inflation, a swelling, and multiplication of everything."[58] By contrast, the masses in the new Soviet metropolis are engaged in a well-organized productive process of building a bright future. Whereas "Kharkiv" includes a purely fantastic episode, this is a different kind of fantasy from the symbolist tales. Rather than being "tortured, sick, and pathological," fantasy appears happy and uplifting, both in a figurative and literal sense. Pain, humiliation, and torture, which were the key methods of the Stalinist terror, are masked as a joyous and purifying public ritual. The symbolic act of transferring power from the old capital to the new one is envisioned as an exchange of gifts between their respective architectural symbols: St. Sophia's Cathedral and Gosprom. The bursting of St. Sophia's bubbled domes with assorted clerics inside can perhaps be interpreted metaphorically as the ultimate collapse of the symbolist mode of storytelling,[59] while the arrival of the strictly rectangular constructivist Gosprom can signify the triumph of socialist realism. The increasingly complex and arcane style of the late symbolist tales gives way to the direct and simple narration of *Hoyptshtet*. And yet, we should not forget that this grandiose vision is nothing more than the delirious fantasy of a lonely drunkard, a familiar figure from Der Nister's symbolist tales.

## LENINGRAD: THE MUSEUM OF THE IMPERIAL PAST

The relocation of Ukraine's capital to Kiev was one of the indications of the conservative turn toward restoration of certain imperial features in Soviet life and politics, which had a

significant effect on Der Nister's writings of the 1930s. In "Leningrad," the second chapter of *Hoyptshtet*, history becomes the
main theme of his writing for the first time. The Russian Empire,
in the guise of the corpulent equestrian statue of Alexander III,
greets the narrator upon his arrival at the October Train Station.[60] The description of that remarkable monument sets the
tone for Der Nister's critical exploration of Russia's imperial past
through the rich landscape of its former capital. For Der Nister,
the statue represents the tsar as "a typical assistant policeman
[*pristav-gehilf*], or a gendarme . . . with the broad comic bottom
of a coachman, which could easily . . . be swapped with his face."
In short, he concludes, "Even its worst enemy could not imagine
a better caricature of autocracy."[61] Der Nister contrasts *Alexander
III* with the famous *Bronze Horseman*, the monument to Peter
the Great, interpreting them as two sculptural bookends of the
imperial period, its early dynamism and later stagnation. This
interpretation was popular among the Russian intelligentsia of
the early twentieth century: "The monuments were perceived as
symbols of the beginning and the end of the St. Petersburg period of Russian history," notes Vladimir Piskunov in his analysis
of space in Andrei Bely's *Petersburg*, a novel that, as I will try to
demonstrate, can be seen as a symbolist foil to Der Nister's "Leningrad."[62] Peter's monument represents the tsar as the personifica-
tion of historical momentum: "Apart from the personal features
of the horseman, the artist has also conveyed here, consciously
or not, the appearance of his young historical class, his wild
expression, his drive to conquer new land and sea routes for trade
with Europe and the world." (Der kinslter hot do—bavust oder
umbavust far zikh aleyn—oyser di perzenle eygnshaft fun rayter,
oykh dem oysdruk fun zayn yung-geshikhtlekhn klas gegebn—
zayn vilde ekspresye, zayn shtrebn tsu velt- un eyrope-handl, tsu
naye yaboshe- un vaser-vegn derobern.)[63] Der Nister's interpretation of Peter's historical role followed the theory of Mikhail
Pokrovskii, the leading authority on Soviet Marxist history up

to the mid-1930s. Pokrovskii's popular book, *Russian History in a Brief Survey,* appeared in several editions, including a Yiddish translation. According to Pokrovskii, Peter's reforms were driven by the energy of Russia's young and vigorous commercial capital, which sought access to new European markets. As a result of Peter's victory over Sweden in 1721, the "mechanism" of the Romanov Empire took its final shape as a "combination of two powers, serf labor and trade capital."[64] Peter's historical role was therefore progressive for the age of emerging merchant capitalism, but that brief period of growth was followed by a long decline of the ruling classes of the Russian Empire.

Unlike Kharkiv, where the past was all but absent from the city's space, Leningrad's streets and neighborhoods are inhabited by ghosts from the tsarist period belonging both to the oppressors and the oppressed. Local residents avoid the formerly aristocratic neighborhood near the Winter Palace, especially at night. It is the favorite haunt of ghosts from the *oylem-hatoyhu* (the Hebrew term for the world of chaos where the souls of the dead must wander until they atone for misdeeds and earn their place in heaven).[65] In the opinion of Der Nister's narrator, the city center ought to be turned into a museum, "because one cannot think of it otherwise" (vayl andersh vi a muzey kont ir zi nit denken).[66] In this dark and eerie part of the city, the ghosts of political prisoners held in the Peter and Paul Fortress across the Neva confront the nobility dancing gaily at balls in the palaces on the embankment. The restless "shadows" of the past hide among the architectural details of the buildings: "They are wandering, and one can see them appear on the roofs, walking between the roofs and building entrances, looking down from cornices, friezes, masks, roof vases, stairs, and balconies." (Zey ruen nit, ot di shotns. Zey lebn umvandlerish un me ken zey, dakht zikh, oft af di dekher zen, fun eyn dakh afn andern umshpatsirn, fun eyn moyer-arayngang tsum andern, un fun di karnizn, frizn, maskes, dakh-vazes, trep un ganikes aropkukn.)[67] The ghosts encountered by the narrator as he wanders the city might be ordinary, nameless people as well as prominent historical personalities.[68]

The prominence of ghosts in a socialist-realist reportage may seem surprising. Der Nister's narrator did not encounter them in Kharkiv, presumably because the city's history had been completely erased by the new socialist construction projects. In Leningrad, the past seems to dominate the present, and its shadows are omnipresent. To better understand the role and function of this unusual imagery, we can turn to Andrei Bely's novel *Petersburg*. First published in three volumes in 1913 in St. Petersburg, it was reissued, in a shorter two-volume version, in 1922 in Berlin and in 1928 and 1935 in Moscow. Like Der Nister, Bely immigrated to Berlin in 1921. In 1923, Bely returned to the Soviet Union, where he was able to publish his works until his death in 1934. It seems possible that at least some of Bely's ideas about symbolism were familiar to Der Nister and his Kiev associates. Bely's name was also mentioned by the editors of *Di royte velt* as an example of a (former) symbolist author whose works were published in the Soviet Union. It is likely therefore that Der Nister was familiar with *Petersburg*, which was regarded as a major novel of Russian symbolism. Leonid Dolgopolov notes in his analysis of *Petersburg*, Bely "simply erases borders between the real and the unreal, between the past and the present, between reality and imagination. Death and birth do not exist for him in the common meaning of these notions." Among Bely's predecessors Dolgopolov lists Nikolai Gogol and Dostoevsky, two Russian writers whose ghosts appear in Der Nister's "Leningrad."[69] But Bely goes further than Gogol and Dostoevsky in making the "unreal" a reality of a higher order: "The unreal, which follows from the general connection of the events described in the novel and thus acquires the meaning and character of a higher, artistic reality— this is the main device which Bely uses in the novel."[70] Indeed, as Bely's narrator tells us, "Petersburg streets possess an indubitable quality: they turn passers-by into shadows; while Petersburg

streets turn shadows into people."[71] Der Nister's use of this symbolist device reveals an ambiguity in his newly invented literary
persona. On the one hand, he conjures the ghosts of prominent
figures of the Russian imperial past to pronounce final judgments upon them from the privileged position of Marxist historical materialism. On the other hand, he is mystified and, by his
own admission, "intoxicated" by the grandeur and beauty of the
former imperial capital.

Confused by this mixture of reality and fantasy, Der Nister's
narrator gets dizzy from the "cinematographic" speed of the
changes to historical names and places. Standing next to the
Admiralty, he feels intoxicated by the overdetermined urban
landscape, desiring to retain "the entire building and its every
detail" (dem gantsn binyen un yede detal)[72] in his memory. The
architectural monuments from the cruel tsarist past, such as the
buildings on Palace Square, also provide "a bit of consolation,"
a "relief from everything that was hard, and a safe promise of a
happy future" (derlaykhterung fun ales shvern un ales gevezenem,
un a zikherer tsuzog af vayterdikn un af shtendik gliklekhn).[73]
Observing the panorama of the city from an embankment on a
light June night, Der Nister's narrator sees the city emerging and
then disappearing with the "light airiness of a dream" (a shtot
antshteyt, a shtot vert farshvundn mit der laykhter luftikayt fun
a kholem).[74] The dream changes as a short stroll across the Neva
to Kadetskaya Liniya on Vasilyevskii Island transposes him into
a different epoch, from the night of the tsarist past to the dawn
of the communist future. It was here, in a red building on a street
corner, on June 4, 1917, that Lenin famously proclaimed the Bolsheviks ready to take power.[75] This juxtaposition of "revolutionary" Vasilyevskii Island with the "tsarist" mainland part of the
city resonates with the apocalyptic warning by Bely's narrator:
"O Russian people, Russian people! Do not admit the crowds of
flickering shadows from the island: stealthily those shadows penetrate into your corporeal abodes; they penetrate from there into

the nooks and crannies of your souls: you become the shadows of the wreathed, flying mists."[76]

The Marxist dichotomy between the slavery of the past and the promise of future freedom is stamped onto every piece of Leningrad architecture. Its stylistic variety reflects the steady decline of the empire, from the imposing originality of eighteenth- and early-nineteenth-century baroque and classicism to the derivative mock-Byzantine, mock-Gothic, and mock-Russian styles of the late nineteenth and early twentieth century.[77] On Nevsky Prospect the narrator runs into an old acquaintance, who becomes his guide. The man was trained as an architect but became a theater director, and the combination of the two professions enables him not only to recount the city's history through its buildings but also to impersonate the character types from its past. Among them are a tsarist officer and the petty official Akakii Akakievich, the protagonist of Gogol's story "The Overcoat." This character evokes the ghost of his creator, who walks along Nevsky and whispers, in Russian, words from his story "Nevskii Prospect": "Our life is an eternal strife between dream and substantiality." (Der Nister uses Gogol's original Russian word sushchestvennost' for "substantiality.")[78] As the narrator explains, Russian literature is essential to our understanding of St. Petersburg because the city exists thanks to its imagination.[79] In other words, the city's historical "substantiality" as the imperial capital is a product of its writers' dreams, an idea which has its roots in nineteenth-century Russian literature from Alexander Pushkin to Dostoevsky and is summed up in Bely's prologue to Petersburg: "If Petersburg is not the capital, then there is no Petersburg. It only seems to exist."[80] Literature, like architecture, becomes a bridge between the past and the future. Both literature and architecture not only preserve the past for future generations but also prefigure elements of the future that may go undetected by contemporaries.

The prefiguration of the future is most vividly embodied in the early Russian revolutionaries, who were premature in their attempt to bring about liberation. They appear to the narrator among other street ghosts, such as the specter of a revolutionary terrorist who slipped on ice and blew himself up before he could deliver his bomb to its destination. The main figure from this spectral set is Dmitry Karakozov (1840–1866), the first Russian revolutionary to make an attempt on the life of a tsar. His shadow appears to the narrator in the hotel room in which Karakozov had stayed before the failed assassination attempt on Alexander II, for which he was hanged. (Revolutionary terrorists also feature prominently in *Petersburg*, whose plot revolves around the attempt to assassinate an elderly Russian senator by his own son; but Bely's portrayals of them are much less sympathetic.) In Karakozov's company the narrator visits historical sites looking for signs of the future revolution. In the Tauride Palace, the seat of the State Duma from 1906 to 1917, he imagines the political debates of the prerevolutionary Russian parliament. He asks his guide, a former worker who had lost his arms in a work accident, to show him the former seat of Vladimir Purishkevich, the infamous leader of the antisemitic monarchist Black Hundred movement. The fascinated narrator is unable to leave this seat, which he compares to the "gravestone (*matseyve*) of a lover." Thinking about the past, the narrator laughs with one eye and weeps with the other, as if mimicking the bifocal vision of history as a two-way avenue.

"Intoxicated" (*shiker*) by Leningrad's beauty, the narrator strolls with Karakozov's ghost to the Smolny Institute building, at that time the headquarters of the regional committee of the Bolshevik Party. While they are admiring the architectural masterpiece from a park bench, they are joined by another prominent phantom from the past, Fyodor Dostoevsky. The seating arrangement, Karakozov on the right and Dostoevsky on the left, places them according to the Jewish mystical tradition, respectively, as the good and the evil inclination (*yetzer hatov* and *yetzer harah*), the two opposite inner drives controlling human behavior. The "one on the right side" criticizes the "one on the left side" for not hearing the future knocking on all the "closed doors and shutters"[81] and accuses him of volunteering to serve the tsarist regime. According to Karakozov, Dostoevsky's love for Russia blinded him to its negative aspects and led to uncritical admiration of its autocratic rule: "One world power, one pan-Slavic empire, one Orthodox faith," with grand military and political ambitions to conquer all the territory between the Atlantic and Pacific.[82] Dostoevsky's reactionary nationalism prevented him from seeing the "world mechanics," the "frictions, contradictions, and conflicts" between the oppressor and oppressed nations and between the declining and rising classes.[83] Karakozov concludes his merciless analysis of Dostoevsky's failures: "Instead of seeing his own ideal as a rising and newly born self in the future, he blindly crawled backward, to the moldy and rotten idolatry of self-enslavement and destruction."[84]

To support this argument, the group of three visits the Hermitage Museum, where they encounter representatives of the Soviet people, including visitors from Uzbekistan. These simple people are admiring works of art rather than destroying them in an act of barbarism, as Dostoevsky supposedly feared. Genuine art needs no protection by the reactionary regime, explains the narrator, and it will be embraced by the future, even if it was originally produced for the enjoyment of the oppressor classes. As Der Nister implies through this episode, "genuine" art will outlive its time and social conditions and retain its aesthetic and practical utility for future ages. The cultural relevance of the prerevolutionary past and its value for the new socialist society were hotly debated in the early 1930s among Marxist literary theorists. The so-called despitists (voprekisty), led by the prominent theorist Georg Lukács, "argued that in the case of a literary genius . . . a writer is liable to produce a telling critique of his society despite his political position or class identity." Their more orthodox opponents, the "thankists" (blagodaristy), "believed that a truthful depiction of reality was possible only thanks to the author's (correct) world-view."[85] The latter position was championed by Der Nister's most prominent supporter, Isaac Nusinov.

But how valuable is a work of art when its creator, even a great artist, voluntarily chooses to put his talent at the service of a reactionary regime? Der Nister attempts to tackle this problem in his original discussion of Dostoevsky's novel *Besy* (Demons, 1871–72), a grotesque satire of the Russian radical nihilists of the 1860s, which is usually regarded as Dostoevsky's most reactionary work. Yet, as Der Nister's narrator recalls, his impression on first reading the novel in the early years of the twentieth century was at odds with the author's explicit intention. Instead of vilifying the revolutionary movement, the novel "revolutionized" its young, presumably Jewish, readers. They wanted to see only what suited their premonition of an imminent radical social transformation and ignored anything "alien" to that sense. On the eve of the 1905 revolution, Dostoevsky's caricature of the first Russian revolutionaries was interpreted as a subversive satire that exposed the weakness of the tsarist regime.[86] Upon his second, more recent, reading, the narrator has a different impression. He feels *blamazh* (embarrassment) for the great writer, who dismally failed to implement the "social directive" given to him by his "spiritual patron, the Russian monarchy," which commissioned him to create an adequate artistic representation of the revolutionaries as a serious threat to the regime.[87] Instead, Dostoevsky produced a grotesque travesty by portraying the revolutionaries as a bunch of "psychopaths, degenerates, sickly-idiotic antisocial types, and a couple of simple criminals,"[88] who could be defeated easily by a capable provincial administrator. The ineptness of the local authorities was a sign of the feebleness of the regime rather than the strength of the revolution.[89]

To illustrate his point more vividly, Der Nister invents a conversation between Dostoevsky and Konstantin Pobedonostsev, the Ober-Procurator of the Most Holy Synod and the chief architect of the reactionary policy of Alexander III. Pobedonostsev accuses Dostoevsky of harboring hidden sympathies for the revolutionaries. Moreover, he continues, "In a different situation...you could have become their greatest advocate."[90] Recreating this imaginary dialogue between Dostoevsky and Pobedonostsev can be seen as another nod to Bely's *Petersburg*. Although these historical figures are not mentioned explicitly in the text of the novel, there are many indirect references to them that contemporary readers would recognize. Pobedonostsev served as a prototype for the reactionary Senator Ableukhov, while Dostoevsky's vision of St. Petersburg as a mirage city left a deep impression on Bely's imagination. No less significant for Bely was Dostoevsky's dialectics of good and evil, which he applied to the revolutionary situation in 1905.[91] For Der Nister, a dialogue between two major Russian conservative thinkers provides an occasion to reflect on the function of art and its relation to ideology.

Ventriloquizing through the imaginary Pobedonostsev, Der Nister suggests that a genuine artist must never compromise his talent, even when he openly complies with the regime's directives. Consequently, an aesthetic flaw in a work of art can signal the artist's hidden unfaithfulness to the dominant regime and its ideology. Der Nister concludes that Dostoevsky ultimately failed as an artist not because he tried to comply with the regime's ideological line, but because he did it poorly, without applying the full strength of his talent. For a keen reader like Pobedonostsev, the crude caricature of the revolutionaries in *Besy* could even raise suspicion of Dostoevsky's loyalty to the regime. But for the Soviet reader, Der Nister suggests, it is precisely the artistic imperfection that rescues *Besy* as a document of its epoch and an instructive example of artistic failure caused by the author's ideological ambivalence. Unlike Lukács or Nusinov, Der Nister was not a theorist, and his primary concerns in these deliberations were not ideological but artistic. After the critical attack of

1929, he could have felt the need to reexamine his position vis-à-vis the Soviet regime and its ideology and was looking for past models. He was particularly interested in works deemed obsolete and reactionary, not unlike his own symbolist tales, trying to find ways of reconciling aesthetics with ideological requirements. Dostoevsky's *Besy* provided him with an instructive example of a highly talented author who ultimately failed to harmonize ideology with art, even though he apparently shared the ideological principles of the regime.

Unlike literature, architecture seemed to provide more promising models of reconciliation between art and ideology as a material embodiment of the link between the past and the future. In contrast to Dostoevsky's novel, the Smolny architectural complex outlived its time intact and reemerged as the symbolic site of a new power. Built originally as the Institute for Noble Maidens in 1806–08, it was appropriated by the Bolsheviks, who moved their headquarters from the Tauride Palace on the eve of the October Revolution in 1917. Reflecting on the Smolny building, Der Nister formulates his view of art and its historical purposefulness:

> Genuine art remains as an enduring masterpiece, regardless of the artist's own intentions and purposes at the time of its creation. If they were artistically thorough, I mean if the artist committed all his energy to his work, then it will outlive his time and his purpose, and it will remain relevant and aesthetically pleasing in other eras, and even for purposes that are contrary to those of the artist.

> (Emese kunst iz un blaybt a langdoyerndiker un tsu bavunderndiker muster, vos far a kavones un vos far a tsiln der kinstler hot zikh in zayn tsayt bam shafn dos verk nit geshtelt, nor oyb er hot zey kinstlerish-oysshepndik geshtelt, kh'meyn, oyb er hot mit zayn gantser im gegebener kinstler-energye getray dem verk gedint, lebt er dernokh iber zayn tsayt un zayn tsil, un es blaybt giltik un a sheferisher genus un fargenign oykh far andere tsaytn un afile far kegnzetslekhe tsum kinstlers tsiln.)[92]

Fifteen years after the October Revolution, the Smolny, now the headquarters of the Leningrad Regional Communist Party Committee, remained as relevant as ever:

> You stand in front of this work in 1932 and see that there is no disagreement with 1932 and the interests which this building serves now. On the contrary, you think: that's exactly what the artist had in mind, he intended his work somehow to pass over the past century and, most importantly, to arrive at the present and fulfill its main purpose.

> (Ir shteyt far dem verk in 1932tn yor un zet, vi s'iz gor keyn stire nit tsu 1932 un tsu di interesn, vos badint itst. Farkert, ir trakht: grod dos take hot der kinstler gemeynt, dertsu, eygntlekh, hot er getsilt, zayn verk zol far yenem yorhundert vi nit iz farbay, un der iker zol tsum iker, tsum itst un zayn hoypt-baruf, ariberkumen.)[93]

Thus, Der Nister claims, a successful artistic creation simultaneously inhabits two different historical epochs, the one in which it was created, and the one for which it was intended and in which it fulfills its purpose. The distance between the two can be as long as several centuries. The contrast between the intended purposes of the Tauride Palace and Smolny is inherently built into their architectural forms and exemplifies the conflict between the old and the new regime:

> Nothing in common! While the former one bends, from old age, to the ground, to calm obliteration and to the stillness of a museum or a cemetery, the latter rises vigorously, with its high entrance stairs, its whole façade and annexes, up into the air, to a dynamic and life-awakening activity.

> (Keyn moshl un keyn dimyen! Ven yents bet zikh shoyn, vi fun elter, opgelebt, tsu der erd, tsu shtil, fartishkevetkayt un tsu muzey-un matseyve-ru, rayst zikh op dos geboy, mit di hoykhe oyfgang-trep, mit gantsn front un mit di zaytn-geboyen—in luft, inderhoykh, tsu muntern un tsu lebnvekndiker tetikayt.)[94]

The dominant horizontal outline of the Tauride Palace is contrasted to the verticality of Smolny. Der Nister's peculiar privileging of the vertical line to the horizontal one echoes an idea that the Ukrainian painter Oleksander Bohomazov proposed in his talk "Major Tasks for the Development of Art in Ukraine," which he delivered in Kiev in 1918. In this talk Bohomazov tried to articulate the basic aesthetic difference between the North (Russia) and Ukraine: "In the North the line dynamics are more horizontal, while in Ukraine they are multidimensional, intersected by vertical lines. . . . All of this has a more powerful effect on the viewer."[95] Der Nister, who may have been familiar with this idea, associates the horizontal line with the past and the vertical line with the future. The Tauride Palace had exhausted its historical potential before the revolution and became a museum (or gravestone) to its age, while Smolny is thriving under the new regime. It is not accidental that the two antagonistic classes, the bourgeoisie and the proletariat, chose these two different architectural structures as their "historical pulpits," the Duma and the Soviet, and in doing so revealed their "class substance" (klasn-mehus).

Of course, the Bolsheviks were motivated in their choice of Smolny primarily by their "social and political strategy" (gezelshaftlekhe un politishe strategie), but post-factum, when "whatever happened did happen" (dos gesheene iz geshen), one could see that "regardless of all the motives, the events had to take place here and only here" (epes oyser ale motivn hobn di gesheenishn take do, un dafke do gedarft geshen).[96] This observation leads Der Nister to a laconic conclusion that captures the essence of his new literary style by linking realism with symbolism: "The fact becomes a symbol." (Der fakt vert a simvol.)[97] According to Pokrovskii's theory, the course of history is fully determined by objective, dynamic socioeconomic forces and class interests without the intervention of human agency. The role of artists in this process, as Der Nister sees it, is to find adequate artistic forms for symbolic representations of the historical "facts" of their time. In the most accomplished works, these symbolic representations of the historical present also prefigure the future. Their symbolic significance reveals itself in full only later, in a more progressive epoch. This way of thinking may have helped Der Nister reconcile the troublesome reality of his time with the larger sense of artistic purpose. By capturing the key progressive features of his own epoch, the artist created an enduring work of art that would be fully appreciated only by future generations.

As Koller puts it, "Der Nister translates these historical dialectics into urban spatial imagery."[98] This action by Der Nister's power of imagination in "Leningrad" finds another interesting parallel in Walter Benjamin's cultural-historical investigation of nineteenth-century Paris in his famous *Arcades Project* of 1927–39. Benjamin speaks of a "dialectical image," "wherein what has been comes together in a flash with the now to form a constellation. In other words: image is dialectics at a standstill. . . . Only dialectical images are genuinely historical—that is, not archaic—images."[99] In these "dialectical images," Benjamin goes on to elaborate, "one could speak of the increasing concentration (integration) of reality, such that everything past (in its time) can acquire a higher grade of actuality than it had in the moment of its existing. How it marks itself as higher actuality is determined by the image as which and in which it is comprehended."[100] Although it is highly unlikely that Der Nister was familiar with Benjamin's writings, he could have been introduced to some of Benjamin's ideas by his friend Meir Wiener, who met Benjamin on at least one occasion, in Paris in 1925.

Like Der Nister, Benjamin encountered ghosts in his dream walks around Paris: "The path we travel through arcades is fundamentally just a ghost walk, on which doors give way and walls yield."[101] For his part, Der Nister's narrator is a kind of Soviet Jewish flaneur, a figure that fascinated some contemporary German thinkers and writers and was central to Benjamin's project. Benjamin's description of this experience closely resembles some of the most animated moments in Der Nister's depiction of the city: "We know that, in the course of flânerie, far-off times and places interpenetrate the landscape and the present moment. When the authentically intoxicated phase of this condition announces itself, the blood is pounding in the veins of the happy flâneur ... and inwardly as well as outwardly things go on as we would imagine them to do in one of those 'mechanical pictures.'"[102] To appreciate Der Nister's "intoxication" with Leningrad, which he visited for the first time in 1932, we have to remember that until 1917 the city was legally closed to him as a Jew who did not belong to one of the privileged categories. Fifteen years later, he could not only freely enjoy the beauty of its architecture but also celebrate his triumph over the tsarist regime by sitting in Purishkevich's Duma seat. As Benjamin writes, "The street conducts the flâneur into a vanished time. . . . It leads downward . . . into a past that can be all the more spellbinding because it is not his own."[103] Der Nister's "Leningrad" ends with Dostoevsky's specter slowly and silently entering the building marked by a memorial plaque with his name, walking up the stairs, turning the light on, and drawing the window curtain, which symbolically closes the imperial epoch in Russian history. By critically engaging with the classical Russian literary tradition, Der Nister produces a new, Yiddish version of its "Petersburg text."[104] "Leningrad" is remarkable in a number of respects. While replete with intertextual references to Russian literature, it has practically no Jewish cultural substrate. Der Nister dogmatically sticks to the Marxist theory of historical materialism in Pokrovskii's interpretation (which incidentally was about to be discarded by the Communist Party when *Hoyptshtet* appeared as a book) and at the same time expands his symbolist repertoire by appropriating Bely's legacy and perhaps trying to imitate his manner of survival under the Soviet regime. And, perhaps responding to the political turn of the early 1930s, he seeks to disassociate himself from the toxic local environment in Ukraine by reorienting his creativity toward Russia and inscribing himself into the imaginary space of its two capitals, the old imperial and the new Soviet one. From the past-dominated Leningrad he moves to the future-oriented Moscow as his ultimate destination. As we shall see in the following section, Der Nister's impression of Moscow fits well with Benjamin's radical statement: "In the final analysis, only the revolution creates an open space for the city."[105]

## MOSCOW: THE DIALECTIC OF REVOLUTIONARY UTOPIA

If we read Der Nister's chapters on the capitals as a dialectical triad, the new Ukrainian industrial capital of Kharkiv represents the thesis of the socialist future; Leningrad, as the former imperial capital turned into the urban museum of imperial history, stands for the antithesis of the past; and Moscow creates the synthesis between the two. Moscow is a space where the old Russian tsarist past and the new Soviet communist future find their dialectical resolution, which is made manifest in the imminent apocalyptic utopia of world revolution.[106] In the opening section of "Moscow," titled "A shvere dermonung" (A heavy memory), the narrator recounts his impressions of the city in 1920, when he was working in a Jewish orphanage in Malakhovka near Moscow. Back then the city was "half-dead, a kind of Pompeii" (halbtoyt in a min Pompeye):[107] its main commercial avenue, Il'inka, looked like a cemetery with empty shop windows.[108] Der Nister's imagery of death and desolation echo David Bergelson's impressions of Moscow as he encountered it on his way out of Soviet Russia in the winter of 1921. In an essay that appeared in the New York communist paper *Frayhayt* in 1926, he recalled: "Back then, as if in the netherworld, lifeless men of property who had lost their property were hanging around in the gloomy winter air on Moscow's winding streets." (Hobn zikh dan, vi in oylem hatohu, gedreyt toyte oysgebalebatevete balebatim in kalemutner vinterdiker luft oyf moskver kaylekhdike gasn.)[109]

By 1920 the young revolutionary state had already eliminated the old tsarist regime but was as yet unable to build a new Soviet society, Der Nister explains. This was a critical historical moment of transition from the past to the future, the twilight between the old dark night and the bright new day. The contrast was strikingly evident in the Kremlin, where the seat of the Soviet government was guarded by revolutionary soldiers but the surrounding areas still belonged to the "bitter enemies" (farbisene sonim) of the revolution: monks and priests of the numerous monasteries and churches, such as Iverskaya Chapel and St. Basil's Cathedral.[110] Equally dire was the situation in education, culture, and especially trade, which was not yet under Soviet state control and was conducted mainly in dirty and dangerous street markets (tolkuchka). Everybody who could left the city, and nobody came in. Food shortages were so severe that even the mice came out of their holes and lived among the people, feeding on their shoes and clothes, causing the price of cats to skyrocket.[111]

Der Nister visited Moscow at the beginning of a grandiose reconstruction project that was initiated by the Communist Party in June 1931 and completed in 1935. This was also the formative period of the doctrine of socialist realism, and both projects were interconnected. As Katerina Clark explains,

In the Stalinist thirties, the transformation of Moscow functioned both in official rhetoric and in many of the novels, paintings and films as a source of the master metaphors legitimizing and explicating the Stalinist political program: the building of a new capital city stood for transforming the society, the practical example of what achieved socialism might look like. Particular buildings in the "new Moscow" were successively cited in speeches and articles as the model for architectural practice. This was similar to the standard practice in Soviet literature whereby particular novels or their positive heroes were singled out as exemplars for writers to follow.[112]

It is appropriate therefore that Der Nister's visit to the new Moscow begins, as in Leningrad, with an encounter with a monument, this time to Pushkin. The great poet looks "much older and more melancholic," not recognizing the busy streets around him, crowded with people and vehicles. Some of the old church buildings, such as Iverskaya Chapel at the entrance to Red Square, have been demolished to create space for parks, streets, and cars, while other church buildings have been converted into museums. Plenty of historical "traditional mold" (traditsioneler shiml) has been removed "to reveal what is valuable from the layers of different epochs" (dos vertfule fun di onshikhtungen fun farsheydene epokhes aroystsushayln).[113] Der Nister's choice of imagery reflects the official Soviet accounts of that time, which "stressed how planners were ridding the city of the clutter of 'minor structures' (melkie stroeniia), by which was meant not so much structures that were small literally as the structures of the capitalist, and particularly petty bourgeois, world, such as booths, market stalls, and small shops and enterprises." Churches and other historic structures such as towers, walls, and city gates were also slated for demolition, to be replaced by new broad and open spaces.[114]

In Benjamin's depiction of Moscow in 1927, churches still dominate the cityscape, although many are already "untended and empty. But the glow that now shines only occasionally from the altars into the snow has been well preserved in the wooden cities of the commercial booths. In their snow-covered, narrow alleyways it is quiet. You hear only the soft jargon of the Jewish clothiers in their stalls next to the junk of the paper dealer, who, enthroned and concealed behind silver chains, has drawn tinsel and cotton-wool-tufted Father Christmases across her face like an oriental veil"[115] Benjamin's impression of Moscow at the end of the period of the New Economic Policy—which revived the Soviet economy by allowing some private enterprise—is almost serene. Past and present, represented by busy Jewish traders and abandoned Orthodox churches, seem to coexist peacefully in the Moscow frost. (Interestingly, while Benjamin occasionally mentions Jews in his *Moscow Diary*, there seem to be no traces of Jewish presence in Der Nister's Moscow. Writing for the Kharkiv

Yiddish magazine, he does not mention any of the numerous Yiddish cultural institutions in the Soviet capital.) Benjamin could still see in the streets of Moscow what he described as "a curious state of affairs: the Russian village is playing hide-and-seek in them."[116] The socialist future existed only in pictures: "Now and again one comes across streetcars painted all over with pictures of factories, mass meetings, Red regiments, Communist agitators."[117] This new emerging socialist city was still invisible at the street level, and "Only from an airplane does one have a view of the industrial elite of the city, the film and automobile industries."[118] As in Der Nister's "Kharkiv," the aerial perspective reveals the view of a future that exists as a potentiality in the present.

This new Moscow is already present in Der Nister's depiction, where it appears to dominate and control the past. By 1932 the last remnants of private trade and commerce had been eliminated, and churches were being systematically demolished as part of the anti-religious campaign and the radical reconstruction of Moscow. In the new international capital of the communist future, East meets West, North meets South. Here one can encounter "all sorts of types, people, garb, [displaying] a wild ethnographic mixture and variety" (tipn, mentshn, kleyder fun a vildn gemish un etnografishn alerley).[119] Having depicted many places he visited, such as educational institutions, museums, workers' clubs, and factories, and bolstering his depictions with impressive statistics on Soviet social and industrial achievements, the narrator describes two street encounters. The narrator meets a German engineer who has left his country and found a new home in the Soviet Union. The other encounter is with the poet Heinrich Heine, upon whom the narrator stumbles at night in a side street between Tverskaia and Herzen streets. In his nineteenth-century dress, Heine looks effeminate and even clownish.[120] In Germany, Heine's monument was repeatedly assaulted by nationalists, but in Moscow he can roam freely around the city and would even be held in esteem by the Society for Cultural Contacts with Foreign Countries if he were to present himself at its headquarters. The narrator assures Heine that the Soviet people can bridge the distance between time and space and "bring over from the other side" someone whom they really need.[121] Unlike the reactionary writer Dostoevsky, who remains forever enclosed in the museum space of Leningrad, the progressive poet Heine could be transferred from the German past to the Soviet present, and even accorded residence in a new Moscow as someone who "looked over from his time to ours."[122] To support his interpretation of Heine's significance for Soviet culture, in a footnote Der Nister refers to the essay "Heine and Communism" by Nikolai Bukharin, at that time a leading Soviet Marxist theoretician who would fall victim to Stalin's purges in 1937. By inviting Heine to settle in Moscow, Der Nister responds to the Soviet claim that German classics form part of the anti-fascist "battle over texts, over who has the right to claim the title of guardian of true culture."[123] Incidentally, this trend was initiated at a major international writers' conference in Kharkiv in November 1930, followed by the establishment of a new German-language publishing house in Moscow.[124] Moscow is reimagined as a repository of all progressive elements from different epochs and countries and the guardian of world culture.

Moscow's multilayered cityscape encapsulates different epochs of Russian history, which are now organized according to the Soviet order. The diverse historical pieces merge together into a "charming harmony of the old and the new" (alt-nayem khen), complementing each other "without any conflict or dissonance, just wonderful harmony and authenticity" (nisht keyn vidershprukh, nisht keyn disonans, nor vunderlekhe harmonie un ekhtkayt).[125] This "harmony and authenticity" find their fullest expression in Red Square, where the large commercial shopping structure opposite the Kremlin, an exemplification of tsarist Russia's merchant capitalism, has been absorbed and redeemed by the new monument of Lenin's Mausoleum, which embodies "hope and security" (hofenung un zikherkayt) for the future.[126] Der Nister's vision of the mausoleum as the new guardian of security complements Benjamin's observation that during the tsarist period, "architectural security" (which he conveys by the Russian word *okhrana*) was provided to Moscow by church domes that were visible from everywhere in the city.

Benjamin was enchanted by picturesque St. Basil's: "If you enter Red Square from the west, its domes gradually rise into the sky line like a pack of fiery suns. The building always holds something back and could be surprised only by a gaze coming from an airplane, against which the builders forgot to take precautions."[127] This imaginary airplane invading the "historical space" of the church again reminds us of the flight of Kharkiv's Gosprom building to St. Sophia in Kiev. But St. Basil's Church has been turned in the new Museum of Atheism, where curious Soviet visitors can see the horrors of medieval religious practices.

Der Nister's narrator observes that as visitors exit the exhibition into Red Square, they look gratefully to Lenin's Mausoleum.[128] As the new spatial focus of the Red Square, the mausoleum attracts visitors from all parts of the country. It is a solemn temple in the midst of the busy square, where people come to worship their new deity. A child of a Chinese family wonders whether Uncle Lenin ("feter Lenin") is alive, apparently formulating the question in Russian because the word *zhivoy* is typeset in Cyrillic. The response comes in the form of an echo—whether from his parents or from the narrator is unclear—a repetition of the same word but this time written in Yiddish script.[129]

The final part of the chapter depicts a night dream of the Kremlin wall. In a series of kaleidoscopic episodes, the wall recalls cruel events that it witnessed when the busy marketplace at Red Square doubled as the site of public executions. Now the wall looks hopefully at the mausoleum where Lenin is summoning people's representatives from around the world to gather in Red Square. In this vision of the apocalyptic phantasmagoria,

> Red Square will be full. Large crowds will come to see the represent-
> atives. The entire city will climb, stand, and lie on balconies, roofs,
> and church domes, and young people will cover every street pole and
> curb like flies. Everybody will want to see those who have triumphed
> in the last struggle, who have cracked down on the last remnants
> of crime, who have erased the last borders between countries and
> united all countries into one and all peoples into one working people,
> and whose representatives have now gathered here, in Red Square.

> (Der royter plats vet ful zayn. Hamoynim, hamoynim veln af di
> forshteyer kumen kukn. Di gantse shtot af ganikes, af dekher, af
> shpits-kloysters vet shteyn, lign, krikhn, ale gasn-stoypes, ale rinves
> mit yungvarg, vi mit flign badekt. Ale veln veln zen ot yene, vos
> hobn dem letstn kamf oysgekemft, yene, vos hobn di letste reshtlekh
> farbrekhn gebrokhn, yene, vos hobn di letste grenetsn fun land tsu
> land opgevisht, un fun ale lender—eyn land, un fun ale felker—ayn
> arbet-folk, un vos di forshteyer fun zey ale zaynen itst do, afn roytn
> plats, farzamlt.)[130]

The celebration of the ultimate victory of the working class would commence with the last-ever performance of "The Internatio-nale," whereupon "it will become quiet, and the entire people will cry from joy, and with crying and rejoicing will contribute their song to the music" (un shtil vet vern, un dos gantse folk vet fun freyd veynen, un veynendik un yoyvlendik der muzik mit gezang tsu hilf kumen).[131] Even though present reality still looks quite different from that future celebration, one must firmly believe that the dream will come true.

Der Nister's vision of the Red Square transformed from the place of public executions to the site of the ultimate Communist redemption evokes another parallel with Nikolai Evreinov's work. To mark the celebration of the third anniversary of the October Revolution in 1920, Evreinov staged a grandiose reenactment of the Bolshevik storming of the Winter Palace in Petrograd.

According to the stage designer Iurii Annenkov, the performance engaged more than eight thousand actors, including ballet dancers and circus acrobats, as well as tanks, machine guns, and the cruiser Avrora, which in 1917 gave the signal to the beginning of the Bolshevik attack. More than fifty searchlights were used for lighting, and about one hundred thousand spectators watched the show. The participants, split into the Reds and the Whites, were situated on two giant platforms at the level of the third floor connected by a bridge. They were divided in small mobile groups that received acting instructions by telephone.[132] Then, as described by James von Geldern, "at the stroke of ten, Palace Square was plunged into darkness. A cannon shot shattered the silence, and an orchestra of 500, placed under the arch and directed by Varlikh, struck up Henri Litolff's *Robespierre* overture, introducing the White (!) platform. One hundred and fifty searchlights mounted on the roofs of surrounding buildings were switched on at once, illuminating the Whites, who opened the action. The *Marseillaise*, orchestrated as a polonaise, was begun as the ladies and gentlemen of high society awaited Kerensky's arrival."[133] Many years after his emigration from Soviet Russia Annenkov reflected in his memoirs: "The Russian Revolution, hungry and barefoot, infused a new mighty link into the chain of open-air performances, a type of art with masses of participants where the quantity creates the form of the spectacle."[134]

To conform with the socialist-realist norm, Der Nister provides an appropriate supporting reference for his daring fantasy in Lenin's brochure "What Is to Be Done" (1902), in which Lenin approvingly quotes from the mid-nineteenth-century radical Russian positivist critic Dmitry Pisarev's essay "Promakhi nezreloy mysli" (Downfall of unripe thought").[135] Pisarev argued that even unrealistic dreams can be useful because they "support and fortify the energy of the working man. . . . A discord between dream and reality causes no harm, if only the dreaming person seriously believes in his dream . . . and works diligently towards the fulfillment of his fantasy."[136] Supported by the communist holy writ, the narrator joins the wall in the dream: "I dream together with it, I dream its great and bright dream of the future that is already close." (Ikh troym mit ir mit, kh'troym mit ir vor, afn bodn vor—ir groysn un likhtikn, shoyn noentn tsukunft-troym.)[137] At this culminating moment of the book, Der Nister resuscitates his symbolist style and casts his narrator as a new communist prophet. He is careful enough to legitimize this revival of visionary symbolism by a quotation from Lenin, but he also implicitly uses the allegory from the Prophet Zachariah's vision of the final gathering of all nations in Jerusalem.

## CONCLUSION

Unlike the abstract landscapes in Der Nister's symbolist tales, the descriptions of the urban spaces in *Hoyptshtet* are highly detailed and accurate in their portrayal of reality. They enable the reader to visualize the physical environment and the narrator's position in it. But the city is also a material embodiment of historical time, a multilayered repository of different epochs of the past in relation to the present. Every building, street, and square is a container of historical memory, which can be unpacked by an attentive contemporary observer. Architecture not only preserves memories of the past, but it also contains seeds of the future, although the proportion between the two can vary. Some new buildings, such as Kharkiv's Gosprom building, carry no weight of the past and therefore can literally float in the air. Others, like the Tauride Palace of Leningrad, carry the full weight of the past, which is reflected in their predominantly horizontal structure. They have already fulfilled their historical mission and have no future apart from becoming museums. Only a few architectural ensembles, such as Smolny or Red Square, can combine a rich legacy and an aptness for the future. The ultimate purpose of a work of architecture is not necessarily known to its creator or patron and may only fully manifest its potential under different historical circumstances in the future; however, a discerning observer can recognize its destiny in some of its formal features. Along these lines, the central squares of Kharkiv, Leningrad, and Moscow are particularly significant as arenas of social and historical struggle, reminding us of Roland Barthes's observation: "The center-city is always experienced as the space in which certain subversive forces act and are encountered, forces of rupture, ludic forces."[138]

Architecture can also serve as a moral compass for the contemporary generation by indicating the direction to the future. Der Nister declares in the opening of the book: "History will judge us according to our buildings: how our order is built, on what kind of moral foundations, [and] what political, socio-economic, and cultural-customary forms it takes." (Loyt undzere binyonim vet undz di geshikhte mishpetn: vi azoy undzer ordenung iz geboyt, vos far a morale gruntn zaynen unter ir untergeleygt, un in vos far a politishe, sotsial-ekonomishe un kultur-shteygerishe formen zi hot zikh ongekleydt.)[139] Socialist construction not only creates new buildings, it also transforms the builders along the way: "By participating in the building process, builders are rebuilt themselves" (boyendik, ze ikh, boyen zikh aleyn di boyer iber), a statement that rephrases the Zionist slogan "livnot ve-lehibanot ba" (to build up [the Land of Israel] and to be built by it). By laying down the contours of their buildings, the Soviet people lay the foundation of their future: "The conviction gave us security to imagine our future reality in fantasy, and to fulfill our fantasies step by step." (Di ibertsaygung hot undz festkayt gegebn vegn undzer tsukunftiker virklekhkayt tsu fantazirn un undzere fantazies trit nokh trit take tsu farvirklekhn.)[140] Here again we find Der Nister's belief in accord with Benjamin's reflection: "Historical 'understanding' is to be grasped, in principle, as an afterlife of that which is understood; and what has been recognized in the analysis of the 'afterlife of works,' in the analysis of 'fame,' is therefore to be considered the foundation of history in general."[141]

For Der Nister, it is architecture that embodies both the sociohistorical reality of society as a whole and the bold creative imagination of its most progressive representatives, which are often
not in harmony. The exploration of the tension between the two
is a main concern of Der Nister's *Hoyptshtet*, which will find its
continuation in *The Family Mashber.*

Many puzzling questions suggested by *Hoyptshtet* will be
addressed in the following chapters. A Warsaw Bundist newspaper reported that at the book's presentation in Kharkiv in
1935 Der Nister spoke of the challenge of "liberating himself"
from his previous literary style and his aspiration to reflect the
"Great Epoch" in his prose writing.[142] Clarity and simplicity were
required attributes of the emerging doctrine of socialist realism,
as was, of course, the enthusiastic embrace of communist ideology and an eagerness to follow the changing party line. The
critical campaign of 1929 made Der Nister painfully aware of the
changing situation and forced him to rethink his place in Soviet
literature. In *Hoyptshtet*, his first attempt to write about "reality," he implemented a variety of elaborate narrative techniques
that enabled him to transpose stylistic elements from his previous symbolist period onto the new realist mode of narration.
Along with detailed depictions of urban and rural landscapes,
each chapter contains elaborate fantastic visions that grow out
of the architectural settings. In such surreal episodes, which are
integrated into the realistic narrative, including the dust storm
in the Crimean steppe, the night flight of the Gosprom buildings
from Kharkiv to Kiev, the appearance of literary specters in Leningrad, and the apocalyptic dream of the Kremlin wall, Der Nister reflects on the questions that were of paramount importance
during his transitional period. One of the questions Der Nister
raised was the ability of an artist to transcend the sociopolitical constraints of time and place and to speak to future generations over the heads of his contemporaries. Der Nister touched
upon this issue in the much-quoted letter to his brother but also

revisited it implicitly in the fantasies that transported his readers to different eras and allowed him to assume a perspective beyond his own historical context.

## NOTES

1. Shmeruk, "Der Nister, khayav veyetsirato," 33.
2. Koller, "Der Nister's 'Leningrad,'" 74.
3. Smolych, "Z 'zapysiv na skhyli viku,'" 167.
4. Shkandrij, "Politics and the Ukrainian Avant-garde," 220.
5. Ibid., 226.
6. Ibid., 227.
7. Koller, "Der Nister's 'Leningrad,'" 75.
8. On Slovo, see Bertelsen, "House of Writers."
9. Smolych, "Z 'zapysiv na skhyli viku.'" 164.
10. Max Kaganovitsh's obituaries in *Le Figaro*, April 8/9, 1978; *Israelitisches Wochenblatt* (Zurich), April 14, 1978; *Naye prese* (Paris), April 13–14, 1978.
11. Letter to Max Kaganovich, no date, RGALI, f 3121, op. 1, d. 37, ll. 1–3.
12. One of the most notable examples that may have inspired Der Nister was Maxim Gorky's series *Po Soyuzu Sovetov* (Across the union of Soviets, 1929).
13. Tretyakov, "Evolutsiia zhanra," 407.
14. Ibid., 408.
15. Mykola Waskiw, "Mandrivnyi narys iak sposib piznannia inshoho i samoho sebe," 149.
16. Der Nister, *Hoyptshtet*, 252.
17. Ibid., 271.
18. Ibid., 265.
19. Wisse, *I. L. Peretz Reader*, tr. Milton Himmelfarb, 20.
20. Shkandrij, "Politics and the Ukrainian Avant-garde," 222.
21. Dekel-Chen, *Farming the Red Land*, 138.
22. Der Nister, *Hoyptshtet*, 221.
23. Dekel-Chen, *Farming the Red Land*, 134.
24. Der Nister, *Hoyptshtet*, 222.
25. Ibid., 228.
26. Ibid., 230.
27. Ibid., 230–31.
28. Tretyakov, "Iskusstvo v revolutsii i revolutiia v iskusstve," 215.

29. Tretyakov, "Dramaturgovy zametki," 240.

30. Fowler, *Beau Monde*, 135.

31. Ibid., 139.

32. Der Nister, *Hoyptshtet*, 243.

33. Ibid., 245.

34. Roskies, *Bridge of Longing*, 227.

35. Der Nister, *Hoyptshtet*, 246.

36. Ibid., 247.

37. Ibid., 250.

38. Ibid., 251.

39. Bertelsen, "House of Writers in Ukraine," 14–15.

40. Der Nister, *Hoyptshtet*, 25.

41. Ibid., 14.

42. Ibid., 8.

43. Ibid., 11.

44. Ibid., 16.

45. Shapiro, *Cross and Other Jewish Stories*, 3–18.

46. Der Nister, *Hoyptshtet*, 28.

47. Ibid.

48. Bechtel, *Der Nister's Work*, 240.

49. The trope of the church lost in time and space after the October Revolution was popular among Yiddish writers depicting the new Soviet reality; see also Murav, "Moscow Threefold," 48–49.

50. Der Nister, *Hoyptshtet*, 43.

51. Ibid., 44.

52. Ibid., 38.

53. Koznarsky, "Three Novels, Three Cities," 99.

54. Der Nister, "Me tantst oyf di gasn." RGALI, f. 3121, op. 1, d. 15, l. 1.

55. Ibid.

56. Der Nister's interpretation of purges as staged performances to be emulated by the audience antedates the contemporary concept of self-criticism as ritual by a few decades. See, for example, Getty, "*Samokritika* Rituals in the Stalinist Central Committee, 1933–38."

57. Bechtel, *Der Nister's Work*, 246.

58. Ibid.

59. Ibid., 253.

60. Created by the sculptor Paolo Trubetskoy, it was erected in 1909 and removed in 1937. Der Nister was able to see it in its original location in the middle of the square.

61. Der Nister, *Hoyptshtet*, 48.

62. Piskunov, "'Vtoroe prostranstvo' romana A. Belogo 'Peterburg,'" 211.

63. Der Nister, *Hoyptshtet*, 50.

64. Pokrovskii, *Russkaia istoriia v samom szhatom ocherke*, 70.

65. Der Nister, *Hoyptshtet*, 50.

66. Ibid., 56.

67. Ibid., 55.

68. Koller points to similar imagery in Sholem Asch's novel *Peterburg* (1927). Koller, "Der Nister's 'Leningrad,'" 74.

69. Dolgopolov, "Tvorcheskaia istoriia," 585.

70. Ibid., 586.

71. Bely, *Petersburg*, 123.

72. Der Nister, *Hoyptshtet*, 79.

73. Ibid., 73.

74. Ibid., 74.

75. Ibid., 59–60.

76. Bely, *Petersburg*, 99–100.

77. Der Nister, *Hoyptshtet*, 60–61.

78. Ibid., 61.

79. Ibid., 64.

80. Bely, *Petersburg*, 49.

81. Der Nister, *Hopytshtet*, 114.

82. Ibid., 115.

83. Ibid., 116.

84. Ibid., 117.

85. Clark and Tikhanov, "Soviet Literary Theory in the 1930s," 117.

86. Der Nister, *Hoyptshtet*, 108.

87. Ibid., 110.

88. Ibid., 111.

89. Ibid.

90. Ibid., 113.

91. Dolgopolov, "Tvorcheskaia istoriia," 592–95.

92. Der Nister, *Hoyptshtet*, 80.

93. Ibid.

94. Ibid., 81.

95. Oleksandr Bohomazov, "Osnovni zavdannia rozvytku mystetstva na Ukraini," manuscript, Bohomazov Archive, Museum of Literature and Art of Ukraine. Quoted in Horbachov, "In the Epicentre of Abstraction," 178.

96. Der Nister, *Hoyptshtet*, 81.

97. Ibid.

98. Koller, "Der Nister's 'Leningrad,'" 76.

99. Benjamin, *Arcades Project*, 463.

100. Ibid., 392.

101. Ibid., 409.

102. Ibid., 419–20.

103. Ibid., 416.

104. On the concept of the St. Petersburg text and its variations in Russian literature, see Buckler, *Mapping St. Petersburg*, 27–60.

105. Benjamin, *Arcades Project*, 422.

106. The chapter "Moskve" first appeared in two installments in *Di royte velt* 7–8 (1932): 125–40; 9 (1932): 124–61.

107. Der Nister, *Hoyptshtet*, 128.

108. Ibid., 131.

109. David Bergelson, "Moskve," 5. I am grateful to Harriet Murav for providing me with this text.

110. Der Nister, *Hoyptshtet*, 131.

111. Ibid., 129–130.

112. Clark, *Moscow, the Fourth Rome*, 96.

113. Der Nister, *Hoyptshtet*, 147.

114. Clark, *Moscow, the Fourth Rome*, 101.

115. Benjamin, "Moscow," 44.

116. Ibid., 41.

117. Ibid., 39.

118. Ibid.

119. Der Nister, *Hoyptshtet*, 145.

120. Ibid., 195.

121. Ibid., 197.

122. Ibid.

123. Clark, *Moscow, the Fourth Rome*, 155.

124. Ibid., 44.

125. Der Nister, *Hoyptshtet*, 148.

126. Ibid., 149.

127. Benjamin, "Moscow," 43.

128. Der Nister, *Hoyptshtet*, 144.

129. Ibid., 209.

130. Ibid., 213.

131. Ibid.

132. Annenkov, *Dnevnik moikh vstrech*, 519.

133. Von Geldern, *Bolshevik Festivals*, 203–4.

134. Annenkov, *Dnevnik moikh vstrech*, 522

135. Ibid., 214.

136. Pisarev, *Sochineniia*, 147.
137. Der Nister, *Hoyptshtet*, 216.
138. Barthes, "Semiology and Urbanism," 417.
139. Der Nister, *Hoyptshtet*, 5.
140. Ibid.
141. Benjamin, *Arcades Project*, 460.
142. Estraikh, "Der Nister's 'Hamburg Score,'" 17.

# THREE

# THE 1930S IN CHILDREN'S POETRY

HOYPTSHTET (CAPITALS) WAS DER NISTER's first and last
attempt to reinvent himself as a contemporary writer and master
of the mainstream Soviet literary genre of *ocherk*, a hybrid of essay
and reportage. He may have realized that his foray into depicting
Soviet reality did not appear to be promising, and for nearly a decade he did not return to contemporary themes. When he did, in the
midst of the catastrophe of World War II, his style and approach
were markedly different. However, in the 1930s he made another
attempt at self-reinvention, this time as a poet for children.

## CHILDREN'S LITERATURE AS AN ESCAPE ROUTE

At the time of the Russian Revolution, literature for children—
both original works and translations—was an important item
on the agenda of the modernist revival of Jewish culture both
in Yiddish and Hebrew. As Kenneth Moss argues, "Both Hebra-
ists and Yiddishist pedagogy aimed at nothing short of cultural
revolution in—and through—the lives of Jewish children."[1] The
most creative and productive period for Yiddish modernist literature for children coincided with the brief and turbulent period
between the abdication of Tsar Nicholas II in 1917 and the final
Bolshevik victory in 1921. Despite political turbulence, material

deprivation, and the unprecedented violence of the pogroms, the Kiev-based Kultur-Lige managed to take control over and sustain the production and distribution of Yiddish literature in Ukraine. Its writers and artists created a new model of the children's book as a piece of modernist art in which text and image formed an aesthetic unity.[2] Kerstin Hoge explains the new role of children's literature in Jewish culture: "Children's books not only provided a vehicle for communicating the new art to children (and their parents), but also, and perhaps more fundamentally, a way of anchoring a tradition of visual art into national awareness and making it a source of collective identity."[3] Experimental in both form and content, these books occupy a prominent place today in the European avant-garde canon, primarily as objets d'art. They are highly valued for their illustrations by such famous artists as Marc Chagall and Eliezer Lissitzky. But the texts by the rising stars of Yiddish poetry, Dovid Hofshteyn, Leyb Kvitko, and Peretz Markish, attract only marginal interest. The Bolshevik takeover of the Kultur-Lige in 1920 severely curtailed its creative freedom and induced some of its leading activists to emigrate, but its children's literature branch remained prolific and creative well into the 1930s. In comparison with the earlier period, children's books published in the 1930s were more conventional in style and design, traditional in literary form, and streamlined ideologically, but many of them remained funny, entertaining, and imaginative. They were produced more lavishly and in much larger print runs than in the 1920s. By the mid-1930s, Yiddish literature for children, especially the poems of Leyb Kvitko, became increasingly popular in translations into Russian, Ukrainian, and other languages of the Soviet Union. The print runs of Kvitko's Russian translations reached several millions of copies, greatly exceeding those of the original Yiddish publications. Kvitko was the only non-Russian children's writer to attain this kind of fame and popularity, and he occupied a prominent place among the Soviet literary elite.[4]

Kvitko's upbeat and memorable verses were familiar to virtu-
ally every Russian-speaking child in the Soviet Union, although
most of his readers did not realize that they had been translated
from Yiddish. Kvitko wrote for children from around 1917, the
beginning of his literary career, but until the early 1930s he was
still perceived predominantly as a poet for adults.[5] His spectacu-
lar transformation from a "national minority" author scarcely
known outside Yiddish literature into a leading Soviet poet during the 1930s was a by-product of the critical campaign of 1929.
After Kvitko was thrown off the editorial board of *Di royte velt*,
he found new employment at the Tractor Factory, the newly built
flagship of Soviet industry that was so enthusiastically celebrated
by Der Nister in "Kharkiv." More than thirty years later, Kvitko's
widow Betty recalled, still with some caution: "In 1931, which was
a difficult year for him, Lev Moiseevich [Leyb Kvitko] considered
it necessary to seek work at a factory. He applied for the position
of apprentice lathe operator at the Kharkiv Tractor Factory, hiding the fact that he was a well-known poet."[6] Kvitko left that job
after a few months, but it had provided him with enough material
to compose the poem "In tsekh" (In a workshop, 1932).

Of interest mainly as a cultural-historical artifact, this poem
reveals Kvitko's painful struggle with the new, rigid rules of proletarian realism. The poem was written in a style radically different from that of Kvitko's pre-1929 works and comes close to
Der Nister's attempts of the same time to master the peculiar
style of Soviet "realism," with its fusion of facts and propaganda.
Gone was the peculiar combination of neo-Romantic revolutionary exaltation, obscure idiosyncratic symbolist imagery, and
gloomy darkness that was the hallmark of his early experimental
poetry. Kvitko's new hero was a humble menial worker awed by
the grandiosity of socialist construction and eager to learn new
skills by imitating exemplary shock workers. The technical reality
of industrial production was infused with a heavy dose of propaganda but largely untouched by poetic inspiration. Despite

Kvitko's best efforts, "In tsekh" did not meet with the approval of Soviet critics, who found that the poem did not sufficiently highlight the leading role of the Communist Party.[7] But after 1932, when the narrowly dogmatic doctrine of proletarian realism gave way to the more inclusive and sophisticated concept of socialist realism, Kvitko's position in Soviet literature improved. The process of organizational and ideological consolidation of Soviet literature was completed by the formation of the Union of Soviet Writers in 1934, and Kvitko was accorded a respectable place in its hierarchical structure. His return to literature was signaled by the publication of the omnibus *Rayzes un poemes* (Travels and poems, 1934), which included both his new poems and previously published ones. However, this collection would be his last major book for adults.

By 1934, literature for children had become an established branch of the Soviet literary system. It had an organizational and institutional infrastructure of its own, including publishing houses, journals, and a special section in the Union of Soviet Writers.[8] For writers with a checkered past of prerevolutionary political activity and cultural engagement, such as Kornei Chukovskii, a well-known liberal journalist, or Samuil Marshak, who in his youth dabbled in Zionist poetry, children's literature became a safe haven in the stormy sea of Soviet cultural politics. Apart from practical benefits, such as respectability and a stable income from mass-produced books, children's literature also offered a certain degree of creative autonomy. The Russian literary historian Marietta Chudakova explains that writing for children provided "freedom from the regulations that were developed for the big form such as the 'adult' novel, and offered a possibility of a relatively free movement of the characters in the literary space."[9] In children's books it was easier to comply with the basic tenets of socialist realism, such as the requirements of simplicity, clarity, and "folkishness" (Russian *narodnost'*/Yiddish *folkstimlekhkeyt*), without feeling guilty for betraying a former commitment to modernist aesthetics.[10] According to Chudakova, this combination of objective and subjective factors allowed for the unprecedented flourishing of Soviet children's literature during the 1930s, which reached its peak on the eve of the war. Although some scholars have recently rejected the hypothesis of children's literature as a "loophole in the system of socialist realism," one can still argue, as Ainsley Morse puts it, that "children's literature offered not so much greater artistic freedom as simply laxer entry standards—writers inclined to formal experimentation usually had no hope of officially publishing books for adults."[11] This insight helps explain Kvitko's success in creating the imaginary space of a bucolic and happy childhood free from fear and separate from the reality of life under Stalin's regime, with its everyday terror and anxiety. At the First All-Union Conference on Children's Literature, Kvitko argued that "not only the tractors in the children's books were 'Soviet,' but also the sun and the animals."[12] In 1939 he was awarded a medal, along with a few leading Russian children's authors, at that time a rare distinction for a writer, let alone for a Yiddish poet for children. By adjusting the dominant Stalinist discourse to a child's level of perception, Kvitko recreated a quasi-religious patriarchal myth of a benevolent father under whose watchful eye animals, children, and adults can roam freely, blissfully unaware of the bars of their cage.[13] But Der Nister's poetry for children offers no bucolic alternative to the cruel reality of the adult world.

## AN END TO FAIRY TALES: DER NISTER'S NEW *MAYSELEKH*

Perhaps inspired by Kvitko's successful comeback as a children's writer and the palpable benefits associated with this status, Der Nister made a similar, albeit less successful, attempt to recast himself as a poet of children's fairy tales. The genre of the fairy tale and its place in Soviet literature became a hotly contested ideological issue in 1929, when it was subject to criticism by the

Russian Association of Proletarian Writers (RAPP): "According to this view, children would only be confused and misled by the fantasy worlds depicted in fairy tales; their natural cognitive development would be misdirected and fundamentally stunted by the likes of talking animals, flying carpets, and other such impossibilities."[14] This campaign even led to the arrests of some writers and artists working in children's literature in late 1931, but the following year saw the demise of RAPP, and in 1933, a party resolution "declared in passing that even fairy tales were a necessary part of children's literature."[15] During the 1930s Der Nister published three books of poetic fairy tales (*mayselekh*) for children, which were illustrated by the leading Yiddish and Ukrainian book artists Moisei Fradkin and Ber Blank.[16] Unlike Kvitko's poetry, none of Der Nister's thirteen poems was translated into Russian or Ukrainian. His contribution to Soviet Yiddish children's literature has been largely forgotten, in contrast to his early works for children published under the auspices of the Kultur-Lige. Der Nister's first experiment in the genre of poetic fairy tales had been the collection *Mayselekh in ferzn* (Fairy tales in verse), with illustrations by Marc Chagall. This book appeared in four editions in the 1920s, in Kiev, Warsaw, and Berlin and became an iconic example of the Kultur-Lige modernist style. In her analysis of Der Nister's early children's poems, Daniela Mantovan points out their dark and pessimistic tone, their focus on death or illness, and, in contrast to traditional folktales, their absence of happy endings.[17] These features remain prominent in Der Nister's books of the 1930s, reflecting the difficulties he had in adjusting to the new regime, which required an optimistic resolution of conflict in line with communist ideology.

The 1934 collection *Dray mayselekh* (Three fairy tales) exemplifies three different attempts at producing a Soviet-style *maysele* (fairy tale). The first poem, "Der toyt fun a khinezer" (The death of a Chinese man), is an attempt to respond to current political events using the form of a children's fairy tale. In fact, the political theme of the poem—the persecution of the communists by the nationalist Kuomintang regime during the civil war that started in 1927—was already outdated by the time of its publication. In the early 1930s, especially after Japan's invasion of northeastern China, the Soviet Union moved closer to supporting the nationalist government. Diplomatic relations with China were restored in 1933, and the Soviet Union tried to maintain a balance between the opposing sides in the civil war. But Der Nister's representation of the conflict remains strictly black-and-white. The hero of his poem is a Chinese worker who is arrested by the Kuomintang secret police and executed for distributing leaflets with communist propaganda. The swift and cruel execution of the Chinese worker is the result of the political terror unleashed in his country: "And a time, my dear ones, / is such now / when terror is wild / and the enemy's sword flashes" (Un a tsayt, mayne libe, / a tsayt aza itst, / ven s'vildevet teror / un soynes shverd blitst).[18] Mantovan reads these lines as a subversive critique of the Great Terror, which started the same year. By moving the action to China, she argues, Der Nister establishes a "distance," "which permits the expression of some open criticism."[19] She supports her argument with the reference to passerby characters, "who, noticing the arrested worker followed by a secret service agent and by a dog, turn their heads," and concludes, unequivocally: "A man followed by a secret service agent was in the Soviet Union something which did not need any commentary."[20]

There is no doubt that the poem depicts a dark atmosphere of terror in which someone can be arrested and shot. But this straightforward interpretation of "Der toyt fun a khinezer" as an allegory of Stalin's terror raises troublesome questions. Was this message supposed to be clear to children but somehow escape the vigilant eye of trained Soviet censors? After all, Der Nister's more abstract symbolist stories provoked ideological accusations even in the relatively mild atmosphere of the late 1920s. Would Der Nister have taken the risk of being accused of anti-Soviet propaganda just when he was trying to make his literary come-back? Did he think that children's literature was not under strict political surveillance, even though a number of its authors and artists had been arrested in 1931 (and more would be arrested in 1937)?[21] And finally, was he truly opposed to the Soviet regime and critical of the terror tactics that were emerging in the early 1930s? His depictions of purges as public spectacles in *Hoyptshtet* (published the same year as *Dray mayselekh*) seemed positive and approving, although somewhat grotesque. While the question of Der Nister's "genuine" attitude toward the Soviet regime and its practices cannot be answered in the absence of reliable sources, we should be skeptical of any attempt to read Der Nister's poetry for children as a straightforward subversive allegory. Some of his poems are morally ambiguous and darkly pessimistic, and the author's stance is often uncertain, which may have been one of the reasons he did not become a successful Soviet children's poet like Kvitko. The ending of this violent tale about the execution of a Chinese worker, like many of Der Nister's other children's poems, does not offer a clear interpretation. In his final words, the worker promises an apocalyptic moment of redemption: "But a day will come, / that day of the days!" (Ober kumen a tog vet, / yener tog fun di teg!) The narrator's conclusion is some-what uncertain, and even the grammar of the final two lines is not clear: "Whether that's what I heard / whether so I was told, / that's how I mourn the death of the Chinese man" (Tsi azoy hob gehert, / tsi m'hot mir dertseylt, / nor azoy hob khinezer / zayn toyt ikh baveynt).[22]

The second poem in *Dray mayselekh* is an abridged version of "A mayse mit a ber" (A tale about a bear) from *Mayselekh in ferzn*. Der Nister (or the editor) simply removed the core part of the tale while keeping the opening and the ending with slight but noteworthy changes. The protagonist, a simple *goy* (in this case, a gentile peasant) in the earlier version, becomes a *mentsh* (man, a more generic and positive term) in his new Soviet incarnation, evidently because the word *goy* was banned from Soviet literary Yiddish as politically incorrect.[23] In the earlier version the tale is a dark mystery. By felling a tree in a winter forest, the peasant accidentally wakes up a bear; the bear frightens the peasant away and jumps onto his sleigh. The terrified horse darts away into the empty snow-covered fields, where an old abandoned *tseylem* (Hebrew word for "cross," with a connotation of idol) stands on a faraway hill. As the horse passes by the cross, the bear tries to get off the moving sleigh by grasping the cross, but the rotten wood breaks, and the bear remains in the sleigh with the cross in his paw: "And from that time on, as people tell, / already for many years, / always in the winter in the fields / one can see the bear ride with the cross" (Un fun demlt on, dersteylt men / shoyn fun kame-kame yorn, / Tomed vinter in di felder / zet men ber mit tseylem forn).[24]

In the concluding part the narrator redirects the reader's attention from the enchanted bear with the cross to the poor goy who is stranded in the forest. Although curious children might ask about his fate, little information is provided. He has remained alone in the forest, unable to write down his story because he has no writing tools: "Had he ink and a pen, / he would have described his life there" (Ven er hot a tint un feder, / volt zayn lebn dort bashribn).[25] Thus, it falls to the Yiddish poet to tell a haunting story of a bear and a goy who has no appropriate means for recording it. The central, uncanny event of the tale—the bear snatching the cross and turning into a ghost that forever thereafter drifts over the fields on its sleigh—is missing in the Soviet version of 1934. The removal of the cross, probably because of its obvious religious connotations—which would be different for Jewish and Christian readers—effectively eliminates the "fairy" component of the tale, leaving only its rather boring narrative frame. The Soviet editorial transformation of "A mayse mit a ber" is a good example of the ideological "taming" of fairy-tale animals by removing eerie and haunting elements and turning them into dull and predictable creatures. The uncanny image of *pakhed-baytsh* (fear-whip), which drove the bear forward in the earlier version, gets changed into an ordinary whip, taking agency away from fear as an independent driving force and replacing it with an instrument of violent enforcement. What remains constant, however, is Der Nister's way of concluding his tales on a note of uncertainty, refusing to offer a simple lesson. The narrator fashions himself as a mediator between the remote world of fantasy and the concrete Soviet reality, leaving the interpretation open to the reader.

The last poem in the collection, "Der fuks un der ber" (The fox and the bear), with the subtitle of "Joke Story," is the most bizarre of the three in its gratuitous violence. Neither an adaptation of an older version nor a direct response to current political events, it ushers in Der Nister's new approach to animal tales by introducing animal characters and motifs that will reappear in his later poems. A fox challenges other animals to wrestle with a bear, warning them that if they lose, they will be cut into halves, one of which will be cooked as a meal for the bear and the other set free. Since no animal volunteers, the angry and hungry bear devours the entire fox raw, "From the fur down to the flesh, / from the flesh down to the bone / and he has eaten it up slowly / without sauce and without horseradish" (fun fel un tsum fleysh, / fun fleysh un tsum beyn, / un gegesn pamelekh / on zanft un on khreyn).[26] Like the previous poems, this poem ends without a clear moral judgment or political lesson. After a few more gruesome details describing the eating of the fox followed by a dotted line, the storyteller merely states: "That's how the bear finished his meal" (hot ber dan zayn sude / farendikt azoy).[27] This macabre and absurdist poem forms a transition between the old and the new way of representing animals in Der Nister's fairy tales. Animals are still the main actors in the fairy-tale world, from which humans are absent, but they behave in senselessly cruel and self-destructive ways. In Der Nister's next two children's books, the animals' natural habitat becomes fully controlled by humans, which largely fits the general Soviet trend, seen for example in Kvitko's poetry. Hunger or illness occasionally drives animals to hostile human settlements, where they are lucky to escape back into nature. This mode of representation stands in stark contrast to our expectation of socialist-realist literature for children, which is supposed to be optimistic and didactic and avoid excessive brutality.[28] Unlike Kvitko, Der Nister never uses a child as the narrator, or even as a character in his *mayselekh*. The stories are told through a somewhat-detached adult voice, occasionally betraying anxiety, insecurity, or fear and offering no clear moral judgment. In one instance the capricious narrator even admits that he is too lazy to tell the story in full detail. The occasional dark irony of the narrator seems more appropriate to adult than to children's literature.

In the collections *Mayselekh* (Fairy tales) and *Zeks mayselekh* (Six fairy tales), published in 1936 and 1939 respectively, the human world more closely resembles the Soviet society of that time. It is tightly organized, strictly controlled, and suspicious of strangers. Some of the *mayselekh* can be read as straightforward political allegories in which a predatory animal personifies the class enemy who tries to pass for an innocent character but is unmasked by vigilant citizens. One example is "A volf in a shofener fel" (A wolf in a sheepskin), in which a wolf puts on a sheepskin in order to steal sheep while the shepherds and guard dogs are asleep. But the sheep manage to wake the dogs, and the wolf is shot by the shepherds.[29] The conclusion stresses the novelty of this tale: "This kind of tale / that was not heard / even by / old men with beards" (A mayse aza min, / vos zi nisht gehert / es hobn afile / keyn zkeynim mit berd).[30] Although it is new, the narrator assures us, "And yet it is true, / not made up" (Un dokh is zi emes, / nisht oysgetrakht iz).[31] In "A mayse mit a fuks" (A tale about a fox), a fox that used to steal chickens from a poorly guarded shed gets shot when the members of a collective farm install a proper security system.[32] The concluding message of this otherwise straightforward tale appears somewhat ambiguous, because it negates the possibility of the *mayse* genre in the contemporary world: "What once was / today is no more. / Out of fashion, / stories about foxes / are also finished." (Vos geven iz amol,/ iz shoyn haynt, iz shoyn nit. / Nito, shoyn nito, / Fun der mode aroys, / oykh mayses mit fuksn / geendikt un oys.)[33] Does this ending mean to suggest that the new regime puts an end not only to the freedom allegorically represented by the wild animals but also to the freedom to tell stories about them? Is this a hidden criticism of a regime that has not merely eliminated wild animals, presumably its masked enemies, but also erased all memory of them? In this case, is the very act of preserving the memory of the regime's victims subversive? Der Nister appears to assert on the one hand the novelty and truthfulness of his animal tales, as in "A volf in a shofener fel," while on the other he pronounces this genre dead, as in "A mayse mit a fuks."

The *mayses* about smaller animals are less cruel. To protect himself from the marten, the squirrel tries to bribe the hunter by buying him new boots and a gun. Having earned some money from selling nuts, the squirrel purchases the equipment but, not surprisingly, is unable to carry the heavy gun and the boots back to the forest. In the end the squirrel decides to stay in the forest where it belongs—"and the squirrel remained / what the squirrel is" (un geblibn iz veverik / vos veverik iz),[34]—and never to come to town again. Instead of nuts, the squirrel sends its greetings to children. As in the previous tales, the meaning remains unclear: is it good or bad for children to receive greetings rather than nuts? In another *mayse*, a toothache forces the hare to seek help from humans in town. One night, overcoming its natural fear, the hare goes to the dentist's office but is terrified by the drilling machine and runs back to its cabbage field. Again, it is the ending that makes the meaning ambiguous: "Khi-khi-khi and kha-kha-kha! / Have you heard such a thing! / That a hare with toothache / should go to a dentist? / No!" (Khi-khi-khi un kha-kha-kha! / Hostu gehert a zakh aza! / az a hozl zol mit tseyn / gor tsum dokter veln geyn? / - Neyn!) [35] Like the tale about the fox, this one concludes with the resolute negation of the possibility of the fairy-tale genre, but, unlike the fox, the hare and the squirrel seem to be safe in their natural habitat. Unlike big predators, such as the fox and the wolf, that can cause damage to human society, small animals are harmless intruders that should be isolated from people. The didactic meaning of these tales remains puzzling. Large predators may be understood to represent the enemies of the Soviet regime who try to pass for innocent "sheep" or take advantage of the lack of vigilance to steal collective property. But why is it impossible for Soviet society to be kind to small animals like the squirrel that want to help people, or are in need of help for themselves like the hare? Do they pose a danger simply because they are different?

### THE SELF ON TRIAL

Der Nister's only *mayse* with overtly political references to Stalinist terror is "Kozekl-royt" (A little red Cossack), which was included in the 1939 collection. It opens with the arrival of a traveling puppet show: "A puppet theater in our courtyard! ... / Hey, kids, a tumult, / a great commotion" (Der lialke-teater / bay undz iz in hoyf! ... / Oy, kinder, a tuml, / a groys ayngeloyf).[36] The actor is hidden in the booth under the stage, but his shadow is visible through the veiled bottom. After prolonged silence, a little puppet in patent leather boots, satin trousers, a red jacket, and a hat, "a genuine Cossack" (an ekhter kozak) appears on the stage. He asks the children if they have ever been to war and seen a battle against an enemy. Following a negative response from the audience, another character comes onto the stage. He has a stick in his hand but "is trembling from fear" (tsitert far shrek): "He would like to run away, but the walls don't let him" (s'volt

ergets antlofn, / nor s'shtern di vent).[37] The children dislike him
at first sight "because he looks like a little demon / who came
from mud, / and he is dressed / entirely in black" (vayl s'zet oys
dos rukhl / fun blote aroys, / un ongeton iz es / in shvartsn nor
bloyz).[38] Interestingly, this is the only occasion in Der Nister's
Soviet *mayses* in which he uses a word from his old symbolist
vocabulary, *rukhl* (little demon), which in this context denotes
a political enemy. The Cossack asks the audience who this "blo-
tiker" (dirty) man is, but the children have no answer. Then he
turns to the *rukhl*: "Who sent you? And who are you?" (Ver hot
geshikt dikh? / un ver du bist?),[39] to which the terrified *rukhl*
responds, stuttering: "Trotskist" (Trotskyist). He further confesses to having been paid to cross the border illegally: "And I
was told, / oh, Little Red Cossack, / to murder / you together
with the children" (Un m'hot mir geheysn / oy, kozekl-royt / i
dikh mit di kinder / dershlogn tsum toyt).[40] The Cossack asks the
audience again: "What does such a person deserve? / ... A cookie
with cream? / Or maybe marzipans? / Or bread with butter? /
And the children respond: / 'No, he deserves death!'" (Vos kumt
aza eynem / ... a kukhn mit krem? / tsi gor martsipanes? / tsi
puter mit broyt? / un s'entfern kinder: / 'neyn, s'kumt derfar—
toyt!')[41] Hearing the verdict, the Cossack takes the stick from the
Trotskyist's hand and beats him to death "until he jerks up his
head" (biz yener dos kepl / farvarft shoyn aruf).[42]

Der Nister adapts the form of the traditional Ukrainian folk
puppet theater *vertep* for his poem. The vertep performance was
divided into two parallel acts, the sacred and the secular, which
played out in the upper and the lower level of the box respectively. The Nativity story in the upper level was accompanied in
the level below by lampoons of different groups of local population represented by the figures of Kozak (Cossack/Ukrai-
nian), Liakh (Pole), Tsyhan (Romani), Moskal' (Russian), and
Zhyd (Jew). Vertep had been a popular form of entertainment
in Ukrainian rural communities since the seventeenth century,

but in the 1930s, it was largely banned in Soviet Ukraine because of its overtly religious message. It was traditionally performed by itinerant students of religious seminaries and had many regional variations, especially in the secular part. The academic study of vertep by Yevhen Markovs'ki, published in Kiev in 1929, included transcripts of several plays that could have inspired Der Nister's appropriation of this medium for his poem. One particular episode, common to all variations, presented a confrontation between the Cossack and the Jew. In one variation the Cossack asks the Jew for a drink of vodka, the Jew initially refuses, but when the Cossack threatens him, the Jew agrees. When the Cossack gets drunk, the Jew tries to strangle him, but the Cossack manages to get up, hit, and kill the Jew. Disgusted by the stench of the Jew's corpse, the Cossack summons Satan and tells him to take away the Jew, whom he calls "your [Satan's] grandfather": "you will have a great roast / such that you've never had in your life." Satan is happy: "At last, I've been long waiting for it! / Now I've got the Jew in my hands"; he takes the Jew's body to hell.[43] In another variation, the Cossack simply kills the Jew instead of paying him for the drink and calls the devil to take the body to hell.[44]

The similarity between the vertep episode and Der Nister's poem is obvious, but the meaning of this parallel is puzzling. To begin with, vertep had not been performed in Ukraine since the late 1920s, so the implied Yiddish-speaking child readership would not be familiar with this form of Ukrainian folk theater. Even more surprising is the appropriation of the crude and violent antisemitic trope for Yiddish literature. By casting the hapless Trotskyist in the traditional role of the Jew murdered by the Cossack, Der Nister seems to suggest (at least to a reader familiar with the vertep conventions) association between Trotskyism, the most dangerous political label in the late 1930s, and Jews. Can this be a hint at the antisemitic character of Stalinist terror, which was carried out by "Red Cossacks"? Yet the Trotskyist is represented as a repulsive character according to the conventions of vertep genre, so it is difficult to see any appeal to mercy or hidden criticism of the terror on the part of the author.

Mantovan argues that the main focus of this tale is not the play itself but the "dynamics between the public and the puppeteer," which highlight the role of the "man behind the boards . . . with his manipulative way of retelling the story (and history) and his threatening message."[45] She describes this "technical strategy" as the art of "cryptic criticism"—"to look like propaganda and be the contrary of it"—a practice that Der Nister "cultivated . . . over a number of years" after his return to the Soviet Union.[46] Indeed, the framing of the puppet show offers many intriguing clues, but the interpretation that they suggest is more complex and ambiguous than "cryptic criticism" of the Soviet regime. Typically for Der Nister, the ending is perplexing. When the *peyger* (derogatory word for "corpse," which is usually used for dead animals) of the Trotskyist is disposed of in a *lokh* (hole) and the performance ends, the puppeteer who played both roles quietly comes out from behind his booth, packs up his stage set, and leaves for the next courtyard. The children run after him, eager to see what will happen there: "How he comes, his face made up, / to plunder and murder us. / And how the Little Red Cossack / will kill him there" (Vi er kumt fargrimirt / undz af royb un af mord. / Un vi kozekl-royt / vet im toytn oykh dort).[47] This ending also calls into question the validity of the story as an allegory, opening up a range of possible interpretations.

The ending draws attention to the fact that the puppet show trial is actually performed by the *same* actor who plays both the accuser and the accused. As Mantovan observes, the show trial motif is present in Der Nister's late symbolist tales, most prominently in "Under a Fence." In that "review," as Der Nister described its genre, the narrator himself played both the victim and the accuser, similar to the puppeteer in "Kozekl-royt." The technique of relocating the trial to a stage goes back to the reportages from the early 1930s. In "Kharkiv" the purge was a public ritual celebrating veteran communists, while in "Eyns a shtetl" (One of the shtetls), the theater performance had a liberating and invigorating effect on the collective farm audience. In "Kozekl-royt," the manipulative puppet show trial is routinely performed before mechanically approving young spectators who ritualistically demand a death sentence after hearing an obviously forced confession from a miserable, dehumanized defendant. In agreement with Nikolai Evreinov's concept of the origin of theater from the archaic spectacle of public execution, Der Nister portrays the Stalinist show trial using the folkloric medium of vertep. This would be in line with other examples that Evreinov drew from the medieval and early modern genres of popular theater, such as Passion plays and performances of tortures in hell. Today it is tempting to interpret this performance as a subversive critique of the Stalinist terror of the 1930s. But considering the historical context, we are left with the same questions as earlier, regarding "Der toyt fun a khinezer" (The death of a Chinese man). Did Der Nister believe that the Soviet censor or editor would not be able to catch the trick, especially at a time when other prominent Soviet children's writers had already been persecuted? Was he trying to reach out to an audience of children over the heads of the adult censors, trying to unmask the cruel absurdity of the Stalinist show trials? And, perhaps most disturbingly, why are the roles of the accuser and the accused performed by the same actor? The show trial in "Kozekl-royt" plays out not between us and them but within the self, between the right and the left hand. It is a painful, repetitive, and ultimately self-destructive process. In the context of the 1930s, this existential condition of the divided self finds its expression in the form of a party purge or a show trial, but its roots can be traced back to the Jewish mystical concept of the inherent conflict between the *yetser-hatov* and the *yetser-hara*, the drive for "good" and the drive for "evil" vying for control of man's free will by addressing him from opposing sides. This ethical and philosophical problem comes to the fore in *The Family Mashber*, in which the trial motif is central to the plot.

CONCLUSION: EACH ACCORDING TO ITS KIND

Unlike Kvitko, Der Nister was unable to secure for himself a place in children's literature. The dark and disturbing world of his *mayselekh* differs from Kvitko's bright and bucolic utopia, in which Soviet people and domestic animals live in happy harmony. Der Nister's human society is tightly organized, strictly controlled, and wary of strangers who come at night from the woods. Any form of "otherness," such as the one represented by wild animals, is no longer tolerated here. The animals, the masters of the universe in Der Nister's early *mayselekh*, have now been pushed back into the wilderness where they belong. The lines dividing the animal and the human worlds are clearly demarcated and closely guarded. If an animal, driven by hunger or pain, crosses the border into the realm of humans, it risks death as an enemy. Smaller and presumably cleverer creatures, such as the squirrel and the hare, learn the rules of the game and retire to their natural habitat voluntarily, whereas bigger predators, such as the fox, the wolf, and the bear, are mercilessly killed as "enemies of the people." But Der Nister does not seem to protest this order. Instead, he simply registers the death of the symbolist mode of imagination, which could freely mix humans, animals, and supernatural creatures.

So who was the intended reader and what was the meaning of Der Nister's bizarre self-negating, if not self-hating, children's poetry? One can hypothesize that his primary addressee was himself. It is possible that Der Nister could also have been speaking above the censor's head to the small and diminishing circle of his devoted admirers who were conversant with his obscure symbolist vocabulary and familiar with Jewish religious tradition and Ukrainian folk culture. Using the deliberately "naïve" form of fairy tale and the format of the illustrated children book as his new vehicle, Der Nister might even have been reflecting on his own position as a "wild animal" in the rigid and strictly disciplined society of the Soviet Union. Yet it would be too simplistic to cast him as a defender of artistic freedom and a critic of the

Soviet regime. Rather, his rare power of imagination enabled him to speak for both the accuser and the accused, the perpetrator and the victim, like the puppeteer in the puppet show trial. The puppeteer is both the manipulator and an object of his own manipulation, doomed to replay the show trial over and over again. Der Nister's works of the 1930s, with all their obvious artistic weaknesses and ambiguities, offer a profoundly disturbing insight into the destructive ability of totalitarianism to split human personality, locking it in a vicious cycle of self-persecution, making circles across winter fields like the bear with a cross on a sleigh.

NOTES

1. Moss, *Jewish Renaissance in the Russian Revolution*, 201.

2. The role and significance of children's literature in the aesthetics and ideology of Yiddish and Hebrew modernism and various artistic aspects of Yiddish books for children at the turn of the 1920s have recently received much scholarly attention in studies by Kenneth Moss, Hillel Kazovsky, Kerstin Hoge, Sabine Koller, and others who examine this phenomenon from historical, literary, and artistic points of view.

3. Hoge, "Design of Books and Lives," 52.

4. Hellman, *Fairy Tales and True Stories*, 392.

5. In his entry on Kvitko in the *Literaturnaia entsiklopediia*, vol. 5, 169, the critic Aron Gurshteyn devotes only one sentence to Kvitko's children's poetry.

6. Kvitko and Petrovskii, *Zhizn' i tvorchestvo L'va Kvitko*, 137.

7. See Estraikh, *Evreiskaia literaturnaia zhizn' Moskvy*, 149.

8. For more detail on the creation of the "industry of children's culture," see Fateev, *Stalinizm i detskaia literatura*, 53–59.

9. Chudakova, *Izbrannye raboty*, 347.

10. Ibid., 347–50.

11. Morse, "Detki v kletke," 128–29.

12. Hellman, *Fairy Tales and True Stories*, 369.

13. For a more detailed comparison of Kvitko's and Der Nister's poetry for children, see Krutikov, "End to Fairy Tales."

14. Morse, "Detki v kletke," 56.

15. Hellman, *Fairy Tales and True Stories*, 368.

16. On Fradkin, see Kotliar, "Obrazy shtetla v grafike Moiseia Fradkina."

17. Mantovan, "Transgressing the Boundaries of Genre," 37–39.

18. Der Nister, *Dray mayselekh*, 6.

19. Mantovan, "Reading Soviet-Yiddish Poetry for Children," 104.

20. Ibid., 105.

21. Morse, "Detki v kletke," 128–29.

22. Der Nister, *Dray mayselekh*, 11.

23. However, a *goy* and a *shiksl* (derogatory term for a gentile peasant girl) do appear as late as 1929 in the poem "Vint" (Wind) by Itsik Fefer, an exemplary Soviet poet (and Der Nister's rival). It was published in a collection that had the same title as Der Nister's. Fefer, *Mayselekh in ferzn*, 14–17.

24. Der Nister, *Mayselekh in ferzn*, 6.

25. Ibid., 7.

26. Der Nister, *Dray mayselekh*, 28.

27. Ibid., 30.

28. Morse, "Detki v kletke," 62–63.

29. Der Nister, *Mayselekh*, 13–23.

30. Ibid., 23.

31. Ibid.

32. Ibid., 24–34.

33. Ibid., 34.

34. Ibid., 12.

35. Ibid., 43.

36. Der Nister, *Zeks mayselekh*, 21.

37. Ibid., 24–25.

38. Ibid., 25.

39. Ibid., 26.

40. Ibid.

41. Ibid., 27–28.

42. Ibid., 28.

43. Markovs'ki, *Ukrayins'ky vertep*, 90-93.

44. Ibid., 179.

45. Mantovan, "Reading Soviet-Yiddish Poetry for Children," 108.

46. Ibid.

47. Der Nister, *Zeks mayselekh*, 30.

FOUR

—ᴍ—

# THE GENERATION OF 1905

DER NISTER'S THIRD, AND BY far most successful, attempt
at creative reinvention was in the genre of historical fiction. His
major achievement is the novel *The Family Mashber*, but, judging by two works that remained unpublished during his lifetime, his plans for this genre were more ambitious. In the letter
to his brother Motl that was mentioned in chapter 2 and will be
discussed in more detail in chapter 5, Der Nister wrote of his
intention to write a book about his "entire generation": "About
what I saw, heard, experienced and imagined" (S'handlt zikh vegn
mayn gantsn dor—fun dem, vos ikh hob gezen, gehert, ibergelebt
un oysgefantazirt).[1] The two works discussed in this chapter were
probably meant to be part of that historico-biographical project,
although their exact place and relation to *The Family Mashber*
remains unclear.

## "PUPE": AN OLD-TIME FAMILY DRAMA

The novella "Pupe: A mayse fun tsurik mit yorn" (Pupe: A tale
from years ago) was published in the Paris journal *Parizer tsaytshrift* in 1956 with a footnote stating that the text was sent by the
writer's widow.[2] The typewritten manuscript with Der Nister's
handwritten corrections, which has been preserved in the Russian

State Archive of Literature and Art,[3] has no date. According to
Der Nister's widow, Elena Sigalovskaia, the novella was written
in the late 1930s; stylistically it also seems to belong to the prewar period.[4] In the 1960s, when the publishing house Sovetskii
pisatel' considered the publication of *Regrowth*, Der Nister's collection of short prose, it was decided, after some discussion, that
"Pupe" did not fit the "thematic unity" of the volume, which was
described as "the tragedy of the Jewish people in the territory of
occupied Poland."[5]

Pupe, which means "doll," is the name of the main character
and is how the novella is referred to in the Russian documents
related to its proposed publication. The novella is set around 1905
in the "aristocratic" residence of a merchant named Shloyme
Sheynfeld, which is located next to a large meadow on the out-
skirts of an unnamed city. The Sheynfeld family has a peculiar
symmetrical composition. Shloyme, a widower, has three sons
and one daughter. The two younger sons, referred to as *bonim*
(a somewhat belittling Hebraism for "sons"), are portrayed as
mentally slow but physically strong, with no aptitude for study
or interest in business. By contrast, Azriel, the oldest son, is an
intellectual who has studied at the Breslau rabbinic seminary,
the premier German center of Jewish scholarship. A widower as
well, Azriel has a teenage daughter named Pupe. His sister, also
widowed, has a son named Muni who is in his early twenties.
The three generations of the family reside comfortably in a large
house surrounded by a beautiful garden, supported by Shloyme's
trading business. Pupe is a lively and clever girl, while Muni is
melancholic and pensive. She enjoys laughter, good company,
and fresh air, while he prefers the solitude of his study, where he
composes learned articles for his own journal. She is beloved by
everybody in the house and is especially good at dancing, which
she performs skillfully, while his favorite pastimes are to visit the
sick and follow funerals to the cemetery. Pupe loves Muni, but
he, "a kind of little grandfather" (a min kleyner zeyde),[6] is cold to

her, probably because of his suppressed *yetser-hore* (evil inclination), as Der Nister ironically refers to erotic desire.[7] Muni's lack of interest in Pupe is upsetting to the family, who would like the cousins to get married and further insulate the household from the surrounding world.

Disappointed in Muni, Pupe befriends boys from the local commercial school who follow her as she walks home from her girls' gymnasium. Eventually one of them—who remains nameless throughout the story—wins the competition for her attention and becomes her permanent suitor and dancing partner at school parties. This lighthearted and easygoing boy comes from a dysfunctional family. His father, a failed broker who sponges from his wealthy acquaintances and former clients, neglects his children. As a good student, his son has a full scholarship, but in the opinion of Pupe's family, which is apparently shared by the narrator, he is an "intellectual hoodlum" (gaystiker hefker), an irresponsible and frivolous person (parshoyn) who takes after his freeloader father. Yet Pupe is attracted to precisely those qualities that she finds lacking in her own family. She spends more time with her new friend in the park and eventually visits him in his rented room. At some point thereafter, her appearance begins to change; she becomes slow and weak, and finally it becomes evident that she is pregnant. To avoid a public scandal and keep the disgrace within the family, Shloyme resolves the problem in a quiet way by making Muni marry Pupe in a private wedding ceremony at home. In the meantime, the unnamed offender disappears from town.

These events, the narrator informs the reader more than halfway into the story, take place on the eve of the 1905 revolution, an event that shook the foundation of the Russian Empire. The story then turns to "Pupe's guy" (Pupe-parshoyn), who resurfaces in town when the revolution is drawing to an end. He is characterized as a "déclassé ruffian" (deklasirt-gekhrasteter), shifting from one political party to another, partaking of the different "social meals" (sotsiale sudes) in the manner of his father, who used to drift from one wealthy home to the next. Eventually he finds his political home among the anarchists. While pretending to preach the lofty ideals of social justice, he is in fact the leader of a gang that extorts money from the city's well-to-do citizens. The anarchists terrorize the prosperous homeowners by sending letters with death threats, which they occasionally make good on when someone refuses to pay. In the meantime, Muni has decided to study in Germany, from which he sends a letter of divorce to Pupe. Shloyme, unable to recover from these misfortunes, spends his days in a wheelchair in his room upstairs, refusing to see his granddaughter and her son, who reside on the ground floor.

One evening, while Azriel is driving home in his droshky with the cashbox holding the day's earnings from the family business, he is attacked and killed by anarchists. In a raid on the anarchist hideout, the police arrest their leader, who turns out to be Pupe's former lover. In a desperate attempt to save him from a death sentence, Pupe pleads with her grandfather to intervene on his behalf, revealing that she still loves him and wants to marry him. Now that her father is dead and Muni has divorced her, this marriage is her only chance to rebuild her life and give her child a father—his real one. Crushed by adversity and frail from old age and illness, Shloyme finally forgives his granddaughter and gives her his blessing, but in this moment he suffers a stroke and loses his speech. In the end, all efforts to rescue Pupe's lover fail, and he is hanged with the other terrorists. Shloyme dies soon afterward, leaving no will. The family business passes to his daughter, Pupe runs the household, the *bonim* marry two sisters of a similar disposition, and Muni stays abroad as an independent scholar supported by his mother. "And that's it. And everything has remained as it used to be." (Un shoyn. Un vayter iz alts geblibn, vi geven.)[8]

It is easy to see how this novella does not adhere to the prescriptions of socialist realism. Permeated by melancholic, if somewhat ironic, nostalgia for the patriarchal lifestyle of the provincial Jewish bourgeoisie, it shows little interest in the revolution. Der Nister suggests that the rogue anarchists were not "genuine" revolutionaries, but he offers no positive alternative to their revolutionary terror, which he portrays as criminal violence. Moreover, the narrator even seems sympathetic to the efforts of the tsarist police to crush the anarchist cell. The novella's setting, a spacious old house surrounded by a large, leafy garden, evokes Anton Chekhov's *Cherry Orchard*, a parallel which is accentuated by the image of an old mulberry tree framing the narrative.[9] In the beginning of the novella, the tree appears as a metaphoric foreboding of troubles to come. One half of it is inside the garden, whereas the other half extends outside the wall, where street boys are free to eat its sweet berries. The tree reemerges in the concluding line of the story, and this time it is old and dry, with no leaves or berries. The decay of the tree symbolizes the decline of the Sheynfeld family, which has been unable to resist the pressures of the new era. Despite their best efforts, Shloyme and his children cannot protect their deteriorating family by keeping the family behind the walls through arranging the marriage of the cousins. Even Pupe's falling in love with the "intellectual hoodlum" seems to be an act of despair caused by Muni's apathy rather than a protest against the patriarchal order.

"Pupe" fits well into the narrative of social decline and biological degeneration that was prominent in European and Yiddish literature in the late nineteenth and early twentieth century. In this view, decay seems to affect men more than women. Shloyme and Azriel prefer to stay widowers and have no interest in women, and Muni prefers the dead to the living. Azriel and Muni have inherited Shloyme's intellectual abilities but not his vigor and business acumen, while the two *bonim* are chronically immature, both intellectually and ethically, despite their physical strength. But the most prominent examples of social degradation are Pupe's anonymous lover and his father, who represent the disappearing social group of brokers and mediators who had once thrived in

Jewish society. Pupe and her aunt, however, seem to be more resilient in the face of social malaise and physical degradation, even though these female characters are less complex and somewhat flatter than the male ones. They jointly run the household after the death of Shloyme and Azriel, supporting and controlling the male family members who remain, Muni and the *bonim*.

It is Pupe, not Muni, who takes the initiative in courting. In a playful reference to the story of Adam and Eve, Pupe buys an apple on the way home from the river on a hot summer day from a street vendor, a "garden Jew" named Henekh, bites into it, and offers it to Muni, but the charm does not seem to work on her cousin. Henekh encounters her again at the end of the story while Pupe is taking her son to the river; his figure may be read as Der Nister's affirmation of the eternal vitality of the Jewish people, a theme that becomes prominent in *The Family Mashber* and especially in his fiction of the 1940s. Yet after giving birth to her son and until the final episode, the cheerful and extroverted Pupe recedes from the narrative . With all her charm and vitality, she remains a doll, an object of manipulation by her family and male-dominated society. The theme of family decline links "Pupe" with *The Family Mashber*, which might serve as a clue as to how the novella fits into Der Nister's larger plan of writing a history of his generation. Yet it remains an isolated episode, a nuanced, somewhat nostalgic but also ironic, psychological study of a traditional family's futile struggle against the pressures of historical change.

### FROM THE YEAR 1905: TACKLING THE SUBJECT OF THE REVOLUTION

According to Leyzer Podriatshik, the literary scholar who published the unfinished draft of a novel by Der Nister under the title *Fun finftn yor* (From the year 1905) in 1964 in the Moscow journal *Sovetish heymland,* Der Nister was preoccupied with the theme of the 1905 revolution from the late 1930s until his arrest in 1949. Podriatshik cites Der Nister's widow, Sigalovskaia, who "confirms that Der Nister began working on the novel *Fun finftn yor* at the end of the 1930s," adding that during his meetings with Der Nister from 1944 to 1948, the writer showed interest in the subject. At that time, Der Nister was "reading memoirs of revolutionary activists, searching for folksongs and folktales from that period."[10] During a conversation with Podriatshik, Der Nister said: "The young people struggle [boren zikh] with 1905, oh how they struggle with it."[11] It is not clear, Podriatshik concludes, whether Der Nister was still working on his 1905 novel during the late 1940s, but there is no doubt that "he had been carrying this theme inside himself for years. He hoped that it would be a song about the generation with which he went hand-in-hand." (Er hot yornlang oysgetrogn in zikh ot di teme. Er hot gehoft, az dos vet zayn a gezang vegn dem dor, mit velkhn er iz hant-ba-hant mitgegangen.)[12]

Podriatshik was one of the most erudite literary scholars and critics associated with *Sovetish heymland* in the 1960s, until his immigration to Israel in the 1970s. A native of Bukovina, he belonged to the group of "Westerners" who began their literary careers outside the Soviet Union and became Soviet citizens as a result of the annexation of parts of Romania, Poland, and the Baltic States, and he played a prominent role in the revival of Yiddish culture in the Soviet Union in the 1960s. Podriatshik received Der Nister's manuscript in 1962 from Nokhem Oyslender, at that time the editor in charge of literary criticism at *Sovetish heymland*, who in turn had received it from Sigalovskaia. Podriatshik describes the manuscript as a working draft dense with emendations, revisions, and variations, some of which were barely readable, as if Der Nister was trying to record at once "the multitude of images and associations" that were produced by his imagination.[13] In addition, some parts of the text were crossed out by the author, but omitting them in the publication would create significant gaps in the narrative. Thus, the published text is a product of

Podriatshik's extensive editorial work and reflects his changes to the original text. In his afterword to the publication, Podriatshik places this unfinished novel at the end of the epic series of novels that Der Nister apparently planned to write.[14] *The Family Mashber* and *Fun finftn yor* were probably intended to be the bookends of this series, but Der Nister's work on its middle part likely did not move beyond a draft of the introduction, which was preserved in Der Nister's archive and was published by Podriatshik in 1967. The introduction focuses on the social and economic transformations that took place in Berdichev in the 1890s under the impact of capitalist modernization.[15] This hypothesis is supported by Der Nister's own words in the 1934 letter to his brother, in which he writes about his desire to produce a novel about his generation.

## THE NOVEL AND ITS MESSAGE

*Fun finftn yor* is set in a nameless city during the spring, summer, and autumn of the fateful year 1905. It has two main characters, Leybl and Milye, whose romantic relationship blossoms against the background of the lead-up to the revolution. They belong to different social classes, and their union symbolizes the solidarity among the members of a new generation of young progressives involved in the revolution. Leybl's father, a scion of an affluent and pious family with an illustrious pedigree, embodies the physical decay and moral degradation of the traditional Jewish elite. The true head and the driving force of the family is Leybl's mother, who comes from a "healthier root, with a healthy head on her shoulders" (fun a gezintern shoyresh, mit a gezuntn kop af di pleytses) but is proud and protective of the social status and reputation for piety of her husband's family.[16] She invests all her energy and ambition in raising and finding an appropriate spouse for her only son, who represents "the meaning of her present and her future" (dem zin fun ir itst un ir tsukunft) (4). She fails to consider the revolutionary spirit of the times, which tended to divide progressive children from their traditionalist parents: "The time did not agree with her" (di tsayt hot mit ir nit ayngeshtimt) (4). In spite of her efforts to shield her son from progressive ideas by surrounding him with religious tutors, Leybl eagerly absorbs new social theories and radical ideas and discards his Jewish education. He also rejects his mother's efforts to arrange a socially appropriate marriage for him and joins the revolutionary movement, where he quickly earns the respect of his comrades for his intelligence, erudition, pedagogical abilities, and oratorical skill.

Leybl joins a small, secretive circle of young Jewish men and women who meet at a discreet location in a side alley far from the city center. This scarcely furnished, inconspicuous house is entirely different from his lavish family home. It belongs to a poor widow with two children. Her elder son is in prison for his political activities and her younger daughter, Milye, is a student in the local gymnasium. The tenants are engaged in clandestine work preparing for the coming revolution: "Their main interest is not here, in the present, but elsewhere, in the future" (Zeyer hoypt-interes ligt nit do, inem itst, nor ergets andershvu, in der tsukunft) (8). The mutual attraction between Leybl and Milye grows as they become more deeply engaged in revolutionary activity, which tears down the social differences between them. Leybl's selfless idealism and love for Milye stand in contrast to his mother's obsession with money and status, whereas Milye's mother is supportive of both the revolutionary work and her daughter's attachment to Leybl.

The narrator tells us that the spring of 1905 marks one of those special historical moments in which the season of rebirth coincides with a "social spring" (gezelshaftlekher friling) (18). The combined awakening of nature and the revolution contributes to the blossoming of the relationship between Leybl and Milye. But their idyllic romance is disrupted by the interference of Leybl's mother, who wants to "turn back the wheel of history" (dreyen di geshikhte-rod aftsurik) (39). Unable to cope with losing her son to the times and blinded by her rage, she denounces the revolutionary circle to the authorities, sending her own son to prison. In the end she commits suicide, unable to forgive herself for the catastrophe that she has brought upon her family.

The summer season is busy with revolutionary activity that leads to violent confrontations with the authorities. Police, the clergy, and Russian nationalists mobilize peasants against Jews and students as the enemies of the monarchy. The attempt by town revolutionaries to dispatch self-defense units to the country ends in a massacre at the hands of agitated peasants (49). This violent episode deepens the rift between the young revolutionaries and the middle-class residents of the town, who accuse the youth of provoking the pogroms. The tension erupts in a scandal in the synagogue during the memorial service for the murdered members of the self-defense unit. The members of the group demand that the name of Blinov, a non-Jewish member of the self-defense unit, be read out together with the names of the murdered Jews, causing outrage among the pious Jews who refuse to commemorate a gentile as a martyr for the sanctification of the Divine Name in the Jewish communal prayer.[17] After an excited young man fires his revolver, the police storm the synagogue and arrest the revolutionaries. At this point, Leybl's mother, agitated and confused by the incident, loses her mind. As if "possessed by a dybbuk" (53), she denounces the revolutionaries to the authorities. The police raid Milye's house and arrest Leybl and other revolutionaries. Milye refuses to part with her beloved and follows him to prison.

The prison then becomes the setting for the narrative. Separated by gender into different cells, prisoners engage in heated ideological debates. Prison forges a new community made up of a variety of people who are in conflict with the regime, ranging from "disheveled religious dissidents" (patlate sektantn) to anarchists: "Here one can sometimes see a rare picture, like in Noah's Ark during the flood, where different kinds of creatures, kosher and non-kosher, were thrown together in one place, each with their own nature and particular attributes" (Do kon men amol zen a zeltn bild, a bild, vi in Noyekhs teyve beysn mabl, ven farsheydene minim khayes, koshere un nit koshere, hobn zikh in eyn eng ort ongeshtupt, yederer mit zayn natur un eygnshaft) (64). In their cells, they debate different visions for the future of society, as "the storm is knocking on our walls" (der shturem klapt shoyn in di vent tsu undz). The political spectrum is represented by the "truly major party" (emese take hoypt-partey) and "little side parties" (kleyne arbl-parteyelekh) (65). According to the official version of Soviet history, the "major party" could only be the Bolsheviks, although their presence in 1905 Berdichev was insignificant, whereas the Bund played the main role in revolutionary events there. This fact was acknowledged even in Soviet publications from the 1920s, before Stalin imposed the Bolshevik narrative on the history of the Russian revolutions. In declining to identify the "truly major party," Der Nister leaves some room for ambiguity: an informed reader might have interpreted it as a gesture toward the recognition of the Bund's central role. We will never know how the Soviet editor or censor would have responded to this ambiguity because the manuscript never reached the publication stage.

After Leybl has been imprisoned, his mother realizes the gravity of her actions and hangs herself. Her death is perceived as a bad omen by many of her social class, who fear "the possibility of a coming catastrophe" (epes meglekh forshteyendikn khurbn) (60) in the impending revolution. The story reaches its climax as a mass protest approaches the prison in order to liberate the revolutionaries on the very day the tsar issues his manifesto promising limited civil liberties. The disoriented soldiers shoot at the demonstrators and kill Milye's mother, who happens to be at the front, holding a red banner. Frightened by the murder, the authorities release the prisoners, and the funeral of Milye's mother turns into a protest by the entire population of the town, "with almost no exception" (on kimet oysnam) (73). The manuscript concludes with two symbolic acts that take place over the open grave and that link Jewish folk traditions and the revolution. The neighbor's newborn son is named after Milye's mother, "Symbolizing the connection between the death of Milye's mother and the life of the newborn child" (Simbolizirndik dermit di shaykhes fun milyes muters toyt tsu ot dem nay-geboyrenem kinds lebn) (73). The other act is the betrothal of Milye and Leybl, who reach for each other's hands over Milye's mother's grave.

The novel's message seems straightforward. The contrast between Milye's and Leybl's mothers symbolizes the irreconcilable conflict between the old and the new social orders, in which there is no possibility of compromise. Wealth and social ambition have blunted the sensitivity of Leybl's parents and prevented them from recognizing the tectonic shift in the foundations of the Russian Empire. As residents of the poorer suburban part of the town, Milye's mother and her neighbors are free from the constraints imposed by middle-class anxiety and are open to the changing times. The forces of history act in harmony with nature, and political freedom has its correlation to spatial openness. Revolutionaries feel comfortable in open spaces such as gardens, river banks, fields, and woods, where they can congregate, educate, and organize themselves, whereas the narrow, enclosed spaces in the town center, such as synagogues, prosperous middle-class homes, narrow streets, and the prison are sites of confrontation and violence. The tension between the closed spaces associated with the past and the open spaces representing the future is symbolically resolved in the final episode. The closed space of the grave where Milye's mother is buried simultaneously serves as the open site of the future revival, suggested by the naming of a newborn baby and the betrothal of a new revolutionary couple.

## HISTORICAL BACKGROUND

An important political turn occurred in Soviet historiography in 1931 when Stalin's personal intervention imposed a uniform version of the historical narrative, stressing the leading role of the Bolshevik Party in the history of the revolution, and Der Nister had to be careful not to deviate from this official line. Yet many of the sources and studies about 1905 published in the Soviet Union during the 1920s had a more favorable view of the role of the Bund and other non-Bolshevik socialist groups in the revolutionary struggle. One of Der Nister's likely sources was a collection of memoirs, *1905 yor in Barditshev* (The year 1905 in Berdichev), which was prepared by local historians and published in Kiev to commemorate the twentieth anniversary of the events (the book was actually published in 1927). The collection acknowledged the leading role of the Bund and praised its heroic struggle and vigorous organizing activities, explaining the weakness of the Bolsheviks by the absence of an organized industrial proletariat. Understandably, Der Nister had to temper the pro-Bundist tone while adapting some of the episodes and characters for his narrative. Thus, the final episode about the death and funeral of Milye's mother has as its prototype the story of *khaverte* (comrade) Gnyessia, a Bundist demonstrator who was killed by the police and buried on October 19, two days after the proclamation of the tsar's manifesto. At the same time, the mother's death at the head of the demonstration is a replay of a similar scene in Maxim Gorky's *The Mother*, the foundational novel of Soviet socialist realism.

Focusing on the grand narrative of the revolution, Der Nister glosses over the internal complexity of the negotiations among the Russian authorities at that critical moment, which made these events possible. According to the documents and memoirs published in *1905 yor in Barditshev*, there had been a disagreement between the Berdichev police and military commanders, on the one hand, and the town mayor, on the other. Unsure how to address the new political situation after the proclamation of the October Manifesto and unwilling to antagonize the population, the mayor asked the police not to interfere with the funeral procession and personally vouched for its peaceful character.[18] In his report to the Kiev governor, however, the police chief presented the funeral procession as a dangerous mass demon-stration threatening public order. This account makes it clear that this revolutionary "victory" was possible because of confu-sion among the authorities, though they soon recovered their strength and crushed the revolutionaries. But Der Nister chose not to extend the narrative beyond this fleeting victory. He also sometimes modified events to make them more dramatic. For example, he mentions an attack on a cruel police officer named Lukashevich by the revolutionaries, who threw acid in his face and blinded him. However, according to the Bund report of Aug-ust 1905, Lukashevich was merely doused with sunflower oil.

One of the most intriguing episodes in the novel is the depic-tion of a secret gathering of representatives from different Jew-ish socialist groups at the house of Milye's mother. Their fierce debate occurs in a form similar to that of a Talmudic dispute. Like the famous discussion of the sages in the Passover Hag-gadah, it goes on until morning. For conspiratorial reasons, the conference is masked as an engagement party for Milye and Leybl, prefiguring their betrothal at the grave of Milye's mother at the end of the novel. At a critical moment, when the lookout suspects a police raid, Milye and Leybl are placed at the head of a table set with meager fare, while the political representa-tives become celebrating guests. Thus the young couple's future union receives a symbolic "blessing" from revolutionary author-ities, though the alarm turns out to be a false one (29–30). Der Nister describes the participants rather generally as "represent-atives of different camps, of different organizations and differ-ent ideological positions, which differed in their assessment of present events and consequently had different projections and outlooks for the future" (fun farsheydene lagern, fun farshey-dene organizatyses un farsheydene ideishe aynshtelungen, vos shatsn op farsheydn di gesheenishn fun haynt, fun velkhe es dringen aroys di farsheydene prognozn un oyszikhtn af der tsu-kunft) (25). Instead of conveying the content of the ideological debates among the representatives of different Jewish groups, he describes the heated emotional and intellectual atmosphere and the characteristics of the participants of the revolutionary "Sanhedrin," as he refers to the meeting.

Only one person is identified by name. His real-life inspiration is Ber Borokhov, the founder of the Poale Zion (Labor Zionist) party. He is described as

> a certain comrade Borekh-Ber, as he was called, still a young man, but overgrown—not so much with the hair on his head and in his beard, as with an excess of knowledge and information. He had been made nearly blind by his penchant, cultivated since childhood, for every kind of book, from which he scooped treasures with full hands, a sharp but an undisciplined and casuistic intellect.

> eyner a khaver Borekh-Ber, vi me hot im gerufn, nokh a yunger mentsh, ober a shtark bavaksener, nit azoy mit hor fun kopf un fun der bord, vi mit fil kentenish un yedies, velkhe hobn im gemakht blindlekh-kurtszikhtik fun hobn tsu ton fun yungerheyt on mit farsheydene bikher, fun velkhe er hot geshept fule oytsres mit fule zhmenyes, a sharfer bal-moyekh, ober nit genug organizirter, a tse-dreyter. (27)

As a high school student, the young prodigy Borekh-Ber has already mastered Kantian philosophy and then moved on to the social sciences. The narrator remarks that Borekh-Ber has also made a remarkable contribution to the study of Yiddish, the language that he, as his real-life prototype Ber Borokhov, did not know and had to learn. He participates in the conference as the leader of "one of the Jewish territorialist parties" and impresses the audience with his powerful logic and erudition.

Writing after his immigration to Israel, Podriatshik identified the description of the political gathering in Der Nister's novel as the Berdichev Conference of December 1905, during which the leadership of the Labor Zionist organization Poale Zion tried to work out a new strategy in light of the evolving revolutionary situation. Two leading activists of the organization, Zerubavel and

Rachel Yanait, remembered that the young Pinhas Kahanovitsh was also present at that conference.[19] For understandable reasons, Der Nister's narrator does not reveal his own attendance, nor does he go into detail about the ideological debates; all the groups were, of course, branded as nationalist and reactionary by the official Soviet historiography of the 1930s. The leading figure at that conference was indeed the young Ber Borokhov, an intellectual prodigy who combined his ideological commitment to Marxism and Zionism with a deep scholarly interest in the Yiddish language. The movement that he initiated on the eve of the 1905 revolution later became a major political force in the creation of the state of Israel and his followers continued to occupy leading positions in Israeli politics until the 1970s.

The Berdichev conference was one of many occasions during which Borokhov engaged in fierce ideological debates. As the historian Jonathan Frankel relates in his account of Borokhov's political career:

> From Poltava, Borochov traveled with Ben Zvi straight to Berdichev for a conference of Poale Zion in the southwest. He arrived, after a train journey much delayed by strikes, with a heavy cold but, nonetheless, he single-handed conducted the battle against the Vozrozhdentsy [members of the Vosrozhdenie (Renaissance) group, later the Zionist Socialist Workers Party] led by Moyshe Zilberfarb. The contest raged, Zilberfarb later recalled, for an exhausting eight days, but always at a "high intellectual level," and although most of the delegates remained loyal to the Vozrozhdenie, it was generally agreed that Borochov had more than held his own.[20]

From the point of view of historical chronology, it is significant that the Berdichev conference took place in December, when the revolutionary wave was ebbing, and the Jewish revolutionaries had to decide what to do next. But as a novelist, Der Nister was more concerned with artistic "truth" than with historical accuracy, so he decided to change the chronology and move the event back in time. In the novel, the conference occurs in the spring, amid the buildup to the revolution, right after the first terrorist attack against the local police.

Der Nister's portrait of Borokhov is interesting both for what it says and for what it omits. Consistent with his nebulous narrative style, Der Nister does not even identify the object of Borokhov's linguistic interest as Yiddish, leaving the nature of his philological pursuits vague. Nor does he mention the word *Zionism*, replacing it with the more neutral term *territorialism*. While the latter omission is perfectly understandable in the context of the 1930s, the former is difficult to explain. Der Nister does not conceal his admiration for Borokhov, creating a vivid image of Borekh-Ber's remarkable personality. Was this a hidden message addressed to those readers whose knowledge of the history of 1905 went beyond the official Stalinist version of events and who were familiar with Borokhov? And how would Der Nister have addressed this episode in a more polished version of the novel? Borekh-Ber and his opponents embody the new wave of springtime energy that revives both nature and people. From this point of view, the ideological differences among them are less significant than the unifying spirit of revolutionary optimism. Because most of the Jewish radicals have come to the revolution straight from the yeshiva bench, they excel in debating the nuances of revolutionary theory. They have adequate organizational skills but are less effective when it comes to actual fighting. The narrator is fascinated by the intellectual brilliance of the Jewish revolutionaries and their commitment to ideological rigor, but his account becomes vague when he describes the details of the disagreements between the unnamed "main party" (perhaps the Bolsheviks) and the rival "splinter groups."

## LOOKING BACK AT 1905 FROM THE 1930S

The 1905 revolution became a popular subject in Yiddish fiction almost instantly and remained so until World War II. However, the representation of the events and the portrayal of characters largely depended on the ideological orientation of the author.[21] It is obvious that *Fun finftn yor* represents Der Nister's serious and likely sincere attempt to harmonize with the dominant Stalinist narrative of the Russian revolution. It is less clear, however, how readers should interpret the deviations from that narrative: as deliberate attempts to subvert it by addressing a certain segment of the readership over the heads of the censors, or simply as an unfinished and incomplete draft in need of further revision. Der Nister was not the only Soviet Yiddish writer who revisited the turbulent events of 1905 from the perspective of the 1930s. Another example is the novel *Dem shturem antkegn* (Toward the storm, 1938), by the veteran Yiddish writer Lipman Levin, who began his literary career in 1900 as a bilingual—Yiddish and Hebrew—writer and, like Der Nister, had to reinvent himself to comply with the terms of socialist realism. Lipman Levin initially worked in Hebrew on his historical trilogy focused between 1905 and 1914 after the October Revolution, but he eventually published two novels in Yiddish, in 1934 and 1938. Like Der Nister, he presented the revolution through the lens of a romance, in his case between a young woman from a wealthy merchant family and a young man from a humble background. There are certain parallels between *Dem shturem antkegn* and *Fun finftn yor* that suggest that Der Nister may have been familiar with Lipman Levin's novel.[22] Both novels end at the moment when revolutionary enthusiasm is at its highest pitch, before the collapse of the movement by the end of 1905, and both authors rearrange the timing of historical events to suit their compositional purposes. But unlike Der Nister, Lipman Levin meticulously adheres to the key tenets of socialist realism by stressing the prominence of the Communist (Bolshevik) Party. His leading characters follow the latest directives of the party before taking action, while the Bundists and Zionists are reduced to caricature. *Fun finftn yor* satisfies only one criterion of socialist realism—namely, "the representation of reality in its revolutionary development"—but fails to convincingly emphasize the leading role of the Communist Party. Instead, Der Nister presents the "will of the people" as the driving force of historical progress, a theory that was subject to explicit Marxist critique by Lenin and his followers.

These nuances in Der Nister's representation of the 1905 revolution largely escaped the attention of critics outside the Soviet Union. Chone Shmeruk dismissed the novel as "unambiguously realistic and . . . marked by an almost hackneyed ideological and artistic conception,"[23] and Elias Schulman, while acknowledging a "mixture of sincerity and cliché," considered the novel (or novella, as he sometimes calls it), written "according to the party line," a "regression [yeride] for Der Nister."[24] Echoing Shulman, Daniela Mantovan surmises that while writing the novel, Der Nister "must have realized that he was walking on a tightrope and that his work, within the limited boundaries of prescribed ideological constraints, could not equate to his artistic truth or to historical accuracy," which explains why Der Nister abandoned the project and decided to relocate to a "less politically 'sensitive'" time in The Family Mashber.[25] While the criticism of the published draft—particularly of its heavy, repetitive, and convoluted style and its ideological engagement—is justified, the critics paid little attention to its most complex and psychologically interesting character, Leybl's mother, Malke Mints. Here Der Nister turns to the problem of a personality divided against itself, closely examining motives and forces that bring a stable and self-confident person to act against her own interests. Malke's erratic behavior, which leads to the denunciation of her son and ultimately to her suicide, might have sounded particularly resonant in the charged Soviet atmosphere of the late 1930s. She is portrayed as a victim of delusions of grandeur that make her blind to the momentous historical changes taking place around her. But she is also a victim of fate: a member of a social class doomed to extinction by the merciless law of history. This type of character trapped in history finds its full development in *The Family Mashber*.

### NOTES

1. RGALI, f. 3121, op. 1, d. 37 (Letter to Max Kaganovich, no date), ll. 1–3.

2. Der Nister, "Pupe," 3.

3. Der Nister, "Pupe," RGALI, f. 3121, op. 1, d. 26.

4. RGALI, f. 1234, op. 19, d. 1966 (Sigalovskaia's letter to the Sovetskii pisatel' publishing house of June 14, 1966), l. 17.

5. RGALI, f. 1234, op. 19, d. 1966 (editorial decision regarding the publication of the collection *Vidervuks* of December 27, 1966), l. 15.

6. Der Nister, "Pupe," 11.

7. Ibid., 17.

8. Ibid., 52.

9. In the original, Der Nister calls this plant "ozhine-boym," which means "blackberry tree." However, blackberries grow on a relatively low bush, while what Der Nister describes sounds more like a mulberry tree.

10. Podriatshik, "Arum dem roman Fun finftn yor," 75.

11. Ibid.

12. Ibid.

13. Ibid.

14. Ibid., 74.

15. Der Nister, "Nokhvort un forvort." It is discussed in more detail in chapter 5.

16. Der Nister, *Fun finftn yor*, 3. Further page references in parentheses are to this edition, and translations are mine unless otherwise indicated.

17. Nikolai Blinov was a Russian student and member of the Socialist Revolutionary Party. During the anti-Jewish violence in Zhitomir in the summer of 1905, he tried to negotiate with the pogromists and was murdered. S. An-sky wrote an elegy for him, and in 2010 the St. Petersburg–based Russian author Aleksander Laskin published a novel with Blinov as a central character. A monument to Blinov has been erected in the town of Ariel on the West Bank.

18. *1905 god v Berdicheve*, 26.

19. Zerubavel, "Di grindungs-peryod fun der YSDAP-poyle tsien"; Yanait (Ben Zvi), *Anu olim*, 286–87. Quoted in Podriatshik, "Genize-shafungen," 105–6.

20. Frankel, *Prophecy and Politics*, 344.

21. More on early Yiddish literary representations of 1905 in Krutikov, *Yiddish Fiction and the Crisis of Modernity*, 67–117.

22. Krutikov, "Writing between the Lines," 212–19.

23. Shmeruk, "Der Nister's 'Under a Fence,'" 286.

24. Shulman, *Di sovetish-yidishe literatur*, 167.

25. Mantovan, "'Political' Writings of an 'Unpolitical' Yiddish Symbolist," 76.

# TEXT AND CONTEXT OF
# *THE FAMILY MASHBER*

MOYSHE LITVAKOV, THE MOST HIGHLY placed supporter of
Der Nister in the party hierarchy of the late 1920s and early 1930s,
would have probably admired *The Family Mashber* as a revelation of Der Nister's hidden genius as a realist writer, something
Litvakov had anticipated in his early articles. But Litvakov perished in the purges of the late 1930s, as did Der Nister's adversaries from Minsk, Khatskl Dunets and Yashe Bronshteyn. The
Stalinist terror of 1934–37 largely eliminated the old Bolshevik
cadre, along with many of the radical champions of proletarian
culture, and thus inadvertently created more favorable conditions for a sympathetic portrayal of the Jewish prerevolutionary
past. In the early 1930s, a historical novel depicting a middle-
class Hasidic environment would have been denounced by the
watchmen of proletarian realism as ideologically subversive. But
Der Nister had influential supporters among the members of the
Soviet literary establishment who, unlike Litvakov, survived the
purges unharmed and played a decisive role in the publication of
*The Family Mashber.* Isaac Nusinov was the editor of the first part,
published in 1939, while the prolific critic and Marxist literary
theorist Aron Gurshteyn served as the editor of the second part,
published in 1941. In the Soviet system of literary production,
the editor bore responsibility not only for the literary quality of

the text but also for its political correctness. The editor's name was always featured on the last page of every Soviet book, along with the print run and the dates of when the typesetting of the manuscript began and when it went to press.

## WRITING THE NOVEL: THE PERSONAL STORY

As mentioned in chapter 2, in 1934 Der Nister wrote a letter to his brother Motl in Paris. He explained the dire straits in which he found himself, due to the capital shifting from Kharkiv to Kiev, and his precarious position as a symbolist writer in Soviet literature. To survive as a writer, he wrote to Motl, "One has to be born anew, one has to turn his soul inside out." Finally, after a long period of reflection and self-searching, Der Nister found himself "on his way" (aruf af a veg): "I have started writing a book, according to my opinion and to the opinion of my close acquaintances, an important one. I want to dedicate all my energy to this book. It's about my entire generation—about what I saw, heard, experienced, and imagined." (Ikh hob ongehoybn shraybn a bukh, loyt mayn meynung un loyt der meynung fun noente bakante, a vikhtikn. Ikh vil dem bukh vidmenen ale mayne koykhes, vos ikh farmog. S'handlt zikh vegn mayn gantsn dor—fun dem, vos ikh hob gezen, gehert, ibergelebt un oysgefantazirt.) Writing this book was for him a matter of life and death: "And I must write my book. If I don't, it will be the end of me as a human being. If I don't, I will be erased from literature and from the life of the living." (Un shraybn mayn bukh muz ikh, oyb nit, bin ikh oys mentsh, oyb nit, ver ikh oysgemekt fun der literatur, un fun lebedikn lebn.) Writing equals living: "What is a writer who does not write[?] . . . it means that he does not exist, he is not part of the world." (Vos s'heyst a shrayber, velkher shraybt nit . . . dos heyst, er ekzistirt nit, er iz nito af der velt.)[1]

Der Nister explained that being distant from the new Ukrainian capital with its publishing infrastructure could be a benefit, because freedom from routine work would allow him to devote all his time to his book project. But he needed money to live on, which was the main reason for writing the letter. He asked Motl for a sum equivalent to fifty pounds sterling, to be paid in installments over two years while he was working on the novel. During this time he hoped to "get on my feet as a writer" (shteln zikh oyf di fis als shrayber). The decision to ask his brother for help was not easy. Der Nister described his whole family as "aristocratic paupers" (aristokratishe kaptsonim) who were not accustomed to asking for help even in dire circumstances. But after much deliberation Der Nister came to the conclusion that their refusal to ask for help was merely "silliness and empty pride" (narishkayt un puste gayve): "Healthy people do not behave like this, because it is not worth losing one's life over vain self-importance." (Gezunte mentshn tuen nisht azoy, vorem iber nishtike gadles iz nisht keday keyn lebns tsu farshpiln.) Der Nister specified that this help should not come at the expense of their mother, and he also insisted that neither she nor their sister Khana, who lived in Kiev, should know anything about his "bad time."[2] Der Nister's poverty was also discussed by his Moscow colleagues; the critic Meir Wiener wrote to Gurshteyn in 1935: "I have received news that Nister is literally starving in Kharkiv. This is a source of shame for all of us."[3]

From the following letters we learn that Motl was indeed sending money to his brother, although not as frequently as Der Nister hoped. Der Nister thanked Motl for the transfers and provided information about his work and their mother's condition, but he refrained from adding much personal detail. He was dreaming of a reunion with his brother: "Oh, how much I would like to see you, to have a long conversation with you after so many years that we have not seen each other: what each of us has been through in his life, what he has done." (Akh, vi s'volt zikh gevolt zayn mit dir, mit dir a groysn shmues ton far azoyfil yorn zikh nit zen: vos yederer fun undz hot durkhgelebt, vos durkhgemakht?)[4] But in his response to Motl's inquiries about life in the Soviet Union, Der Nister dutifully stuck to the official party line: "I would recommend you read our press, *Pravda* and *Izvestia*, every day. Every issue is a song, a poem. They tell about our truly colossal successes in all areas." (Ikh volt dir gerotn leyenen undzer prese tog-teglekh. Di "Pravda" un di "Izvestie." Yeder numer iz a lid, a poeme. S'vert dort dertseylt fun undzere virklekhe kolosale derfolgn af ale gebitn.)[5] This letter appears to have been written around the spring of 1935, since Der Nister recommended that his brother follow the International Writers' Congress for the Defense of Culture, which took place in Paris in June 1935. Der Nister also reported that the publication of the first chapters of the novel was well received by Kiev writers: "The entire Yiddish press reported on it as my great success, pointing out that it will play a significant role in the new Soviet Yiddish literature." (In der gantser yidisher prese iz geven gemoldn derfun vi fun may-nem a groysn derfolg un az dos vet opshpiln a hipshe rol in der nayer sovetisher yidisher literatur.)[6]

The beginning of this correspondence between the brothers coincides with several important events that not only made the publication of the novel possible but also contributed to its critical success. The formation of the Union of Soviet Writers in 1934 consolidated the ideological monopoly of the Communist Party over literature, while also providing consistent material support for many writers. Although Der Nister continued to occupy a relatively low rung in the Soviet literary hierarchy, he did benefit from his membership in the writers' union: soon after the migration of the Ukrainian literary elite from Kharkiv to Kiev, he was able to move into a free apartment in the writers' cooperative, Slovo. He could also make use of the union's recreation facilities, where writers would get subsidized board and lodging. Yet his financial situation remained dire even after the publication of the novel, aggravated by the deteriorating health of his daughter, Hodl, who lived in Leningrad.

The publication process of the novel, which appeared initially as individual chapters starting in 1935, and eventually in two book editions of 1939 and 1941, created a great deal of anxiety for Der Nister. Immediately after the publication of the first part as a book in the summer of 1939, he began preparing the second, expanded edition. On August 31, 1939, he wrote to Gurshteyn, asking for assistance with the second edition:

> I have a request for you. You are aware of my financial circumstances: they are so dire that they could not be more so. The only thing that can save me is the second edition of *Mashber* (the first one, I was told by Finkelshteyn, is already sold out). . . . Ask Nusinov, Markish, and so on for help. Tell them that without it my life is not a life. I am already tired of poverty. Prices go up every day, and that edition is my only possible source of income.

> (Ikh hob tsu aykh a bakoshe. Mayn materieler shtand is aykh bavust: shofl, vos shofler kon nit zayn. Dos eyntsike, vos kon mikh rateven, iz aroysgebn a tsveyt-oyflage fun "Mashber" [di ershte, hot mir gezogt Finkelshteyn, iz shoyn tsegan]. . . . Tsit tsu dem eysek Nusinovn, Markish, u. a. v. Zogt zey, az on dem iz mayn lebn keyn lebn. Ikh bin shoyn mir mid fun kaptsones. Der yakres vert vos a tog greser un mayne fardinstn kon ikh aroysbakumen nor fun ot der oyflage.)[7]

In case Der Emes press in Moscow refused to publish the second edition, Der Nister intended to turn to the Ukrainian National Minorities Press (Ukrnatsfarlag). He planned to add eight new printer's sheets, counting on a substantial honorarium of up to one thousand rubles per sheet.[8] The intercession of prominent figures like Nusinov and Markish likely helped, and Der Emes took on the publication of the second edition. In November 1939, Der Nister promised to send Gurshteyn eleven new printer's sheets for editing, urging him impatiently:

> You don't know what a state I am in now. I rely on your steady hand, [hoping] that you will not touch the edifice that has cost me so much labor and marrow. I rely on your clear conscience, which will tell you

that if someone creates problems for me now, then my entire future work is in danger.

(Ir veyst nit, in vos far a shtand ikh bin itster. Ikh farloz zikh af ayere getraye hant, az ir vet nit onrirn dem binyen, vos hot mikh gekost azoyfil mi un markh. Ikh farloz zikh af ayer tsikhtikn gevisn, vos vet aykh unterzogn az oyb m'vet mir itst makhn shverikaytn, shteyt in a gefar mayn gore vayterdike arbet afn gikh.)[9]

Der Nister was apprehensive about the possible actions of his enemies:

I am so wildly wrought up—from all the long and hard work alone, but especially from those bastards and careerist graphomaniacs who want to attribute to me something that I never had in mind. Remember one thing, my dear friend: for those like Orshanski I will never be innocent. They don't care about ideology, they care about my existence; I am a thorn in their side. Never in their life will they forgive you, Markish, Kvitko, Bergelson, or anybody else from our lot, but they are too weak to reach the others; but where I am concerned—what does it cost them to drop a line to the "right place" [the secret police] that I allegedly idealize what should not be idealized, and so on.

(Ikh bin azoy, oykh vild arufgeshroyft—aleyn nor fun der doyern-dikier un mifuler arbet, bifrat fun dem, vos oysvufrn un karyeristn-grafomanen viln mir tsushraybn dos, vos kh'hob in lebn nit in zinen gehat. Gedenkt eyns, tayerer: far azoyne vi di Orshanskis, vil ikh shoyn keynmol nit yoytse zayn. S'geyt zey nit in ideologie, s'geyt zey in mayn ekzistents, vos iz zey azoy a dorn in oyg. Zey voltn gevolt nisht farginen dos lebn nisht aykh, nisht Markishn, Kvitkon, Bergel-sonen un keynem fun undzere, nor benegeye ale andere iz zey geven tumpik, benegeye mir—vos kost zey onshraybn vuhin me darf az ikh idealizir, klompersht, vos m'darf nit, u. a. v.)[10]

Der Nister clearly feared a repeat of the ideological campaign that had silenced him ten years earlier, which had been initiated by the Minsk camp of proletarian writers. Ber Orshanski was one of a few veterans of that camp to have survived the purges of 1935–37. In the letter, Der Nister clearly identifies with the Kiev group as "our lot" (undzere) and appeals to group solidarity. The political climate in 1939 was markedly different from 1929, and the Kiev group now dominated Soviet Yiddish literature.

A sign that the ideological change had occurred was the rehabilitation of Y. L. Peretz, a peculiar side effect of the Molotov-Ribbentrop Pact's granting the eastern parts of Poland to the Soviet Union. As the historian Shimon Redlich observes, "In spite of the continuing decrease of Soviet-Yiddish publications during the 1930s, the annexation of new territories in the west, with a two-million strong Jewish population, resulted in a revival of Yiddish publishing. . . . Almost 700 books in Yiddish were published in the years 1939–1940."[11] In the new geopolitical situation, Yiddish culture was mobilized to Sovietize the Jewish population in the new territories, and the promotion of Peretz as the third founding father of Yiddish literature helped incorporate the Polish Yiddish literary tradition into the Soviet canon.[12] Responding to the news of the upcoming celebration of Peretz's ninetieth birthday, Der Nister wrote to Gurshteyn on the last day of 1939:

> An end to the ban [*kherem*] on such a mighty force as Peretz! No more fake sociology, and no more demands that one deliver something he does not have instead of appreciating what he does have! . . . For twenty years the literary pests of Evsektsiia [Jewish sections of the Communist Party] have kept such a great writer under lock and key!

> (An ek mitn kherem af aza gvaldiker kraft, vi Perets! Oys bafelshte sotsiologie, un oys monen bay eynem dos, vos er hot nit, un nit bamerkn, vos er farmogt yo! . . . tsvantsik yor hobn farshidene idsekishe shlek in literatur gehaltn unter a shlos aza shtik shrayber!)[13]

Der Nister interpreted the rehabilitation of Peretz as the official repudiation of the "sociological" approach to literature practiced by the proletarian critics. Though the proletarian critics routinely labeled Der Nister as Peretz's follower, his relationship with Peretz was not unproblematic, as we have seen in the introduction. When Gurshteyn asked him to write an article about Peretz, Der Nister responded positively: "I certainly owe it to Peretz." (Kh'bin avade shuldik Peretsn.) But he was slow to deliver, explaining that he was too exhausted and depressed to take on any other work in addition to finishing the novel.[14] Der Nister relied on Gurshteyn's support for the novel and eagerly awaited his review of the first part. Der Nister urged Gurshteyn to publish the review not only in the Yiddish press but also in the Russian *Literaturnaia gazeta*: "That's the best place. Everyone reads it." (Dos iz dos beste ort. Ale leyenen zi.)[15] Der Nister was pleased when the review appeared, in June 1940, and mentioned it to Gurshteyn, referring to a letter from Markish saying that it had made a positive impression on Moscow writers except for David Bergelson, for whom the praise of Der Nister's novel apparently created some "emotional distress" (shvere iberlebung).[16] Der Nister was especially pleased that the review was addressed to a general Russian readership.

Despite the apparent intrigues of the "graphomaniac informer" (grafomanisher moser) Orshanski and the "butcher boy" (katsevyung) Fish, a staff member of Der Emes, who "feed on denunciations like worms on cheese" (vos zey darfn fun mesires tsien zeyer khayune vi verim fun kez),[17] and the problems with paper shortages,[18] the publication of the second edition proceeded, thanks to the support of Nusinov, Gurshteyn, and "hundreds and thousands of readers" who, according to reports from various libraries, were reading the novel with great interest.[19] But the final composition and the size of the second edition were probably affected by the interference of people such as Orshanski and Lev Strongin, the director of Der Emes. Der Nister was upset that not all of his finished chapters were included in the book. In February 1941 he discussed another denunciation (*mesire*) by Orshanski, whom he refers to as "Berl":

> Somehow literature senses me as a foreign body that it has to spit out and set aside. Otherwise I cannot explain my literary fortune....

Maybe it comes from Kiev—from Fefer's Kiev gang, which is thirsty for Nusinov's blood and wants to get at him through me.

(Epes filt mikh di literatur, vayzt oys, vi a fremdkerper, vemen zi darf oysshpayen un opsharn in a zayt. Andersh kon ikh zikh mayn literarishn mazl nit derklern.... un efsher geyt es fun Kiev—fun der Fefer-Kiever bande, velkhe iz oyfgetrogn biz blut af Nusinovn un vil im durkh mir derlangen).[20]

Der Nister again surmised—supporting Gurshteyn's assessment of the situation—that the attacks were directed not merely against him but against "the entire Moscow bunch of writers" (dos gantse Moskver bintl shrayber), among whom he apparently counted himself. This time the attacks originated not in Minsk but in Kiev, from the circles around the poet Itsik Fefer, who in 1929 joined the chorus of Der Nister's critics and wrote a satiric epigram ridiculing the mystical obscurity of his writing.[21] Der Nister repeatedly complained about his poverty, which bordered on starvation and general destitution: "A question: what do I live for? Who needs such a life? And even if I were a giant, how could I carry such a heavy load and not break down?" (Fregt zikh, iz tsu vos leb ikh? Ver darf aza lebn? Un oyb ikh zol afile zayn a riz, vel ikh den aza mase ibertrogn un zikh nit unterbrekhn[?])[22]

The second edition of the novel came off the press a few days before the German invasion of the Soviet Union. According to the publication data on its back page, it went to press in Vilnius on June 13, 1941, and had a print run of six thousand copies. Der Nister did not see this edition until the liberation of Vilnius in 1944, when it turned out that a few hundred copies of the book had survived the German occupation. This edition is not listed in the comprehensive bibliography of Soviet Jewish publications and is absent from libraries outside the Soviet Union.[23] In his last letter to Gurshteyn, which was written in Russian ten days after the outbreak of the Soviet-German war, Der Nister asked Gurshteyn to take the advance copy of the second edition from the press, deposit it in the Moscow Literary Museum, and arrange for the honorarium to be sent to his daughter in Leningrad. He concludes: "Don't forget about me, write frequently and in detail about everything and everybody. I especially ask you to reply to this letter within the next few days, in Russian."[24] A month later Gurshteyn enlisted in the Writers' Volunteer Unit and soon was killed in action defending Moscow. Der Nister managed to escape from Kharkiv and was evacuated to Central Asia.

In the fall of 1943, Der Nister settled in Moscow, where his wife was an actress at the Moscow State Yiddish Theatre. The same year the first part of the novel had appeared in New York, published by the Yiddish Cultural Association (YKUF) Press, as a reproduction of the 1939 Moscow edition in the Soviet (phonetic) spelling. This publication enjoyed an enthusiastic reception among American readers. The Moscow newspaper *Eynikayt*, the official organ of the Jewish Antifascist Committee (JAC), reported that literary events dedicated to the publication of the novel were held in Pittsburg and other American cities in 1944.[25] The connection between JAC and YKUF, a left-wing cultural association closely but not directly affiliated with the American Communist Party, was established around 1944. In an undated letter, Itsik Fefer thanked Nakhmen Mayzel, the head of the YKUF, on behalf of the JAC for a letter sent on January 14 (1944?): "Very good that a normal communication has been established between us. I believe that our organizations will benefit from it." Fefer discussed the possibility of exchanging books and periodicals, adding, "We will send the last chapters of Nister's second book [second part of the novel] when the author has finished them. . . . They are not ready yet." [26] Mayzel was Der Nister's old acquaintance from the Kiev group, and Der Nister reintroduced himself in a private letter:

> Dear Nakhmen! Here writes to you . . . I, an old acquaintance of yours, also known as Nister, whom you do not want to acknowledge now, not even to send greetings, even though you are well aware that I am in Moscow. Well . . . so be it.

(Liber Nakhmen! Dos shraybt aykh . . . Ikh—ayer amoliker bakanter, hamekhune nister, tsu velkhn ir vilt zikh nit [der]kenen[?], afile nit lozn grisn, khotsh ir veyst gut az ikh gefin zikh in Moskve. Nu sheyn . . . nu meyle.)[27]

Der Nister informed Mayzel that he was sending the first of the eleven chapters of the second part of the novel. Further chapters would be sent, "for a particular reason," in batches of two or three. Correspondence about that matter would be conducted by the official representatives of the Jewish Antifascist Committee, Shakhne Epshteyn and Itsik Fefer (the latter, as we have seen, was not a good friend of Der Nister's). In conclusion, Der Nister touched upon a sensitive matter, inserting: "Concerning the honorarium for the first part, I will write to you later in detail." He asked Mayzel to send him no money at that point; later he would let him know what he needed. Der Nister concluded his letter in a friendly manner: "With greetings, respect, and friendship" (Mit grusn un akhtung un khavershaft).

In subsequent letters, perhaps sent through more official channels, Der Nister's tone became more assertive. He complained that Mayzel had not consulted him before reprinting the first part of the novel and asked for his honorarium to be transferred to him in Moscow. He reported that for the 1939 edition he had received an honorarium of 25,000 rubles, which had been sufficient for him to live on for two years, and he requested an adequate compensation for the American publication. He repeated the request to send him "goods"—probably items of clothing or household objects—instead of cash. His tone was firm:

> In short: I demand my author's rights. First, you shouldn't publish without my permission; second, for what has already been published—an honorarium equivalent to what I would have received if the book were published here, in the Soviet Union. And I want to have a written contract for the second part: how many copies you want to print and what I shall receive for it.

(Mit eynem vort: ikh mon oytor-rekht. Ershtns, ir zolt nit drukn on mayn derloybenish; tsveytns, far dem, vos iz shoyn opgedrukt—aza sume honorar, vifl ikh volt bakumen, ven di zakh volt gedrukt zayn bay undz, in ratn-farband. Vegn tsveytn teyl vil ikh hobn fun aykh a geshribenem opmakh: vifl denkt ir drukn un vos vel ikh derfun hobn.)[28]

Der Nister further promised to send the text of the second part chapter by chapter, contingent upon receiving a detailed response to all his demands, and concluded: "It's difficult for me to write about myself: we haven't seen each other for about 25 years, so where does one start?" (Vegn zikh perzenlekh iz mir shver tsu shraybn: mir hobn zikh shoyn nisht gezen a yor 25, iz fun vos heybt men on?) [29] In later letters Der Nister's tone softened somewhat, but he remained reluctant to offer information about himself: "In our days it's impossible to write to you as to an old friend. Because we live now through the greatest catastrophe of our history." (Vegn shraybn aykh a yedidey-brivl, vi ir zogt, iz bimeynu oysgeshlosn. Vayl vey-vey, mir lebn dokh itst iber dem grestn khurbn fun undzer geshikhte.) The conclusion of the letter sounded vaguely upbeat: "It would be the right thing to do for us to see each other some time and to get a load off our minds, after so many years have passed. Is it possible—why don't you, Nakhmen, try and get over here, overseas." (S'volt geven a yoysher mir zoln zikh a mol konen zen un zikh oysredn far azoy fil yor. Tsi iz dos ober meglekh—anu, pruvt, Nakhmen, un khapt zikh ariber fun ayer meever-leyam.)[30]

Der Nister's attempts to publish the new edition of the novel in the Soviet Union were not successful. In a letter to the writer Itsik Kipnis, sent to Kiev in December 1947, he openly discussed his problems:

You want a copy of *Mashber*. I would have given it to you with pleasure, but I don't have one myself. Just think: the book has been in the publication plan of Der Emes since [19]44. So it's been 44, 45, 46, 47, and soon it will be 48, and my book is still in Der Emes, and God knows when it will crawl out.[31] There must be some "good friends" who are taking care of me, and their efforts are crowned with success. They have brought me to a state where I have said: all right, now it's like in the days of VUSPP [All-Ukrainian Association of Proletarian Writers]. Let it be. As to a copy of the second expanded edition of *Mashber*, which came out in Vilnius in 1940 [sic!], and of which not more than a few hundred copies are left, which are already, naturally, sold out—I don't want you to have it. Because I am not happy with the three additional chapters in this edition, "Then It Was That," "Two Deaths, One Marriage" and "Bankrupt." I have reworked them completely. If I could have bought up all the remaining copies, I would have gladly done so.

(Ir vilt a ekzemplyar "Mashber". Mit fargenign volt aykh gegebn, nor kh'hob aleyn nit. Batrakht: in plan fun farlag "Emes" gefin ikh zikh shoyn fun 44tn yor on. Ot iz aykh 44, 45, 46, 47, un itster iz bald dos 48te un ikh bin nor alts in dem "Emes," un hashem yoydeye ven ikh vel aroyskrikhn. Faran, heyst es, gute fraynt, vos mien zikh far mir, un zeyer mi vert gekroynt mit derfolg. Zey hobn mikh derfirt tsu dem, az ikh hob gezogt: moykhl, kimat vi bimey VUSPP. Zol zayn azoy. A ekzempliar fun "Mashber" tsveyte fargreserte uflage, vos iz aroys in Vilne 1940 [sic!], un vos fun ir iz geblibn nisht mer, vi a por hundert ekzempliarn, velkhe zaynen shoyn, natirlekh, oysfarkoyft— vil ikh nit ir zolt hobn. Vayl dos tsugekumene tsu der uflage di dray kapitlen "demlt iz getrofn," "tsvey toytn, eyn khasene" un "bankrot" bin ikh itst klal nit goyres. Kh'hob zey ingatnsn ibergearbet. Ven ikh zol konen oyskoyfn di farblibene ekzempliarn volt ikh es gern geton.)[32]

The director of the Der Emes press, Lev Strongin, announced the forthcoming publication of a new, three-part edition of *The Family Mashber* in one volume in *Eynikayt* on February 1, 1947,[33] but the actual contract was signed by Strongin only on March 23, 1948. Presumably, Der Nister intended to restructure the two books of the New York edition in three parts, to be published as one volume with some editorial revisions. The new edition, with a print run of fifteen thousand copies, was to include twenty-five printer's sheets from the previously published edition along with twenty-five printer's sheets of new text. The contract stated that the manuscript had been submitted: the honorarium was calculated as 4,000 rubles per each new printer's sheet and 2,400 per each previously published one. It also annulled the previous contract of May 22, 1941, and the agreement of August 13, 1945.[34] After the closing of Der Emes press in November 1948, Der Nister submitted a request to the liquidation committee: "Because my book *The Family Mashber* has been typeset, composed, and signed off by me before the liquidation of Der Emes, I request my honorarium to be paid in full, 100%."[35] Most likely his request was not granted, and the proofs of that edition have not yet been found. The full version of the novel never appeared in the Soviet Union. The posthumous Soviet editions of 1974 and 1985 represent a compromise between the Moscow 1941 edition and the New York version, with one additional chapter added to the 1941 Soviet edition.

### PUBLICATION HISTORY

The long and dramatic history of the novel's writing and publication shows that its concept and composition underwent significant revisions between the publication of the first chapter in 1935 and the final New York edition of 1948. The first Moscow edition of 1939, with the subtitle *Part One,* consisted of twelve chapters. It was followed by the second edition in 1941, which contained fifteen chapters and was divided into two parts: part 1 included chapters 1–9, and part 2 had chapters 10–15 (that is, the last three chapters of the 1939 *Part One* edition were now moved to part 2).[36] This text now reads as a straightforward story of Moshe's bankruptcy. Part 1 depicts the course of events leading up to his misfortune, whereas part 2 describes his economic downfall.

As his letters to Mayzel make clear, Der Nister continued working on the novel after his return to Moscow in 1943. In its final published version, the New York edition of 1948, part

1 reproduced the twelve chapters of the 1939 Moscow edition (apart from adapting the spelling to the norms established by the YKUF, similar to the YIVO standard), while the extended part 2 consisted of ten chapters. In other words, after the 1941 publication, Der Nister added seven more chapters to his novel, substantially revised some of the chapters already published, and restored the initial division between the two parts (although this may have happened without his knowledge, because part 1 was apparently reprinted in New York without his authorization). At some point before the war, he had probably intended to write a three-part novel. In the May 1941 issue of the Kiev journal *Sovetishe literatur,* which turned out to be its last because of the outbreak of the war, there appeared a fragment of what was later to become chapter 5 of part 2 of the New York edition. It followed the chapter "Fraudulent Bankruptcy" (Beyzviliker bankrot), which was meant to be the last chapter of the 1941 Moscow edition but in the end was not included. This publication was provided with a footnote: "From the third part of *The Family Mashber.*"[37] One can assume that in the end, what was intended to be part 3 became part of the extended part 2 in the American edition.

The novel ends with a promise: "And now we take the narrative back from Mayerl and we undertake to report what is to come in our own fashion and in the style that is unique to ourselves. . . . And with this, we believe that our first book is finished."[38] As Chone Shmeruk suggests, *The Family Mashber* could have been planned as the first of a series of novels that was to cover the second half of the nineteenth century up to the revolution of 1905.[39] Nakhmen Mayzel's brief introduction to the 1948 edition of part 2 concludes on an optimistic note: "We await further volumes of this interesting and inspiring work. Let us hope that the delay this time will not be as long as it was between the first and second volumes."[40] A handwritten list of unpublished works in Der Nister's archive includes two items related to the continuation of the novel: "Nokhvort un forvort" (Afterword and foreword),

consisting of fifty-four typewritten pages, and "A kapitl fun a vayterdikn teyl 'Mashber'" (A chapter of a following part of *Family
Mashber*), consisting of twenty-six handwritten pages with addi-
tions.[41] A possible sequel, of which only a few fragments survived
and were published posthumously in *Sovetish heymland*, probably
depicted the period of the 1890s.

The exact plan for the ambitious multivolume project remains
unclear, and even less uncertain is its feasibility under the strict
Soviet ideological regulations of the time. The Yiddish critic
Yehoshua Rapoport speculated provocatively that had Der Nister actually written a further installment of *The Family Mashber*, it
would most likely have turned out to be a "profanation," because
he would no longer have been able to maintain the same delicate
balance between his creative imagination and restrictive self-
censorship that was possible in his depiction of the more remote
and ideologically safe period of the 1860s and 1870s.[42] The published version of *Fun finftn yor* (From the year 1905) shows that
Rapoport's insight was not far off the mark. In the final analysis,
we should consider *The Family Mashber* as an essentially complete novel, although perhaps not quite finished to the author's
satisfaction. Der Nister would probably have revised his text
again if it had been published by Der Emes, but his life was cut
short by the new wave of Joseph Stalin's terror, which destroyed
Soviet Yiddish culture.

### THE CITY OF N.

*The Family Mashber* opens with a city portrait that remains unsur-
passed in Yiddish literature in its precision, richness, and depth.
The narrator depicts the town of N. with great care, building up
step-by-step the symbolic structure of the urban space. The city
that emerges is divided into three concentric rings, each one with
a distinct architectural look that reflects its social character. The
first ring encloses the commercial center, which is the heart of

the town's life. The second ring includes the middle-class residential areas, and the third ring is the realm of the poor underclasses. Money reigns supreme in the first ring, where profit is sought by all possible means, including "lying labels, false seals" (E 39).[43] Numerous synagogues and houses of study in the second ring reflect the variety of spiritual dispositions of the prosperous and established segment of society. Theirs is the religion of "a wandering and an exiled God" (E 43), rooted in the state of permanent anxiety in which Jews of the Diaspora existed, as a result of the tension between the illusory stability of everyday life and the profoundly insecure existential condition of exile. But on the everyday level, religious mysticism coexists with crude capitalism. Der Nister's concept of history in *The Family Mashber* retains traces of the influence of Mikhail Pokrovskii's rigid socioeconomic Marxist scheme, which identified the main driving force of history between the Middle Ages and the modern period as "commercial capital" and regarded all institutions of state and society as merely its functions. According to Pokrovskii, the economic foundation of the eighteenth- and early nineteenth-century Russian state was the export of grain that was produced by large feudal estates using serf labor, but by the mid-nineteenth century mercantile capitalism was forced to give way to more advanced forms of industrial capitalism.[44]

Read from Pokrovskii's perspective, the story of Moshe Mashber's bankruptcy presents a case study of the transition from a feudal to a capitalist economy. Elements of this scheme are still visible in the structure of the last Soviet edition of 1941, when Pokrovskii had been officially condemned as an "anti-Marxist" "vulgar sociologist."[45] Chronologically, the two parts of the novel in that version are separated by the autumn holiday of Rosh Hashanah (Jewish New Year). This symbolic moment of drawing up a spiritual balance of the sins committed during the past year can be interpreted from a materialist Marxist socioeconomic point of view as a religious foil for mundane stocktaking of material goods. The focus on Moshe's economic downfall and ensuing imprisonment highlights the deterministic view of history as a struggle of economic forces, to which the moral and spiritual aspects are subordinated.

By and large, the economic mentality of N. remains mercantile and precapitalist. Investors are interested not in seeking new areas of investment and developing industry but in ensuring the safety of their deposits. Money still carries a mystical aura, which is supported by the unquestionable link between business and religion: "Their faith in these financial establishments was on a par with their faith in God" (E 290). Inspired by nineteenth-century French realist novelists such as Honoré de Balzac and Émile Zola, Der Nister lingers over the minute details of commercial and financial operations, chronicling with great care the effects of capitalism on the everyday life of the town. The influence of Balzac (whose marriage to the Polish countess Éve-lina Hanska, which took place in Berdichev's cathedral in 1850, shortly before the great writer's death, left a lasting impression on the town's collective memory) is particularly evident in the representation of the entangled net of personal and commercial interests in the business community of N. After the suppression of the Polish uprising of 1863–64, Berdichev, like Paris after the fall of Napoleon, was undergoing a transition from a feudal economy dominated by the landed aristocracy to the capitalist system based on the circulation of money and investment in profitable new enterprises. Another possible source of influence is Nikolai Gogol's prose "poema" *Dead Souls*, which is set in and around the anonymous Russian town of NN. As Roland Gruschka reminds us, "This Gogolian abbreviation became an established means in Russian literature to mark the scene of a novel as a provincial any-town, removing it from any specific geographic context."[46] Der Nister's choice of name for his fictional town, Gruschka argues, suggests the marginality of Jewish experience in the grand historical scheme of things. Berdichev may be an important Jewish commercial, religious, and cultural center known as the "Jerusalem of Volhynia," but from the larger historical perspective, it is merely one of the anonymous provincial "towns of N." in the vast Russian Empire.

No less significant is the influence on Der Nister of the classics of Yiddish literature, in particular the works of Mendele Moykher Sforim (Sholem Yankev Abramovitsh), who resided in Berdichev during the 1860s.[47] In his portrayal of N., Der Nister draws on the symbolic imagery of Glupsk, the fictive counterpart of Berdichev in the cycle of Mendele's novels. Mendele satirically portrays Glupsk as a quintessentially commercial and Jewish town, since trade has been the main preoccupation of Jews in exile from time immemorial. "Where there are Jews, there is Mercury the angel, the overseer of trade," Mendele informed the reader of his most comprehensive Glupsk novel, *The Magic Ring*.[48] Der Nister takes up this ironic reference to Greek mythology in the first chapter of *The Family Mashber* by telling his reader that, after a prolonged delay, the wandering god Mercury, the symbol of commerce, "has finally arrived here [in N.] out of ancient times" (E 42). The forgotten image of Mercury has recently been reinvented and popularized as a symbolic figure of Jewish modernity by the historian Yuri Slezkine in his well-known book *The Jewish Century*. But in contrast to Slezkine's celebration of Jewish "mercurianism" as a precursor of neoliberal globalization, Yiddish writers, in accordance with the ideology of the Haskalah (Jewish Enlightenment), tended to view the commercial activity of Glupsk negatively because its inhabitants were not involved in productive activity and had no understanding of the mechanisms of trade and commerce. Dan Miron explains the main problem of Glupsk in his introduction to the translation of Mendele's works: "In Glupsk, the connection between cause and effect, effort and product, gesture and response, has been severed. People run but they do not get anywhere; they buy and sell but they do not prosper; they act but they do nothing."[49] As a representative of the old business culture, Moshe Mashber has no understanding of the modern economy. He cannot see the advantages of a business partnership over a family-owned business and has little interest in new investment or business opportunities beyond traditional enterprises, such as the wholesale grain trade and lending money to Polish noblemen. His downfall comes about when Polish landowners lose their economic and political power in the western provinces of the Russian Empire after the liberation of the serfs in 1861 and the suppression of the 1863–64 uprising.

The culmination of commercial activity in N. is the Prechistaya Fair, which takes place around Assumption Day, during the harvest season. Since the late eighteenth century, when Berdichev emerged as an important grain trading center, peasants and squires from the surrounding area have come to this fair to sell their produce, make purchases, and arrange loans. During the days of the fair, the whole town seems to be devoted to the worship of mammon. The synagogues and *kloyzn* (private prayer houses) are nearly deserted, and little or no time is devoted to prayer and Torah study. Rabbis are busy resolving disputes between partners, using the opportunity to supplement their meager income. "But the fair was something more than a fair. It served as a sort of holiday for everyone" (E 223). During the fair, the town is filled with people and merchandise, the air is laden with strong odors and "thousands of voices" (E 221). Ukrainian folksingers are as busy making money as Jewish merchants and Polish gentry are. Despite its apparent anarchy, the commercial carnival, with its gluttony, cheating, swearing, and merrymaking, does not affect the hierarchical structure of the town. The fair runs according to a strict order of its own, whereby each market is dedicated to a special kind of business. The upper and lower classes, Jewish traders, Polish nobles, and Ukrainian peasants interact economically but do not mix socially, even in moments of great excitement. Each group has its own taverns for socializing, where it follows its own carnival customs.

The social and economic transformation of the city of N. in the following two decades is the subject of the introduction to the unwritten sequel to *The Family Mashber*: "And here we put the last period to mark the end of our first book. Moving to the next one, we reckon that we should start in the same way as we did previously, that is, providing, by way of introduction, the background, against which we will paint the picture."[50] But unlike the opening chapter of *The Family Mashber*, this introduction pays little attention to the architectural and structural aspects of the city and their effect on people's lives. Instead it focuses on the impact of capitalist modernization on the lifestyle and customs of the city dwellers. The narrative tone alternates between a melancholic nostalgia for the good old days when Jewish merchants adhered to the high ethical standards of Judaism and were well versed in the teaching of the Torah and a Marxist-style critique of capitalist exploitation. The old, stable social order is disrupted by the railway, which has brought more competition in commerce and trade. Bankruptcies become more frequent, and trust among merchants weakens. The static hierarchy of the three concentric rings is affected by the new means of transportation, pushing individual wagon drivers out of business. Now residents could easily move from one part of town to another by horse-driven streetcar in a short time. New water pipelines have made water carriers redundant, and their attempt to rebel against the new technology is ruthlessly crushed. Leather factories mercilessly exploit formerly self-employed artisans who are unable to compete with industrial production. New characters represent the new generation in a somewhat allegorical fashion. A cosmopolitan banker with Zionist convictions, ironically named Himelman (man of heaven), embodies the new Jewish liberal bourgeoisie, while his antithesis, Erdman (man of earth), stands for the future revolutionary intelligentsia.[51] In his brief introduction to the publication, Leyzer Podriatshik describes this fragment as Der Nister's "aesthetic and artistic credo" (ani-maamin), which affirms his successful transformation from symbolism to realism.[52] Indeed, the fragment treats religion as a mere product of economic relationships and describes, with a touch of regret, the deterioration of spiritual life under the conditions of capitalism. Whereas in *The Family Mashber* the seeds of resistance and sparks of social protest were situated on the margins of the Hasidic community, now they take the form of direct acts of defiance against religion. When a poor woman openly sells boiling water from a samovar, thus publicly violating an important Sabbath restriction, the communal leaders fail to hinder her, either by threats or bribery.[53] The word *crisis* features prominently in the text, perhaps accentuating the connection with the Hebrew meaning of the name Mashber.

## POLITICAL AND IDEOLOGICAL CONFLICTS IN THE NOVEL

An important ideological dimension of *The Family Mashber* has to do with Russian-Polish relations. The age-old conflict between Russia and Poland did not end with the collapse of the 1863 uprising. When the Polish Republic was finally reconstituted in 1918 through the Treaty of Versailles, it quickly became the key segment of the so-called cordon sanitaire, which was meant to separate Europe from Soviet Russia. In the summer of 1920, the Red Army conquered large parts of what is presently western Ukraine and Belarus and nearly captured Warsaw in an ambitious attempt to spread the revolution, but it was soon outmaneuvered and repulsed by a Polish counterattack. This defeat of the Red Army led to a radical revision of the ambitious plans of Bolshevik leadership to spread the revolution by military means. Eventually the Soviet leadership abandoned Leon Trotsky's radical doctrine of "exporting the revolution" in favor of Stalin's more pragmatic concept of "socialism in one country." Nevertheless, during the two interwar decades, Poland was a painful reminder to Stalin of the dramatic defeat for which, as a military commander, he was partly responsible. The "Polish question" was "solved" once more in September 1939, when Poland was again divided, this time between Adolf Hitler's Germany and Stalin's Soviet Union.

Not surprisingly, Poland had a bad name in prewar Soviet literature. One of the earliest and most famous examples of this anti-Polish bias is Isaac Babel's *Red Cavalry* (1926). Yiddish literature generally followed suit: such novels as David Bergelson's *Midas hadin* (Measure of judgment, 1929) and Note Lurye's *Der step ruft* (The steppe calls, 1935) depicted Poland as a political and military threat to the Soviet state. Following this trend, *The Family Mashber* also projected a strong negative image of Poland. The suppressed Polish past looms over the ruins of the fortress and the town hall, which are material reminders of the "important government function for which in its time the ancient city has had a need" (E 196). The glorious image of Old Poland lives in the memories and fantasies of Polish owners of family estates around N. Even though Volhynia was not the main battlefield of the 1863 uprising, the narrator tells us that the local nobles "manifested considerable sympathy for the anti-government movement and aided it with money and various other forms of help" (E 229). Der Nister's grotesque depictions of the Polish landowning class border on caricature, which was not unusual in Soviet historical fiction. The catalog of the vices of the Polish squires in chapter 7 reads like an anamnesis of a social and biological pathology. Degradation runs in families such as that of Count Kozeroge: "It was enough to know the old man to guess at the sort of man the son was" (E 232). The narrator's diagnosis is clear: "All of them noble parasites" (E 235). The only clear-minded person among this collection of degenerates is Lisitsin-Sventislavski, a man of no definite ethnic identity who provokes an incident involving shooting at the tsar's portrait, an act which gets the drunken Polish nobles into trouble and eventually brings about Moshe Mashber's downfall. The ambiguity of this character is highlighted by his double Russian-Polish name, the Russian part of which means "fox man." This frightening agent provocateur of the secret police could have been more than historically significant for Der Nister's readers in the Soviet Union in the 1930s, reminding them of the daily danger of denunciation that was the backbone of Stalin's terror, in which members of ethnic minorities, including Poles and Jews, figured prominently, mostly as victims but sometimes as perpetrators.

The shooting episode in *The Family Mashber* brings to the fore the age-old mutual dependency of Jews and Poles. After this episode, the town rabbi Reb Dudi, who is introduced in the opening chapter of the novel along with the warden of the Polish Catholic Carmelite cathedral, reminds the Jewish community leaders of the ancient link between Polish security and Jewish prosperity: "If the noblemen are carried off, you may as well say good-bye to the sums they owe you" (E 248). Remarkably, the Russian investigators of the incident show no hostile feelings toward the Jews. Der Nister is careful to portray the Russian authorities not as anti-Jewish but as anti-Polish, demonstrating a keen sense of the political climate of his time. Indeed, as the Lithuanian historian Darius Staliunas has demonstrated, such was the attitude of Mikhail Murav'ev, the Vilnius governor general notorious for his cruelty to Polish rebels. He specifically ordered "an end to the unwarranted use of the Polish idiom among the Jewish population" and pushed for educating Jews in an anti-Polish spirit.[54] In Der Nister's novel, the Russian authorities regard Jews as mere accomplices, not the main culprits in the political crimes of the Poles. The lesson is that familiarity with the Poles can be dangerous for Jews, as is the case for Moshe Mashber and his family. The Polish landowner Rudnitski's refusal to pay his debt undermines Moshe's financial stability, and Moshe's urgent need to contribute to the bribing of the Russian officials involved in the investigation further drains his resources. And finally, "The best and the wisest doctors in town" (E 362), as the narrator ironically characterizes the two Polish doctors Yanovski and Pashkovski, who first treat Moshe's daughter Nekhamke and then Moshe himself, turn out to be as worthless as their noble compatriots—they can merely confirm the fatal illness of their patients but cannot cure them. The overall negative representation of Poles in the novel seems consistent with Der Nister's personal dislike of Warsaw, which he expressed in his letter to Niger back in 1909.[55]

The Polish-Russian conflict occupies an important place in the narrative, yet the historical event that provided the factual base of the novel had little to do with this issue. Indeed, as Gruschka remarks, "Der Nister's references to actual historical events are not only highly selective, but he also often disregards central aspects or even deliberately modifies them."[56] One of the most significant cases of such modification is the central episode of the novel. As the Yiddish literary scholar and critic Dov Sadan has shown, the plot of *The Family Mashber* is based on an episode that took place in Berdichev in the first half of the nineteenth century, when the struggle within the Jewish community between the maskilim, adherents of the Western-oriented ideology of Haskalah, and the traditionally minded Hasidim reached its peak. According to the local Hasidic chronicler Rabbi Osher Pritsker, the wealthy Hasidic banker Yankev Yoysef Halpern mounted a successful counterattack against a group of radical Galician maskilim and nearly drove them out of town. But when his banking business experienced temporary financial difficulties, the maskilim bribed Halpern's accountant to disclose his commercial secrets and then deliberately pushed him into bankruptcy by setting his creditors against him. Unable to pay back all the deposits at once, Halpern was sent to prison, where he soon fell ill. He was eventually released but died at home shortly after. Rabbi Pritsker portrays him as a martyr: "He died as a saint, the victim of the Berlin Haskalah."[57] The powerful personality of Yankev Yoysef Halpern (in Russian sources he was known as Izrail or Iosif Izrailevich Gal'perin) commanded respect beyond

Hasidic circles. In the essay "Polish Jews" in the July 1858 issue of the progressive Russian journal *Sovremennik*, the Russian mayor of Berdichev, Stepan Gromeka, wrote: "This is the only Jew in the world who is addressed by his first name and his father's name. He holds no official position, no authority is delegated to him personally, yet his power is very strong. . . . I have not seen another Jew who loves his coreligionists more than he does and takes a greater part in their public interests and needs. During cholera epidemics, fires, and other mass calamities, his house is always surrounded by the victims, and not one of them goes away without help."[58] Menashe (Mikhail) Morgulis, a prominent Russian maskil, left a lively portrait of Halpern in his memoirs: "Having studied the spirit of the masses and their psychology, he [Halpern] realized that in order to enjoy mass popularity one has to be an inveterate supporter of *tsadikism* [Hasidism]. As a secular protector of Hasidism, he became very useful. The *tsadikim* of the entire South-Western Region, who commanded a tremendous religious authority among the masses, showed him their respect: all kinds of capital . . . were directed to his cash-desk."[59]

Halpern's bank was one of the biggest in Berdichev, a city that by the mid-nineteenth century had become the financial capital of the Russian southwest. Polish landowners used the services of Jewish financiers in their dealings with Russian and foreign customers: "Although there was neither telegraph nor railway, the capital [Berdichev] knew about everything ahead of time. All political information was very accurate. Keeping track of trade and exchange rates, one had also to follow politics—and each broker was a walking newspaper: while making a deal, he talked about politics, the coming war, the power of Napoleon [the Third], and about everything that was of interest for the business world."[60] The porch of Halpern's house on Berdichev's main thoroughfare, called "Golden" Street, was the focal point of business life in the city. When he made his appearance on that porch, the whole street stopped and followed his minutest gestures. As a maskil, Morgulis was critical of Halpern's conservative stance in the conflict between the Haskalah and traditionalism, but he had as much compassion for the outcome of Halpern's last days as Rabbi Pritsker: "Nobody except me can understand the whole tragedy of that situation. I. I. [Halpern] died as heroically as he lived."[61] Morgulis could not forgive his fellow maskilim for pushing Halpern into bankruptcy: "Who was guilty of such an end of a man who deserved a wreath of laurels, not of thorns? Of course, the enlightened party! One of its members and his business companions in Kiev cunningly spread rumors that his [Halpern's] situation was shaky; everyone immediately began to demand their payments and deposits back. He repaid as much as he could, but then the machine stopped. The fall of such a pillar caused the collapse of many businesses and bankruptcy of thousands of people. I. I. was declared insolvent, and merciless creditors threw him into prison."[62]

Der Nister moved this episode, which must have taken place in the late 1850s, to the early 1870s, when the confrontation between the Hasidim and maskilim in Berdichev had already cooled down. In his fictionalization of Halpern's story, the maskilim have nothing to do with the downfall of the pious Hasid Moshe Mashber, which was due to a combination of objective social, economic, and political causes as well as an inner spiritual crisis. In contrast to the real story, the Haskalah become a side issue in the novel. The marginalization of the Haskalah in the novel was noticed early on by Nakhmen Mayzel. He expressed surprise that Der Nister left out the significant group of maskilim who were active in Berdichev during the 1860s and 1870s, among them Abramovitsh (Mendele) and Morgulis.[63] The chief maskilic figure in N. is Yosele "the Plague," an independently minded and rather well-off young man who has established himself as a public figure, a moral critic of the community. The Haskalah is shown as an ideology of the liberal middle-class intelligentsia, which has little to do with the concerns and aspirations of the masses. Indeed, it can even be dangerous for the lower classes, as is demonstrated in the example of the Hasid Mikhl Bukyer, whose decision to join the followers of the "man from Dessau" (Moses Mendelssohn, the founder of the Haskalah) leads eventually to mental illness (E 333). Mainstream Soviet Yiddish culture of the 1930s, including such figures as Meir Wiener and Max Erik, interpreted Jewish Enlightenment not just as a positive and progressive movement but also as the ideological precursor of socialism among East European Jews.[64] By sidelining the Haskalah in his novel, Der Nister seems to follow Moyshe Litvakov, who criticized the maskilim for being aloof from the concerns of the Jewish masses. Like Litvakov, Der Nister portrayed the Haskalah as the ideology of the Jewish bourgeoisie, an ideology that was alien to the simple folk. Instead of enlightening the medieval mentality of a simple Jew like Bukyer, the Haskalah brings about a violent spiritual upheaval with disastrous consequences for his mind. The novel seems to convey the message that the spontaneous protest of the masses found its authentic expression not through the rationalism of the Haskalah but through the anarchic mysticism of radical Hasidic sects, such as the Bratslav Hasidim.

## THE FAMILY MASHBER AND THE SOVIET HISTORICAL NOVEL

Der Nister was working on his novel during a period of transition in Soviet ideology, when, as the historian of socialist realism Evgeny Dobrenko explains, "The principle of class character [klassovost'] that was central in revolutionary culture . . . was replaced by the principle of national character [narodnost']."[65] This change took place gradually between 1934 and 1938 and left its mark on the text of the novel. Soon after Mikhail Pokrovskii's death in 1932, his concept of history was criticized for its "abstract sociologism" and replaced by a new Stalinist concept that emphasized the role of great leaders and the "people."

The new historiography, Dobrenko explains, had to be "concrete" and "entertaining," consisting of "the illustrations of individual ideologemes that were specifically formulated in the Party's invectives addressed to historians."[66] The new scheme of Russian history presented "an attempt to resolve the main problems of Stalin's epoch: the problems of personal power, coup d'état, the economic leap, the strengthening of state power, centralization and expansion of the state, its internal unity, and the struggle against internal and external enemies."[67] Many works of historical fiction, film, and drama produced after 1935 were merely "historical masquerades," representations of contemporary ideological issues in historical guises. "During the second half of the 1930s the image of the past is being filled with such values as heroic spirit, state, patriotism," Dobrenko continues.[68] This new statist concept of history, which highlighted the continuity of state power between the Russian Empire and the Soviet Union, pushed out the previous revolutionary scheme with its emphasis on class struggle and the radical break between the Soviet and the tsarist regimes.

In the mid-1930s the historical novel came to occupy a prominent position in the genre system of socialist realism. Without openly violating the general socialist-realist guidelines regulating the representation of history in Soviet literature, Der Nister was able to adjust them. Indeed, as Shmeruk admits, "The changes in Party policy in the thirties enabled him to find a new writing pattern by which to remain true to himself."[69] Der Nister's own notion of the mission of the Jewish writer was a peculiar fusion of socialist realism and Romantic nationalism. He would express this idea in his 1940 essay "Letter to David Bergelson," in which he declares that the writer's mission is to use his gifts to unearth and give form to the people's most profound experiences. Der Nister believed that the artistic work was a mirror in which people were permitted to contemplate their collective reflection, with all its merits and defects. The artist was not merely the creator of his people's collective portrait, but also a spiritual leader who envisioned the way into the future.

Der Nister regarded the writer as a prophetic figure, a visionary capable of conveying his vision to his readership by way of verbal images. This notion bridges Y. L. Peretz's neo-Romantic celebration of *folkstimlekhkayt* (people's spirit) as the source of artistic inspiration with the concept of "plebeianism," which was developed by Georg Lukács in the mid-1930s and applied to the historical novel. Lukács believed "when a writer is deeply rooted in the life of the people, when he creates on the basis of his familiarity with the decisive questions of popular life, he can penetrate through to the genuine depths of historical truth."[70] The concept of *narodnost'* or *folkstimlekhkayt*—the most appropriate English equivalent for Lukács's use of the term is *plebeianism*—became core to socialist-realist theory in the historical novel. It required each moment in history to be represented artistically as an episode in the incessant struggle of the masses against their oppressors, a struggle predestined to culminate in the final victory of the proletariat over the bourgeoisie. Lukács's idea of the centrality of crisis and conflict in the historical novel finds a direct correlation in the title of Der Nister's novel: *mashber* in Hebrew means "crisis" or "breakdown." Lukács articulated this idea in an article about Sir Walter Scott published in *Literaturnaia gazeta* (which Der Nister held in high respect, as we know from his letter to Gurshteyn) in 1937. Harriet Murav suggests, "Whether he was reading Lukács or not, Der Nister seems to have taken this characterization as a prescription for the plot of *The Family Mashber*, in which ideological divisions and the contradictions of nascent capitalism come to a head in the quarrel between the brothers Luzi and Moshe and in Moshe's financial crisis, with its far-reaching implications for the entire family."[71] The critical success of *The Family Mashber*, unthinkable in the polemical atmosphere of the early 1930s, reflected the radical change in Soviet literary theory, which was largely determined by the intervention of Lukács and his followers.

In his 1936 book, the critic Mark Serebrianskii called upon Soviet writers of the historical genre to present the "genealogy of the revolution."[72] In apparent agreement with this demand, Der Nister formulated the "essential goal" of his novel in his 1939 preface: "to reveal the hidden strength" of the "vital seed" from which "would emerge first enlightenment and then the revolutionary movement" (E 32). In his novel, Der Nister explains, the doomed classes will "proceed quietly on their historically necessitated way toward the abyss," while revealing "the hidden strength of those who lay, profoundly humiliated, in the 'third ring'" (E 32), the lower-class suburbs in which the "vital seed . . . was already ripening." As Shmeruk perceptively observed, Der Nister avoids describing his realist method as "critical," let alone "socialist." Instead, he declares his adherence to "the principle of artistic realism" and pronounces himself a follower of Goethe (E 31). As Der Nister states in the preface, the seeds of the future were hidden in the rebellious and anarchic underworld and in the marginal Hasidic sects of the third ring. The latent discontent of the poor could occasionally transform into an open confrontation between courageous individuals and the financial-religious oligarchy, but it would never lead to anything more serious than a public scandal, let alone threaten the foundations of the political order. Moreover, the spontaneous social protest of the Jewish masses does not appear in the novel to be connected with the broader Russian revolutionary movement, as was required by the doctrine of socialist realism. A social conflict among Jews seemed to follow certain rules of the game: plenty of shouts and threats, but little violence. Both the communal oligarchy and the masses are represented as politically reactive rather than proactive, as if remaining in the static medieval world in which politics was the prerogative of the nobility.

The representation of the Jewish community as a static corporation outside the mainstream of political progress of society at large has its roots in Karl Marx's essay "On the Jewish Question," as interpreted by Litvakov in application to nineteenth-century Russia. Litvakov argued that the Jews' lack of social development precluded them from active participation in the Russian revolutionary movement. According to him, Jewish social protest expressed itself in the medieval forms of religious heresies and messianic movements, one of which was Bratslav Hasidism, rather than as open rebellions of the poor against the rich.[73] At the beginning of chapter 3, Der Nister portrays the Bratslav congregation as a protocommunist cell, whose members share their meager possessions and earnings "because, as they put it, money 'is neither mine nor yours, but God's'" (E 100–1). But the impulse toward social protest is quelled by the strict Hasidic religious discipline that regulates their lives down to the minutest detail. The narrator clearly disapproves of their fanaticism, calling it "frumkayt un meshugas" (literally "piety and madness," translated as "fanatically religious," E 101).[74] This reduction of the spontaneous feelings of social protest to futile religious sectarianism may indicate that Der Nister still followed Litvakov's historical scheme at a time when Litvakov himself was likely no longer living. The novel contains only vague references to the future time when "the finest youth of the town" (E 59) will come to the third ring to teach the poor and to learn from them. Jointly they will "participate in historically pleasing events" (E 59), but this prediction is left unsubstantiated. "That will happen much later" (E 59), the narrator promises at the end of chapter 1, leaving this development for another story. As the novel progresses, the narrator's vision of the future of N. and its inhabitants becomes increasingly pessimistic, while his attitude toward the characters grows more tender. Der Nister's realistic perception of his own time grew ever gloomier as Europe sank into the abyss of World War II—following the same pattern of gradual darkening as his symbolist fiction during the 1920s.

## BETWEEN HISTORY AND FAMILY

The genre of the family novel became particularly prominent in Yiddish and Hebrew literature during the 1930s and 1940s. It counted among its practitioners such prominent authors as I. J. and I. B. Singer, David Pinsky, A. A. Kabak, and Yehoshua Bar-Yosef. In discussing the genre, the Israeli scholar Malka Magentsa-Shaked remarks: "The sense of catastrophe was a central impetus in the creation of family saga novels, whether or not they described its direct influence on the family. The sense of catastrophe developed in these authors a capacity for observation and summing up the history of the Jewish family."[75] She further argues that in those novels, among them *The Family Mashber,*

> The historical background is very much in evidence. . . . Here the story becomes a kind of paradigm of what actually happened in history, undisguised by the fiction. . . . Here history does not serve as the background behind the family chronicle, mentioned from time to time in order to give it credibility. Rather history directs the entire development, in general and in the details. . . . The foreground position occupied by the historical narrative in Jewish family saga novels apparently derives from the shock of history which overwhelmed Jewish authors at the time of writing, for all these novels were written after the advent of Nazism, during a total change in Jewish history.[76]

While this perceptive observation is certainly true for the Singer brothers, the case of Der Nister seems to be more complicated. It is clear that history plays an important role in the novel, but it is less clear what that history is. Was it the socioeconomic history of Berdichev in the aftermath of two momentous historical events, the liberation of serfs in 1861 and the Polish uprising of 1863–64, which profoundly affected the Jewish economy but can hardly be described as catastrophic? Or was it the ideological and political changes in the Soviet Union during the 1930s, which forced Der Nister to change his literary style but also eventually helped to produce one of the finest Yiddish novels? Or was it indeed, as

Shaked suggests, the rise of Nazism and the imminent destruction of East European Jewry?

Der Nister's available letters and writings show little concern
with that particular issue until the German invasion of the Soviet
Union, even as Poland fell under the Nazi occupation in 1939. One
can of course assume that Der Nister felt it unsafe to touch upon
these themes in light of the Molotov-Ribbentrop Pact. But would
discussing the situation of Jews in Poland be more dangerous
than the subversive critique of the totalitarian regime that some
interpreters today try to read into his work? After all, other Soviet
writers, such as Peretz Markish, did respond to the catastrophe
that was unfolding across the western border in their works.
One can also speculate that, given Der Nister's negative attitude
toward Poland, he did not have much interest in what happened
there. In any event, the situation changed dramatically after June
1941, when Der Nister produced a series of stories "From Nazi-
occupied Poland," reworking the information he received from
Jewish refugees in Central Asia in a highly stylized manner. The
"shock of history" becomes visible in chapters of *The Family Mashber*, part 2, that were written during and immediately after the war.

In the review of part 1 that appeared in the June 30, 1940, issue
of the prestigious Russian periodical *Literaturnaia gazeta* and
apparently made a strong impression on Der Nister's colleagues,
Gurshteyn interpreted the book as moving in the direction of the
historical novel: "On the outside, Der Nister's novel is the history
of one family, but this history is given against a wide background
of different social groups and their interactions. Der Nister draws
a vivid picture of the lifestyle, social relationships, and spiritual
quests of that time. The author paints a really large historical can-
vass."[77] Yet, Gurshteyn continued, this task could not be accomplished within the limits of the family novel genre:

> Whether the author likes it or not, the novel that has come out is a
> historical novel! Having tackled this sort of theme and problems, the
> author *must* (if he wants to remain a significant artist) provide the

correct historical solution to the questions that he touched upon. He must clarify for himself, and show to the reader, the moving forces of the depicted age. When Engels wanted to define the characteristics of future art, he identified, among other things, "the awareness of the historical meaning." And this requirement of the "awareness of the historical meaning" we are especially justified to apply to a work which portrays a large and completed historical age.[78]

However, Der Nister did not agree with this interpretation. In a letter to Gurshteyn, he argued: "You say there . . . that the novel is a historical one. I think it is not. You know my motivations: there is not a single historical figure [in the novel]. Only the air, the coloring are historical." (Zogt ir dort . . . az der roman iz a historisher. Ikh halt, az neyn. Mayne motivn zaynen aykh bavust: s'iz keyn eyn historishe figur nito. S'iz nor do historishe luft, kolorit.)[79] Der Nister is in agreement with Serebrianskii's statement that any work of historical fiction must have real historical characters, "Otherwise a novel or a novella should not be called historical."[80]

A somewhat more nuanced interpretation of part 1 as both historical epic and family saga was suggested by the prominent Yiddish critic Melekh Ravitsh, who at that time resided in Montreal. Welcoming enthusiastically the publication of the first part by YKUF, he compared its multilayered text to a precious etrog (a citrus fruit that receives a special blessing during the festival of Sukkoth), "wrapped in so many coats of silk paper." Ravitsh read this novel as a compressed "epic of a generation" that was "the root and the stem" of the present generation of Russian Jews, and he looked forward to the following parts of the larger historical chronicle. Ravitsh praised Der Nister's innovative narrative technique, his intimate tone of speaking directly to the reader, loquacious and reserved at the same time, as "someone who has much more to say than he says to you."[81] Although on the surface there appears to be little action in the novel, in reality "sensational things are happening here," and only the meticulously crafted and elaborately complex construction of the novel sustains the intensity of feelings and inner resolve of the characters. Despite Der Nister's declared commitment to social criticism, he is milder in his judgment of the previous generation than Mendele, a member of that generation, was.[82] Ravitsh was likely the first critic to appreciate Der Nister's ability to combine a critical distancing from the past as required by the rules of socialist realism with close attention to the subjective, psychological, and spiritual experience of his characters.

In accordance with his concept of the novel as a family history, in the American version Der Nister shifted the focus from the historical narrative to family. He restored part 1 according to the 1939 Moscow version, which ends on the eve of Alter's engagement, an important family event that foreshadows the final disaster, rather than on the Rosh Hashanah holiday, as in the second (1941) Moscow edition. Whereas the second version (which, as we have seen, Der Nister disliked) emphasized the socioeconomic aspect of the family relationships, the later expanded version of part 2 in the American edition was organized around a period in the family story. It brought that period to a logical closure—with one of the protagonists, Moshe, dying peacefully after having suffered and atoned for his sins, and the other, Luzi, leaving N. for good. The seven chapters that were added in the American edition tell the story of Moshe's imprisonment and repentance, softening the harshness of objectivist socioeconomic critique and offering sentimental reflection on the futility of worldly aspirations. In the final version, the novel reads like an elegy for the past rather than a condemnation. As early as 1934, Der Nister described the future novel in a letter to his brother as a story of his "entire generation—of what I have seen, heard, experienced, and imagined." Factually speaking, this is not accurate: Der Nister was born some fifteen or twenty years after the events that are described in the novel, so he could not have known them directly, even as a child. However, the dark and catastrophic mood that becomes especially prominent in part 2 certainly reflects Der Nister's perception of the unfolding catastrophe of the Holocaust.

## VOICES OF NARRATION

In a brief digression in chapter 8, the narrator explains the logic of the two-part structure of the novel. In part 1, "We have undertaken to describe only people," and only in part 2 is it that "we intend to describe events" (E 264–65). Indeed, the novel starts slowly. The actual events that set the story into motion— Rudnitski's refusal to pay his debt to Moshe, Zisye's work accident, and the resulting quarrel between the brothers—do not occur until chapter 5, by which time we are already thoroughly familiar with the setting and the main characters. According to the dual logic, there are two different narrative perspectives in the novel. One is represented by the collective "we," which identifies the narrator with his contemporary readership for whom the narrated events are part of the old historical past. The "we" narrator often sees the past through the eyes of a "stranger," a ghostlike figure who helps the reader to visualize the lost world in the smallest detail. The "we" narrator is mostly omniscient, in conformity with the conventions of nineteenth-century realism, but occasionally he gets confused about the motivations and personal reasons for the characters' actions, bringing in elements of a modernist style. In full command of the story, he tells it according to a definite plan, which, as the reader gradually becomes aware, includes some degree of manipulation of the chronology and the speed of the narration.

These manipulations become evident, for example, in chapter 5, in which the narrator chooses to pass over important events, such as conversations between Luzi and his enigmatic friend Sruli Gol, because, as he explains, retelling them now "would delay us for an unnecessarily long time" (E 175). The missing part is revealed only at the end of chapter 6, when the reader is already prepared for it by the long digression about Sruli's origins. The other narrative perspective is established in chapter 2 through the childhood memory of Moshe's grandson Mayerl, the future family chronicler. The inner life of the family is shown through the eyes of this sensitive and intelligent teenager, who, as Shmeruk argues, has a lot in common with Der Nister.[83] On the realistic plane, his vision is limited and fragmented due to the natural constraints of his age and his position. But these limitations are overcome by Mayerl's remarkable intuition, the "gift of foreknowledge," which runs in the family (E 358) and occasionally manifests itself in the dreams and forebodings of its most sensitive members. Mayerl's perspective adds a symbolist layer to the dominant realist narration, revealing events from the inside.

By adopting a position outside of the historical frame of narration, the "we" narrator can claim the privilege of the wisdom of hindsight, which enables him to pass stern definitive judgments about the meaning and significance of events from the perspective of historical materialism. Yet as the narrative progresses, this objectivist critical mode becomes more subjective and personal, and the narrator shows more sympathy for his characters and their problems. Roland Gruschka interprets Der Nister's narrative technique as "a way of constantly dismissing the authority of an omniscient narrator, of the primacy of the narrator's perspective or any prerogative of interpretation of the action or the figures involved in it."[84] Occasionally the undercurrent tension between the objectivist, authoritative, and omniscient voice and the subjective, subversive, and uncertain one come to the surface of the novel. Thus, in a short digression at the end of chapter 8, the narrator appears to evoke the mood of Der Nister's early symbolist tales by visualizing with great expressive force "all those things that are mentioned in books," such as fairy-tale animals and creatures, "prophets, seers, wanderers, pilgrims with ashes on their heads and dust in their eyes. In a word, everything that is touched on in those marvelously begun and incomplete tales and half tales, forming a fantastic arabesque of God's Name braided with flowers and with the dead" (E 273–74). But this homage to Der Nister's early style is interrupted by the censoring voice of the 1930s, who feels obliged to condemn all "those wildly imagined writings whose authors, with evil intent or because they are themselves misled, have written to blind or to deceive the world" (E 274). These occasional lapses into a judgmental tone notwithstanding, the tone of sentimental nostalgia prevails in the later parts of the novel. In Rapoport's opinion, the narrative voice acquires distinctly *yidishlekh* (sentimentally Jewish) intonations at times when the narrator addresses the reader directly.[85] The turn toward a tenderer mood is evident in small stylistic revisions that Der Nister introduced for the American edition (or perhaps they were made by an American editor): for example, "Fort iz dokh demlt dos lebn nokh primitiv gegangen" (The way of life in those days was still primitive)[86] was changed to "Fort hot men zikh nokh demlt gefirt a hipsh bisl urfoterish un altfrenkish"[87] (But in those days people still maintained the archaic manners of their ancestors–even in business matters) (E 478). The replacement of the harsh and judgmental adverb *primitiv* with the quaint *altfrenkish* in the later version illustrates the shift in the narrative tone that reflects the overall revision of the novel's concept that took place during the war. This tragedy could also have had its effect on the style, transforming the novel from a critical historical account into a eulogy for a world lost to the destruction of the Holocaust. The second part, published in New York in 1948, bears a dedication to "My child, my daughter, Hodele, tragically dead. Born in July 1913 in Zhitomir, died spring 1942 in Leningrad. May your father's broken heart be the monument on your lost grave. Let this book be dedicated as an eternal and holy memorial to you. Your *tate*—the author" (E 29, translation slightly adapted).

Although *The Family Mashber* is not an autobiographical novel—after all, Mayerl must have been born more than twenty years prior to Der Nister—it contains reflections on the role of future generations in preserving the family memory. Mayerl, initially a passive observer, matures during the eventful nine-month time span of the plot into an active and responsible character. The prewar 1941 Soviet edition ends with Mayerl joining

hands with Moshe and Gitl, as if symbolically accepting responsibility for the future of the Mashber family and stressing the
active aspect: "It was then that Mayerl, finding himself between
them, took his grandfather's hand and joined it to Gitl's, uniting
them both in their mute sorrow" (E 509). The last section of the
novel in its final, postwar form, in which Mayerl takes over the
narration as the family chronicler, recasts him as the more passive
figure of the custodian of the past, and the story concludes on a
more pessimistic note. In a fragment that can be placed chronologically between the published part 2 and the introduction to
its unwritten sequel, Mayerl is described as a vulnerable boy who
was deeply affected by Moshe's death and Luzi's departure. He
would often burst into tears during his lessons, unable to explain
the reason. Alter would respond to the family misfortunes in his
own way, by attempting to commit suicide.[88] The autobiographical aspect of the connection between Mayerl and his brother
Alter, from whom Mayerl inherited his gift of storytelling, is mentioned by Shmeruk in a footnote to his introduction. According
to Der Nister's brother Motl, Alter may have been based on Uncle
Tsadek, their mother's mentally unstable brother, who lived in
their house in Berdichev and with whom Pinhas and his brother
Aron spoke a "common language."[89]As Dov Sadan points out,
the main characters in the novel are psychologically out of tune
with the historical period in which the author has placed them:
"Whereas the town and the events are firmly embedded in the
remote past, a few generations back, and reflect that historical
situation, the characters—and the main characters most of all, all
their connections to the historical framework notwithstanding—
belong to a more recent time, one generation ago [Sadan was born
in 1902] and reflect the author's half-native, half-adopted family,
his brothers, and even the author himself."[90] Sadan's insight cor-
responds to Der Nister's own concept of the novel as a story of
his own generation.

## BETWEEN SYMBOLISM AND REALISM

The "stranger" figure appears as early as the second paragraph of chapter 1 and accompanies the reader through the entire narrative. A detached and objective observer, he occasionally offers a critical opinion, explaining the meaning of events in the light of the Marxist theory of historical materialism. This "supposititious stranger," as the English translator Leonard Wolf calls this narrative device, is dismissed by some critics, including Wolf, as a mere "loyalty oath": "The price Der Nister paid so that he could get on with the work at hand."[91] In fact, the stranger is a more complex artistic construction, which enables the author to infuse conventional realism with elements of symbolism. On one level, the stranger operates as a realistic feature, a repository of critical historical consciousness, which, not unlike the didactic voice in Tolstoy's novels, enables the author to produce the effect of objectivity by creating a sense of distance between the reader and the event. But on another level, the stranger can be seen as a new guise for the traditional symbolist figure of the "wanderer," a guest from the future or from the world to come who sees but is not seen, not unlike the Messenger in S. An-sky's *The Dybbuk*. Placed in the midst of the events, the stranger alone has the ability to foresee the "disaster, hanging over the place" (E 48), as well as to discern the first signs of the dawn of redemption arising from the third ring. This wandering stranger was a popular figure in early twentieth-century Yiddish modernism, including S. An-sky's *The Dybbuk* or the works of Y. L. Peretz. Dan Miron traces the origins of that figure, which sometimes appears as a "minor messiah" in shtetl fiction, harkening back to biblical prototypes.[92] In *The Family Mashber*, the realistic-critical and the symbolist-messianic aspects merge, creating a fusion of Jewish religious mysticism, Yiddish modernism, and secular communist messianism.

Shmeruk sums up the connection between Der Nister's symbolist and realistic periods: "The anonymous images which had
populated his previous fantastical visions and tales descended in
*The Family Mashber* to the real world, acquiring historical presence."[93] By historicizing the abstract images of his symbolist fiction, Der Nister achieves the desired synthesis between realistic
veracity and symbolic generalization. Yet this synthesis is also
a compromise. Each major character in the novel experiences a
profound psychological and spiritual crisis, which is caused either
by external socioeconomic circumstances (Moshe, Sruli) or by
internal psychological and spiritual problems (Luzi, Alter). For
portraying the inner world of his characters, Der Nister employs
elements of the technique he used in his visionary symbolist
tales. A detailed realistic depiction of an environment prepares
the ground for a deeper introspective exposition of the character's troubled self through symbolic means. Firmly situated in a
concrete place and time, the characters often reveal their most
intimate thoughts and feelings in long monologues addressed
to an imaginary listener. Der Nister's perplexed characters bear
more resemblance to turn-of-the-twentieth-century Jewish intellectuals than to provincial mid-nineteenth-century middle-class
Jewish businessmen.

The action of the novel revolves around two poles embodied
in the brothers Moshe and Luzi Mashber. As a character firmly
immersed in his socioeconomic reality, Moshe, by contrast to
Luzi and Sruli, has no obvious predecessors in Der Nister's symbolist writing. Yet his realistic nature notwithstanding, Moshe
inhabits a world that is saturated with symbolist meanings. Bad
omens accompany him as soon as he is introduced in chapter 2,
in which he is depicted visiting a cemetery in order to acquire
a burial plot. Moshe's story, as much else in the novel, can be
interpreted on two levels. On the material level he is sentenced to
economic extinction as a representative of the old feudal order by
the objective laws of social development, whereas on the spiritual

level he bears responsibility for his punishment because of his sinful attachment to wealth. Unlike Moshe, Luzi has a number of prototypes among various "dispersed and wandering" types that captured Der Nister's imagination during his symbolist period.[94] In contrast to his well-established brother, Luzi is permanently on the move, searching for a more spiritual environment. He also personifies the family's illustrious genealogy (*yikhes*) and carries on the tradition of learning and asceticism that goes back to the age of the exile from Spain. After the death of his beloved rebbe, Luzi is driven by his spiritual quest from one Hasidic court to another, until he finds his place among the Bratslav Hasidim of N. His arrival and his unexpected elevation to the position of the leader of the Bratslav Hasidim coincide with the beginning of his brother's economic decline. From the beginning of the novel, the two brothers represent two different paths in life. Moshe seeks the stability and respect that would place him in the center of the Jewish community of N. In the conceptual scheme of the novel, this path leads to death, first spiritually and then physically. In contrast, Luzi's restless discontent with his own personality and his unquenchable spiritual thirst keep him constantly alive and on the move. Spiritual alertness enables him to anticipate the destruction soon to descend first upon his brother and then upon the whole town of N. In the end Luzi leaves the doomed place and heads into a perpetual exile, returning to the social and geographical periphery.

The third brother, Alter, has only a small role in the action, but he is, as Murav perceptively suggests, "the embodiment of the crisis and rupture that has already taken place and will take place again in the Mashber family and in the Jewish community more generally."[95] His main quality is his supernatural sensitivity, which makes him a barometer of imminent changes in his family and society, as well as in weather. Alter is the most "symbolist" figure in the novel, and his fantasies and dreams evoke the mystical landscapes of Der Nister's early tales, filled with esoteric erotic

references to the Song of Songs and kabbalistic texts. Alter's lust
for Gnessya is the only motif in the novel that can be remotely
associated with love in a romantic sense. In this, *The Family
Mashber* differs from the European novel tradition. A love story,
the traditional backbone of the European novel, cannot be as
prominent in a Jewish novel drawing on the traditional life of
the Jewish middle classes because of the highly ritualized form of
relationships between the sexes in Judaism. On the whole, Alter
may be the saddest figure in the novel, the innocent victim of the
punishment inflicted on the family. Alter's passivity, dependence,
and weakness are counteracted by Sruli Gol's activity, willpower,
and apparent strength. Sruli fancies himself as a Jewish Robin
Hood, a noble savage who terrorizes the rich and is benevolent
to the poor. His mesmerizing power over people finds its expression in music and dance. And yet, in spite of all his apparent con-
fidence, he is a deeply troubled personality, "a somewhat mad,
contradictory person" and difficult to understand (E 140). Sruli
is a Dostoevskian type, a man of extremes who longs for spiritual
heights but is drawn to the depths by certain flaws in his character. As Gruschka notes: "Within the ensemble of characters,
Sruli frequently acts as the opponent of the most powerful figure
in a scene,"[96] which is vividly manifested in his role as the agent
of fate in Moshe's life. Confrontational and sometimes aggressive, Sruli at the same time operates as a mediator between different social and religious groups. He is the only character in the
novel who feels equally at ease among wealthy Jewish merchants,
lower-class artisans, Jewish villagers, and Ukrainian peasants.
A vagabond with no place of his own, Sruli resembles a kind of
*talush* (an uprooted and alienated man), a type that acquired
prominence in both Hebrew and Yiddish literature at the turn of
the twentieth century.

The only well-developed folk character in the novel is Mikhl
Bukyer, a lower-class version (and something of a caricature) of
a symbolic type of spiritual searcher. His association with the

biblical Job introduces a motif that has key significance for the philosophical concept of the novel. A product of his time and social environment, Mikhl is ill-prepared for the challenges of modernity. His transformation from a Hasid into a maskil turns into a painful and violent spiritual upheaval. As an innate mystic, he interprets the Haskalah as a new variety of the radical folk myth. Objectively, from the point of view of Marxist historical materialism, Mikhl's progress from religious prejudice to rational skepticism should have positive implications as an example of the awakening class consciousness of the Jewish masses. Instead, Der Nister portrays Mikhl as a mentally disturbed man. This deviation from the normative socialist-realist line may indicate Der Nister's skepticism regarding the value of the Haskalah for the Jewish masses. In Mikhl, Der Nister shows us both the light and the dark aspects of the folk psyche: on the one hand, the quest for social justice and a better life, and on the other, the dark, destructive impulse. Stylistically, Gruschka notes, the portrait of this character is reminiscent of the dark grotesque of "Under a Fence."[97]

Some female characters also serve as mediators between the different male-dominated groups within the family as well as in the world at large. Devoid of any social or religious authority of their own in a traditional, male-dominated world, women possess considerable resources of emotional power, the skillful use of which can make them more efficient than men in times of crisis. Women are the glue that holds social structures together. A carefully crafted collective portrait of women in the community of N. in chapter 9 highlights their role as keepers of tradition and of the family. Gitl's dance with her two daughters in chapter 2 conveys her determination to keep her family intact. In an attempt to mend the rupture among the brothers, she brings Luzi back to Moshe and restores contact with Alter. In her final heroic act, she rescues her bankrupt husband from an angry crowd of creditors. The purpose of her life was serving her husband, and with

Moshe gone nothing is left for her in this world. Gitl's lower-class counterpart is Malke-Rive, the mother of Moshe's poor employee Zisye, whose illness initiates the chain of Moshe's misfortunes. Having lost her husband and five sons, she, similar to her class brother Mikhl Bukyer, develops "a diminutive Job in her character" (E 176). This reference to the biblical Job suggests a spiritual dimension in Malke-Rive's tragedy, yet her social behavior is far from meek and submissive. Her forceful demand for social justice from Moshe initiates a series of public outbursts of social protest, which eventually bring about Moshe's downfall. In accordance with the structural pattern of the novel, the initially positive motif of the woman leading social protest is reversed in the text. In chapter 7 of part 2, we see Pesye, the wife of a poor Bratslav Hasid, lead the mob against Luzi in an outburst of protest, which turns out to be orchestrated by the crook Yone, the tavern keeper (E 608–11). Here again, Der Nister sends us a veiled warning of the destructive potential of the unleashed energy of the masses.

The family-centered narration unfolds slowly, interlaced with flashbacks, dreams, visions, and other digressions that add symbolic depth and illuminate the characters' inner worlds. The author deliberately limits his use of the full repertoire of the European realistic novel, especially when it comes to the relationships between the sexes. The erotic energy that middle-class propriety does not allow to be expressed is either sublimated through symbolic imagery or it is displaced to the lower-class reality of the third ring. The slow pacing is achieved by the intensive use of repetitions at several levels: the repetitive syntactic structure of phrases, the duplication of images (such as the tsar's portrait in a tavern and in a brothel), and the duplication of events (for example, Sruli first helps Malke-Rive and then Mikhl in the same fashion; Mikhl comes twice to Reb Dudi to reaffirm his renunciation of the community; Sruli pays two visits to Brokha, etc.). Some events replicate others, creating the sense of symmetrical order in the novel, and certain details stress this aspect of repetition and duplication. For example, when Sruli comes to Moshe's house for the second time, now as its owner, he sits down, looking into the same corner of the dining room where he had put his knapsack during his previous visit to this house, when he was driven out (E 447). Sruli's installation of Mikhl Bukyer's widow and family in Moshe's house represents a compensation for Moshe's expulsion of Sruli in the beginning of the novel. The same logic is also visible in the chronological structure of the novel. The Yom Kippur season in chapter 9 of part 1 is mirrored by the Purim season in chapter 9 of part 2 (in the American edition), and Moshe's fall is offset by his release. This structural scaffolding organizes the narrative and adds certain symbolic gravity to the realistic story. Der Nister, as Leonard Wolf puts it, "has created a realistic novel and compelled it to serve his symbolist imagination."[98]

## FIRE, EXILE, AND REDEMPTION

One of the key structural features bringing together realism and symbolism is the fire motif through the entire novel. Fire is first mentioned in the preface, where Der Nister speaks about the generation of children "who later would turn away from the ancestral traditions and would destroy by fire the mold accumulated in previous centuries," and then reappears in several dreams and visions, which bear great symbolic importance for the overall concept of the novel. In chapter 2, Moshe sees his late father in a dream, come to his house with a message: "A spark has been kindled. Part of your house is on fire" (E 79). Indeed, Moshe sees a small fire but does nothing to put it out or cry for help. Within the novel's symbolic framework, this dream augurs Moshe's imminent bankruptcy, but in the larger historical scheme it can be interpreted as a sign of the future destruction of the entire commercial community of N. in the fire of revolution and civil war. Fire spreads in Mikhl Bukyer's dream (part 1, chapter 3), where it envelops the entire town, until it reaches apocalyptic dimensions in Luzi's vision (part 1, chapter 8), where people voluntarily go into the flames to die for the sanctification of God's name (E 272–73), evoking the medieval Ashkenazi tradition of martyrdom. Although both scenes belong to the first part of the novel published in 1939, in retrospect they may seem like a premonition of the mass murder of Berdichev's Jews in 1941.

As Dan Miron has demonstrated, the motif of fire devouring a town is a core element of the comprehensive metaphor of the Jewish shtetl. The multiple fires in Yiddish literature "are presented as reflections and duplications of the one great historical fire that lay at the very root of the Jewish concept and myth of *galut* (exile): the fire that had destroyed . . . both the First and Second Temples of Jerusalem."[99] The concept of galut links the fire motif with the motif of exile and wandering, which appears in Der Nister's earlier works, such as "A Bove mayse" (A tale of kings, 1920), based on Rabbi Nahman's tales, in which an abstract wanderer comes to a large town and leaves it again, while the townspeople go about their business. Although in *The Family Mashber* the town and the wanderer are depicted in a realistic manner, their symbolic core remains essentially the same as in Der Nister's earlier tales. In Luzi's vision, the town of N. appears as a replica of the archetypical eternal city, an East European mock-up of Rome. Der Nister refers to the medieval Jewish legend in which the messiah sits at the gate of Rome disguised as a stranger, a leprous beggar. The inhabitants, preoccupied with their business, pass by and spit at the man, without noticing his radiant features (E 271). This symbolic vision turns into reality in the final chapters of part 2, in which the mob, instigated by criminals in the service of the town's oligarchy, drives Luzi and Sruli out of town. Exile, Der Nister suggests, can be both curse and salvation. It becomes a curse if we become too deeply involved with the vanity of the world as represented by bustling city life.

But it can also save us, once we disengage from worldly pursuits and set off on the eternal quest for truth.

By endowing the architectural imagery with the symbolism of exile and redemption, Der Nister incorporates the first two rings of N., inhabited by the commercial and middle classes, into the traditional concept of Jewish history as passive waiting for redemption in exile. But the third ring, populated by the poor underclass, does not fit so neatly into this narrative. Its inhabitants have religious concepts of their own, which in many respects deviate from the strict normative Judaism of the first and second rings: "Their customs are the same, but their laws are not those of the town" (E 54). Here, observance is lax knowledge of the law, superficial at best, and the yearning for redemption in Jerusalem is weak. Despite their visible material insecurity, the third-ring Jews seem to be more at ease with their present condition. Their religious creativity takes forms that differ from the normative middle-class Judaism of the city center, and its most authentic product, Bratslav Hasidism, had long fascinated Der Nister. The young Der Nister, David Roskies argues, "was able to reclaim the Hasidic master thanks to the prophets and poets of Russian renewal."[100] Following the trendsetters of Russian modernism in literature and art, Der Nister drew his inspiration from folk mythology and religion, harnessing the religious Hasidic imagination for his symbolist tales. The young Der Nister was not alone in his attempts to apply the general aesthetic and philosophical principles of Russian modernism to the specific Jewish case. Another prominent representative of this trend was Hillel Zeitlin, a Jewish thinker whose return to Judaism was facilitated by his interest in Russian religious philosophy, in particular the works of the existentialist philosopher Lev Shestov. (Shestov, like Der Nister, also lived in Kiev before the revolution, but his family belonged to the Jewish commercial elite.) But unlike Der Nister, Zeitlin was soon to renounce modernism in favor of neo-traditionalism. In the 1911 essay "Among Bratslaver Hasidim," Zeitlin reflected on his visit to the Bratslav synagogue in Berdichev:

> If someone wants to hear a melody that comes after the deepest and hardest *grief*; ... if someone wants to see ecstasy that comes not from enthusiasm and excitement, but from the deepest and clearest *knowledge*; if someone wants to see for real how people can walk around on earth and yet be not here—let him make an effort and measure Berdichev's mud with his feet, follow all the little crooked streets, pass by the Old Cemetery, the large and desolate field where night-shadows lie on the orphaned little hills. ... Let him then pass by the "Living Synagogue" ..., let him absorb all of Jewish forlornness and the Jewish broken spirit that one feels especially acutely in Jewish towns when the Sabbath *shekhinah* is about to part with its children, and dark reality comes out with its staring eyes. Let him then turn to the *shtibl* of the Bratslav Hasidim, bringing with him his whole brokenness, and stand in a dark little corner, listening to *krekhts* after *krekhts* of a few Bratslav Hasidim who sit around the table and listen to the words of Torah, let him feel in their *krekhtsn*, as their speaker puts it, "a yearning for God so strong that it becomes unbearable." ... Let him hear the *essence*, hear the *tone*: the greatest *humility*, which has merged with the greatest *knowledge*. ... Let him hear the world-grief, which, when the inner redemption comes, must turn into the world-joy. Let him sense the hovering spirit of the great Reb Nahman, which elevates people from the deepest and darkest hell to the brightest eternal light, let him thereafter see how the Hasidim quietly leave the table one after another, take one another's hands, make a circle and start dancing. One cannot notice a single coarse movement because every turn, every touch, every bow is polished, refined, and sanctified to the highest degree. ... These seemingly simple people, Jews of little or no learning, who look like artisans and porters, show such inner strength, such depth of feeling, such clarity of thought, such spirituality in every movement, in every position of their foot, in every sound of melody that cannot be found anywhere else.[101]

Der Nister's naturalistic depiction of the Bratslav sect gathering in the same Living Synagogue at the entrance of the Old

Cemetery differs from Zeitlin's neo-Romantic representation: "It was there that they were already gathered very early on Saturday morning, when the sun had just risen and the town was still pleasantly sleeping. All of them had been to the ritual bath, and their heads and beards were still damp and uncombed; they were pale from a whole week of poor nourishment (nor was what they had on the Sabbath any better or more pleasing). They all wore their one vaguely black Sabbath caftan, faded from its original hue and frayed from long years of use (E 109)." In contrast to Zeitlin, Der Nister de-aestheticizes the Bratslav Hasidim, highlighting their physical ugliness, dire poverty, and the crudeness of their manners. In his realistic stylistics the neo-Romantic clichés are replaced by concrete details that stress the heavy materiality of the Hasidic way of life. There is little beauty in their movements and behavior. During prayer, some Hasidim clap their hands, some stamp their feet, some scream, some tremble in silent ecstasy. The contrast between Zeitlin's neo-Romanticism and Der Nister's realism comes clearly through in the depiction of the Hasidic dance in the novel: "And then, as was their custom, they danced. For a long while and on empty stomachs, and until they forgot themselves in the residue of the pure joy they still felt from their prayers. Forming a circle around the reading desk, the whole congregation danced heartedly, passionately, hand in hand, head to shoulder, unable to tear themselves away from each other—engrossed as if there were no real world (E 111)." While the dance of the poor Bratslavers is ecstatic and passionate, the dance of middle-class Hasidim at Moshe's party is orderly and controlled: "The Hasidim danced with each other, hand in hand, or head to shoulder or clinging to their neighbor's waistband with their hands. Merchants danced apart: prosperous, polite and quiet folk. It was easy to see that the paces of dance did not come easily to them" (E 87). Thus, the manner of dance reveals not only the dancers' inner feelings but also reflects their social status.

In Jewish literature, the discovery of dance as an artistic link between the material and spiritual worlds belongs to Peretz. In his story "The Teaching of Hasidim" (Hebrew 1894, Yiddish 1902), he depicts the dance of a Hasidic rebbe as a mystical revelation, a way of mediating the mysteries of the Torah without words. Der Nister developed Peretz's vignette into a full-scale literary device. Through their individual dancing styles, major characters in *The Family Mashber* reveal the deepest aspects their person-alities. The traditional Jewish way of life, highly ritualized and restricted, left little room for the external expression of emotions and feelings, which, in turn, imposed limitations on the literary repertoire available to the realist writer for the representation of strong passions. Der Nister's extensive and detailed depictions of dances convey the nuances of social behavior, the intensity of spiritual quest, and the tenderness of romantic sentiment while staying true to a realist representation of Jewish life. Dances take place at critical moments in the characters' lives, offering a sym-bolic commentary on the events.

## CONCLUSION

As we have seen, in *The Family Mashber*, Der Nister creatively employs various devices of duplication and multiplication of images and motifs, such as mirroring, repetition, and splitting and merging of events, characters, and dreams, and in so doing he carves out an enchanted space within the concrete histor-ical reality of the Russian Empire in the aftermath of the Great Reforms and the Polish uprising. The two narrative planes, the symbolist and the realist ones, are densely interlaced, creating an ambiguous and complicated epic tale of decline. As Harriet Murav has convincingly demonstrated in her analysis of time in the novel, "The text circles back on itself, like the characters in it, who begin in the 'abyss,' undergo reanimation at the hands

of the author, and end back where they started, in the abyss."[102]
The mythological, cyclical time of Der Nister's symbolist tales
meets the unidirectional linear time of social realism, with its
requirement of "representing reality in its revolutionary development." The contradiction is not resolved or eliminated but rather
produces what Murav describes as "temporal forks": "Der Nister
suspends the single axis of historical necessity, replacing it with
a vision of open-ended potentiality, most importantly, including
the potentiality for redemption."[103]

This uneasy symbiosis between realism and symbolism, which
are closely intertwined and yet distinctly separate, enabled Der
Nister to overcome the artistic impasse that he had reached by
the end of 1920s. By attaching his imagination to historical reality, he found the way out of the "forest of symbols," where he,
according to Delphine Bechtel, was lost "without the possibility
of transcending them."[104] Wandering on the margins of history,
following Luzi as he leaves the doomed city of N., the reader is
promised a vague "potentiality of redemption," personal and perhaps even collective. In *The Family Mashber,* Der Nister resolves
the conflict between imagination and reality that plagued his
work during the 1930s and produced the bizarre and sometimes
macabre imagery of violence, pain, persecution, and merciless
show trials that is particularly striking in his Crimea reportages
and children's poetry. History, which first enters Der Nister's
writing in "Leningrad," becomes a realm in which symbolic
imagination can find protection from the violent assaults of reality. But whereas in "Leningrad" and "Moscow" one-dimensional
historical time has a clear directionality, leading from the capitalist past to the socialist future, and only select heroic personalities, such as Karakozov and Heine, have a place in that future,
while others, like Dostoevsky, are doomed to extinction, *The
Family Mashber* offers redemption to all characters. The past has
disappeared, but, in Murav's words, it "remains unfinished and

undead; the futures it contains are virtual realities which may yet be realized."[105]

## NOTES

1. RGALI, f. 3121, op. 1 d. 37 (letter to Max Kaganovich, no date), ll. 1–3.

2. Ibid., l. 4.

3. RGALI, f. 2270, op. 1, d. 104 (letter from Wiener to Gurshteyn of May 20, 1935), l. 22.

4. RGALI, f. 3121, op. 1, d.37 (letter to Max Kaganovich, no date), l. 15.

5. Ibid., l. 21.

6. Ibid., l. 18.

7. RGALI, f. 2270, op. 1, d. 154 (letter to Gurshteyn of August 31, 1939), l. 8.

8. The official fixed exchange rate was 5.3 rubles per US dollar.

9. RGALI, f. 2270, op. 1, d. 154 (letter to Gurshteyn of November 3, 1939) l. 10.

10. Ibid.

11. Redlich, *War, Holocaust and Stalinism*, 53.

12. This development is discussed in more detail in Krutikov, *From Kabbalah to Class Struggle*, 187–89.

13. RGALI, f. 2270, op. 1, d. 154 (letter to Gurshteyn of December 31, 1939), l. 14.

14. RGALI, f. 2270, op. 1, d. 154 (letter to Gurshteyn of January 28, 1941), l. 33. Der Nister's memoir "Perets hot geredt un ikh hob gehert" appeared in the New York communist newspaper *Morgn frayhayt* in September 1945 and was reprinted in *Yidishe kultur* in 1951. The undated manuscript, likely written after 1943, is preserved in the archives of the Jewish Antifascist Committee. GARF, JAC Collection, f. P-8114, op. 1, d. 486 (Der Nister, "Zikhroynes"), ll. 91–103.

15. RGALI, f. 2270, op. 1, d. 154 (letter to Gurshteyn of August 31, 1939), l. 9.

16. RGALI, f. 2270, op. 1, d. 154 (letter to Gurshteyn of July 22, 1940), l. 30.

17. RGALI, f. 2270, op. 1, d. 154 (letter to Gurshteyn of March 15, 1940), l. 18.

18. RGALI, f. 2270, op. 1, d. 154 (letter to Gurshteyn, early June 1940), l. 26.

19. Ibid.

20. RGALI, f. 2270, op. 1, d. 154 (letter to Gurshteyn of February 18, 1941), l. 36.

21. Ibid.

22. Ibid.

23. In the early 1980s, I was lucky to find a copy of this book among discarded Yiddish books in a Moscow synagogue

24. RGALI, f. 2270, op. 1, d. 154 (letter to Gurshteyn of July 2, 1941), l. 38.

25. "Kultur-khronik," 4.

26. GARF, JAC Collection, d. 830 (letter to Nakhmen Mayzel, undated), l. 325. This letter was confiscated, together with other JAC documents, by the Ministry of State Security as part of an ongoing criminal investigation and translated into Russian on November 2, 1948, more than two months before Der Nister's arrest.

27. YIVO Archives, RG 1226, box 1 (letter from Der Nister to Mayzel, undated).

28. Shmeruk, "Arba igrot shel Der Nister," 237. Apparently Der Nister did not receive a satisfactory contract because in a letter written around 1948 he raised the same issue again. See p. 242.

29. Ibid., 238.

30. Ibid., 241.

31. The forthcoming publication of the novel by Der Emes press was announced in January 1947 by the Warsaw newspaper *Yidishe shriftn* and in August 1948 by the Moscow newspaper *Eynikayt*. See Shmeruk, "Arba igrot shel Der Nister," 229, n. 16, 17.

32. RGALI, f. 3121, op. 1, d. 38 (handwritten copy of the letter to Kipnis of December 7, 1947), l. 2. This letter was published, with significant lacunae, in Shmeruk, "Arba igrot shel Der Nister," 243–45.

33. Strongin, "Dos yidishe bukh in 1947 yor," 3.

34. RGALI, f. 3121, op. 1, d. 43, l. 2.

35. Ibid., l. 1.

36. Four chapters of part 2 appeared in Soviet periodicals between 1939 and 1941. See Gruschka, "Symbolist Quest and Grotesque Masks," 157.

37. This fragment, titled "Luzis tsoymen oyfgebrokhn" (Luzi's fences broken), differs slightly from the final version titled "Luzis vog in vaklung" (Luzi off balance). This publication did not reach most of its subscribers abroad and therefore escaped the attention of foreign scholars.

38. Der Nister, *Family Mashber*, 688.

39. Shmeruk, "Arba igrot shel Der Nister," 230.

40. Mayzel, N., "Tsum leyener," 8.

41. RGALI, f. 3121 op. 1 d. 41, l. 6.

42. Rapoport, "Notitsn vegn Dem Nisters 'Di mishpokhe Mashber,'" 69.

43. The page numbers in parenthesis refer to the English translation of *The Family Mashber*, by Leonard Wolf, unless otherwise indicated.

44. Pokrovskii, *Russkaia istoriia*, 75–83.

45. A two-part collection of critical articles against Pokrovskii's theory appeared around the same time as *The Family Mashber*: Boris Grekov et al., eds., *Protiv istoricheskoi kontseptsii M. N. Pokrovskogo* (Moscow: Academy of Sciences of USSR, part 1, 1939; part 2, 1940).

46. Gruschka, "Symbolist Quest and Grotesque Masks,"146.

47. On the significance of Berdichev in Jewish literature, see Krutikov, "Berdichev in Russian-Jewish Literary Imagination."

48. Moykher Sforim, *Dos vintshfingerl*, 131.

49. Miron, introduction to *Tales of Mendele*, lv.

50. Der Nister, "Nokhvort un forvort," 104.

51. Ibid., 104–23.

52. Ibid., 98.

53. Ibid., 122.

54. Staliunas, *Making Russians*, 208.

55. See note 15 of the introduction

56. Gruschka, "Symbolist Quest and Grotesque Masks," 146.

57. Sadan, "Vegn Dem Nister," 64–65.

58. Quoted in Morgulis, "Iz moikh vospominanii," 114.

59. Ibid., 115.

60. Ibid., 116.

61. Ibid., 127.

62. Ibid., 128.

63. Mayzel, N., *Forgeyer un mitsaytler*, 357. Gruschka notes the absence of any reference to Abramovitsh (Mendele), who resided in Berdichev in the 1860s. Gruschka, "Symbolist Quest and Grotesque Masks," 148.

64. More on the Soviet interpretation of the Haskalah in Krutikov, "Soviet Yiddish Scholarship in the 1930s."

65. Dobrenko, "'Zanimatel'naia istoriia,'" 892.

66. Ibid., 876.

67. Ibid., 883.

68. Ibid., 886.

69. Shmeruk, "Der Nister's 'Under a Fence,'" 285.

70. Pike, *German Writers in Soviet Exile*, 282.

71. Murav, "'Feast Has Ended,'" 165–66.

72. Serebrianskii, *Sovetskii istoricheskii roman*, 54. Serebrianskii specifically points out that historical novels had to be written in the various national languages of the Soviet peoples.

73. Litvakov, *In umru*, pt. 1, 41–42.

74. Der Nister, *Di mishpokhe Mashber*, part 1, 99.

75. Magentsa-Shaked, "Singer and the Family Saga Novel in Jewish Literature," 28.

76. Ibid., 29

77. Gurshteyn, *Izbrannye stat'i*, 156.

78. Ibid., 159.

79. RGALI, f. 2270 op. 1 d. 154 (letter to Gurshteyn, early June 1940), l. 26.

80. Serebrianskii, *Sovetskii istoricheskii roman*, 13.

81. Ravitsh, "A khronik fun a mishpokhe," 457.

82. Ibid., 458.

83. Shmeruk, "Der Nister, khayav veyetsirato," 39.

84. Gruschka, "Symbolist Quest and Grotesque Masks," 158.

85. Rapoport, "Notitsn vegn dem Nisters 'Di mishpokhe Mashber,'" 74.

86. Der Nister, *Di mishpokhe Mashber* (Moscow: Der Emes, 1941), 480.

87. Der Nister, *Di mishpokhe Mashber*, part 2, 144.

88. Der Nister, "Nokhvort un forvort," 100–1.

89. Shmeruk, "Der Nister, khayav veyetsirato," 52, n. 4.

90. Sadan, "Vegn Dem Nister," 60.

91. Wolf, translator's introduction, in *The Family Mashber*, 24.

92. Miron, *Image of the Shtetl*, 31.

93. Shmeruk, "Der Nister: khayav veyetsirato," 36.

94. Ibid., 36–37.

95. Murav, "'Feast Has Ended,'" 166.

96. Gruschka, "Symbolist Quest and Grotesque Masks," 151.

97. Ibid., 153.

98. Wolf, translator's introduction, in *The Family Mashber*, 17.

99. Miron, *The Image of the Shtetl*, 18.

100. Roskies, *Bridge of Longing*, 196.

101. Zeitlin, *R. Nakhman Braslaver*, 296–97.

102. Murav, "'Feast Has Ended,'" 168.

103. Ibid., 171.

104. Bechtel, *Der Nister's Work*, 266.

105. Murav, "'Feast Has Ended,'" 172.

# THE LAST DECADE, 1939–1949

*Revealing "The Hidden"*

THE PUBLICATION OF THE FIRST volume of *The Family Mash-ber* brought Der Nister from the margins to the center of Soviet Yiddish literature, in the midst of a turbulent period during the first two years of World War II. The swift German occupation of western and central Poland, combined with the Soviet annexation of the eastern parts, dramatically changed the situation in Soviet Yiddish literature. In addition to eastern Poland, which became part of Soviet Ukraine and Belarus, the Soviet Union annexed parts of Romania and the Baltic republics of Estonia, Latvia, and Lithuania in the summer of 1940. After a slow but steady decline in Yiddish culture during the preceding years—due to the combined effects of successful assimilation, changes in Soviet minority politics that resulted in the closure of most Yiddish educational institutions, and Stalinist purges—there was a sudden revitalization. Yiddish was suddenly needed as a linguistic and cultural tool for the "Sovietization" of more than one million new Soviet citizens in the "Western" territories for whom it was the native language. Leading Soviet Yiddish writers were dispatched as cultural organizers to the new centers of Soviet Yiddish culture in Vilnius, Kaunas, Riga, Bialystok, Lviv, Chernivtsi, and Kishinev.

Due to his reclusive temperament and relatively insignificant rank in the Soviet literary hierarchy at that time, Der Nister was not highly suitable for such a task. But the changes in the cultural landscape improved his situation. One of the peculiar side effects of the Molotov-Ribbentrop Pact was the ideological "rehabilitation" of Y. L. Peretz, who had been practically banned in the Soviet Union since 1935.[1] Der Nister correctly interpreted this as a repudiation of the "sociological" approach, which had given him so much trouble ten years earlier.[2] In his memoir "Perets hot geredt un ikh hob gehert" (Peretz spoke and I listened, dated 1940), which describes his visit to Peretz in Warsaw in 1910, Der Nister declared his "immense admiration and reverence" (gvaldike farerung, der yires-hakoved) for the great Yiddish writer.[3] The conversation between the two was one-sided, but the topic of Peretz's monologue was Der Nister's first literary experiment, and the latter writes that he felt exposed under Peretz's keen insight, as if Peretz was undressing him and would soon leave him completely naked. Der Nister was so gratified by Peretz's mere proximity that he did not care to remember the exact words that he spoke. As a sign of special respect, Peretz had written Der Nister a rejection letter, with a comment: "You should know that I rarely write letters, but for you I made an exception." In that letter, which Der Nister kept for many years, Peretz explained the reason for refusing to publish Der Nister's submission: "Perhaps I am too grey for you, or you are to green for me."[4]

This memoir was unusual for Der Nister, who had cultivated his assumed "hidden" persona, carefully avoiding any revelation of personal details about himself. In this memoir, however, he not only proudly, though not without self-irony, declared his literary genealogy but also set himself against the Warsaw *kibitsarnye* (gossipy company) of Yiddish literati who dismissed Peretz as old-fashioned and irrelevant.[5] Peretz invited him to stay in Warsaw and translate his works into Hebrew, but Der Nister declined, believing—"rightly or not"—that his place was in provincial "hiding" (oysbahaltenish). Der Nister for many years continued to have a deep admiration for Peretz, whom he compared to the sun in the world of Yiddish literature, where Mendele Moykher Sforim was "black earth" and Sholem Aleichem, "ripe ears." Over time, his admiration and respect for Peretz developed into a sense of duty and responsibility. Peretz's mental image commanded: "Remember to whom you are responsible."[6]

The issue of the writer's responsibility to the people is central in another essay, "A brivsu Dovid Bergelson" (A letter to Dovid Bergelson), published in the same year. Here, Der Nister formulates his understanding of the writer's mission: "Everything that the people have experienced at a certain time [in history], the most joyful [moments] as well as the most painful, should be recorded and embodied in types and half-types that are created by the artist's writing. This writing is the people's witness, which is unearthed from the people's deepest, innermost treasures, polished and clarified with the help of any and all means that the people's artist and plenipotentiary representative is endowed with."[7] Thus, Der Nister argues, the writer's task is to create characters in the form of Jungian archetypes that reflect and personify the key features of the nation's collective existence in history. These embodiments of different aspects of the national character simultaneously belong to their time and transcend it, and the writer must speak both from within and outside his time, revealing through these archetypes his people's essence. The writer, Der Nister continues, must be not only an artist but also a "national leader" (folks-firer), who provides the people with a "truthful mirror," both for the present and for the future.[8]

This somewhat convoluted understanding of the writer's role and mission is useful in understanding Der Nister's own approach to writing, which he was developing at that time. Was this statement his way of responding to the beginning of the war and the Nazi occupation of Poland? He did not touch on this subject in his letters to Aron Gurshteyn, but it is possible that the tragedy unfolding on the other side of the new Soviet border directed his attention to broader historical concerns. Der Nister was looking for new artistic means to express the immediate experience of historical time and to create characters possessing a special sensitivity to historic changes. By altering and stretching the historical chronology of events, as we have seen in *Fun finftn yor* (From the year 1905) and *The Family Mashber*, and by depicting the characters' extraordinary actions, passionate feelings, and intimate thoughts both within and outside the confines of the space and time that they inhabit in reality, the writer is able to highlight what he regards as essential and eternal in the national character of the Jewish people. As Der Nister explained to Gurshteyn in the letter discussed in the previous chapter, historical settings merely provided him with atmosphere (*kolorit*) for portraying what he deemed essential and eternal.[9] As we shall see, this understanding of the role and mission of the writer as the people's voice and consciousness would be crucial for the development of a new style that Der Nister used in his stories written after the German invasion of the Soviet Union in response to news about the unfolding Holocaust.

## VICTIMS OR SACRIFICES? 1941–1943

As mentioned in chapter 5, the second part of *The Family Mashber*, edited by Aron Gurshteyn, went to press in Vilnius, now under Soviet rule, only a little more than a week before the German invasion. In his last postcard sent to Gurshteyn from Kharkiv on July 4, 1941 (after the invasion), Der Nister asked him to deposit a copy of the new edition at the Moscow Literary Museum and to send the honorarium to his daughter, Hodl (Olga), in Leningrad. A few months later, Gurshteyn was killed in action defending Moscow, and Hodl died in 1942 in besieged Leningrad. Der Nister was fortunate to escape Kharkiv with his wife and son, likely as part of the group of writers who were evacuated to Central Asia.

Der Nister would later describe his "thorny way" (derner-veg) to the evacuation in Central Asia: "From my home in Ukraine I traveled thousands of kilometers to the Caucasus, from there across the Caspian Sea to Turkmenia and further to Uzbekistan, where I am now."[10] On the way through the Karakum Desert, he meets a ragged refugee engaged in selling contraband of vodka, tobacco, and food, commodities that were in short supply but in high demand due to the large number of evacuees. Hearing that one of the passengers on the train was a writer, the man comes to meet him. In a "heavily Germanized Polish Yiddish," he informs the author that he is from Brno in Czechoslovakia and begins to speak Hebrew. Realizing that the author understands Hebrew, he excitedly tells his story. Before the war he worked for an American firm, earned a large salary in US dollars, and lived in a comfortable apartment with his wife and daughters. When the Nazis arrived in his city, he rushed away from his office and never said good-bye to his family, whose fate remains unknown to him. Without any means or personal connections, he wandered through Poland and ended up in Lviv, which was occupied by the Soviet Union after the outbreak of World War II. During these years he barely eked out a living, doing odd jobs, and, if it were not for his documents, he would have forgotten who he was and where he was from.

Even the precautions that he had taken, anticipating the "stormy weather" in Europe by purchasing a piece of property in the Land of Israel, seem futile now. In his despair, he is afraid to look into the mirror or at his own photograph, which he carries with his documents: "It seems to him that he is not himself."[11] He takes out his picture to show it to the narrator but turns away himself to avoid looking at it. He says in Hebrew: "This is my picture, with my wife and two daughters." When the narrator, surprised by the scant resemblance between the image and the real man, searches the man's features, the spontaneous gesture makes the man break into tears. He paraphrases Ecclesiastes: "I, Solomon, was the king in Jerusalem" (and his real name is Shloyme, the narrator adds), referring to the legend in which Ashmedai once carried King Solomon to a far-away place in which nobody knew him and nobody believed that he was a king. But the case of the contrabandist is even worse, because he does not even believe himself, and this disbelief drives him to the brink of suicide.

When the narrator asks Shloyme why he does not find a job, because, "our state offers everybody an opportunity to work" in industry or in agriculture, Shloyme replies that he is on his way to a collective farm. However, the narrator feels that the answer comes not "from inside" but from the "upper part of the throat," an indication that he is not telling the truth. And indeed, at the next station Shloyme continues his black-market trade. The narrator reflects that Shloyme does it not out of greed or love of speculation but because of his pain and grief, which will not let him return to a normal, productive life. Shloyme recalls his Galician grandfather's custom of walking around the Passover table with a wanderer's staff in hand and a sack on his back, in memory of the exodus from Egypt, and says that if he were to survive the war, he would put the clothes that he is wearing now on every Passover and walk around the festive table in memory of "goles hitler" (Hitler's exile).[12]

This story—which as far as I am able to establish, remained unpublished and has been preserved in the archive of the Soviet Yiddish newspaper *Eynikayt*—shares features with Der Nister's prewar writing. The central image of the wanderer links the new refugee of Hitler's exile with the age-old Jewish condition. The meaning of Passover as the celebration of liberation is turned on its head and becomes the commemoration of exile. The war turns a typical modern middle-class Central European Jew—a "semi-intellectual interested in politics, [who] speaks German, Czech, and Hebrew [and who is] half-nationalist and half-religious"[13]—into a "tumble grass" (vandl-groz), reducing him to the archetypical Jewish wanderer.[14] In this story, Der Nister takes a twofold ideological risk by imbuing the precarious situation of Jewish refugees from Central Europe, a topic not discussed in the Soviet press, with Jewish religious symbolism.

In Central Asia, Der Nister met other Jewish refugees from Nazi-occupied Europe and heard their stories. Using them as his source material, he composed three novellas that were published in December 1943 by the Moscow publisher Der Emes. The collection *Korbones*, which in Yiddish and Hebrew means both "sacrifices" and "victims," had a print run of eight thousand copies, an impressive number for a Yiddish publication. Each story bears a subtitle identifying it as an "Occurrence in Present-Day Occupied Poland," but the actual location is specified in only one of them. Like most of Der Nister's works of that time, the stories were reprinted in the New York monthly *Yidishe kultur* and later included in the collection *Dertseylungen un eseyen* (Narratives and essays, New York, 1957), which contained Der Nister's works from 1940 to 1948. Two of the stories, in their 1943 Soviet versions, were included in the collection *Vidervuks* (Regrowth), published posthumously in Moscow in 1969.

Heshl Ansheles, the eponymous hero of the first story, dated August 1942, is a brilliant but somewhat mentally disturbed and emotionally unstable young intellectual who lives in comfortable seclusion with his father and a manservant, Shamai, after his mother's suicide. After the Nazi invasion, a German officer moves into their house and orders Heshl to carry a bag with his teeth. The intensity of this critical moment is indicated by Heshl's eyes changing color from gray to white, "as if his mother's milk had entered into them."[15] The shock, which can be partly attributed to the psychological infirmity that he inherited from his mother, makes Heshl mute and unable to close his mouth, and "from that point on, Heshl didn't know what was happening around him."[16] After the family is forced out of their house into the ghetto, the health of both Heshl's father and Shamai rapidly deteriorates, but Heshl himself remains in the same transfixed state. One day, encountering three German soldiers on the street, one of whom is carrying a bag, he suddenly bends down as if to repeat the earlier order, but instead bites off the soldier's finger—and closes his mouth for the first time since that traumatic incident. Heshl is instantly killed by the Germans, and, after prolonged negotiations, his body is finally released for burial. At this final point, a bizarre complication arises: when the burial society prepares Heshl's body, they are unable to pry his mouth open and extract the finger. The learned members of the burial society are split in their opinions of how to proceed. One side argues that it is wrong to bury a corpse with a body part from a gentile in its mouth, whereas "others—the more pious ones, precisely—pressed for the opposite: especially *with* it [the finger], let them [up] there see in what situation we are (dafke *mit* dem un zol men *dort* zen, vu me halt)."[17] This Yiddish quote follows the Moscow editions of 1943 and 1969; in the 1957 New York edition, the appeal to heaven is more pronounced: "un zol men oybn dort visn . . . zol men dort zen un zikh mien" (and let them up there know . . . let them there see and try to do something).[18] The story concludes on a hesitant note: "Presumably, he was buried like that—with the bone, which couldn't be taken out."[19]

In her analysis of this story, Harriet Murav elaborates on the symbolic significance of the striking and disturbing synecdoche, the image of Heshl's mouth as "the sign of injury": "His open mouth cannot speak, cannot provide testimony, but it can inflict violence."[20] Murav concludes: "The story does not absorb the violence it describes into a comfortable narrative of loss and restoration but instead reinflicts it."[21] Indeed, Heshl's macabre response to the inflicted trauma, which the author explains as a hereditary psychological instability, is the central theme of the story. It has immediate and powerful resonance for any reader, regardless of his or her familiarity with the Jewish tradition. There is, however, another layer of reference, which brings Der Nister into dialogue with Peretz. Following Peretz's model, Der Nister uses the ending to prompt the reader to reread the story and rethink the obvious meaning.

Reading the story in a psychological or a symbolist mode does not explain the somewhat enigmatic legalistic debate regarding the eligibility of Heshl's corpse for a Jewish burial. Did Jews in the ghetto not have more pressing problems than arguing over whether gentile body parts could be buried in a Jewish cemetery? According to the basic position in Judaism, a Jew is to be buried as he or she was born, which makes Heshl's case problematic. Moreover, according to the medieval commentator Rashi, Jews may involve themselves in the burial of gentiles if the later have been killed along with Jews, which is clearly not the case here.[22] And yet, as we see in the story, what prevails is the opinion of the "more pious" party, which argues that the German's finger in Heshl's mouth should be buried with his body to serve as a message sent *up there*, presumably to inform heaven about the desperate situation of Jews down here (interestingly, *dort* is italicized in the first Moscow edition but not in the second, which deemphasizes the metaphysical element).

This unexpected and macabre plot twist calls into question one of the basic tenets of Judaism: divine omniscience. It also brings to mind Peretz's classic story "Three Gifts," in which the soul of a modern Jew is expected to offer gifts as a kind of bribe for admission to heaven. On the command of the heavenly tribunal, a soul travels through time and space, collects three objects that are associated with Jewish martyrdom for kiddush hashem (literally, sanctification of the Divine Name), and delivers them to the guardians of paradise as the price of admission. When these precious objects are put on display in heaven, "a connoisseur's voice is heard to say: 'Ah, what beautiful gifts! Of course, they're totally useless—but to look at, why, they're perfection itself!'"[23] This provocative ending (which was sometimes omitted

in publications for children) questions the old Ashkenazi tradition of glorifying suffering for the sake of piety. It appears that
Der Nister is evoking Peretz's critique of the tradition using a
similar subversive device. What was an obsolete memory of the
medieval past for Peretz, has now acquired new relevance for Der
Nister. In his story Jews, at least in Poland, remain loyal to the
legal letter of the tradition, but by breaking the law under emer-
gency circumstances, they send a desperate message to heaven,
which has abandoned them.

The second story, "Der zeyde mitn eynikl" (Grandfather and
grandson, 1942) is set in the Galician town of Mielec, in south-
eastern Poland. Its protagonists belong to different generations
of one family and represent opposite worlds. The pious ascetic
grandfather Rabbi Aaron is fully immersed in studying the holy
books, while his teenage grandson Itsikl becomes involved in
the underground communist movement. The rabbi is concerned
about the spiritual decline of Jews and is envious of his great
predecessors, such as Isaak Abarbanel, who refused to convert
to Christianity and led his people to exile from Spain, or the
medieval German Jews who chose to slaughter each other rather
than betray their religion. But he ponders whether his generation
would be ready to sacrifice their lives "if, God forbid, even now
a time of evil decree and persecution were to come and martyrdom might be demanded"?[24] Rabbi Aaron's only weakness is his
love for his remaining family, Itsikl, whom the rabbi should have
rejected for his atheism and communism. When Itsikl makes
fun of his grandfather's devotion to the study of obsolete laws
for ritual sacrifices, the grandfather retorts: "And who told Itsikl
that there is no Temple and that neither priests nor sacrifices are
needed? Here, after all, is Itsikl himself, also, it would seem, a bit
of a priest in a temple that no one sees, and there he offers sacrifices that one sees quite clearly: the years of his youth which are
passing him by and that will be difficult to snatch back later."[25]
At this point the relaxed and slightly ironic voice of the narrator

takes on a somber tone, foretelling the coming martyrdom of both grandfather and grandson, who, "though from different sides, ascended the same sacrificial altar to be slaughtered by the same knife."[26]

In the following section the narrator switches to the story of their future executor, the Gestapo officer Heinrich Dreyer. A frustrated World War I veteran from Altona, near Hamburg (where Der Nister spent his last two years in Germany, 1924–26), Dreyer had worked for a Jewish firm for a salary so meager it did not allow him to marry his fiancée. Angry with the socialists and the Jews, whom he blames for his misery, he joined the Nazi party and made a professional career in its paramilitary forces. He had participated in the Kristallnacht and the persecution of Jews in Austria and Czechoslovakia, and now his Gestapo unit is following Wehrmacht into Poland. The Jews of Mielec attempt to flee the advancing German army to the Soviet border but are surrounded and forced back to the shtetl. They return on the eve of Yom Kippur, with no time left to eat before the fast. As the congregation starts the Kol Nidre prayer, a Gestapo unit appears in the shtetl, and when the service moves to the Shmone Esre prayer, one can hear the sound of gallows being built on the market square near the synagogue. That night Itsikl is arrested and beaten by the Gestapo.

Early the next morning the entire community is back in the synagogue, and when the precious old Torah scroll is taken out of the arc for the reading, the Germans come in and order Rabbi Aaron to go with them. Holding the scroll like a baby, he walks to the market square, followed by the entire congregation. From the opposite side of the square Itsikl is led, with Lenin's portrait hung on his chest. A German soldier orders Itsikl to spit at the Torah scroll in his grandfather's arms, which he refuses to do; similarly, the grandfather refuses to spit at Lenin's portrait. They are both hanged in front of the terrified Polish and Jewish population. Their dying bodies turn toward each other, and when the Nazis roar "Heil Hitler!" the Rabbi shouts "Shma Yisroel!" The congregation responds, according to the custom, "Blessed be the Name of his glorious majesty," while Itsikl seems to utter, "Long live the liberation of the world" (*velt-oysleyzung*, which can also be translated as "redemption").[27] They are both buried in the Jewish cemetery, but their graves are neglected by the community in the tragedy that follows. Addressing the reader in the present time, the narrator concludes with a promise that "when better times come we shall see a tombstone erected there, clearly marked with an explicit inscription composed in Hebrew in the traditional Jewish manner."[28]

As Ber Kotlerman notes in his analysis of this story, Der Nister likely heard of what happened in Mielec from a Polish Jewish refugee in Central Asia and decided to adapt it for his story. According to the account in the Mielec memorial book, the massacre of Jews happened on the eve of Rosh Hashanah in 1939. When the shooting began, Rabbi Naftoli Meilekh Vassershtrum was seen pressing a Torah scroll to his chest. "Rabbi Vassershtrum also had a shofar close to his chest, and when the shooting began he blew it. By chance the executioners' bullet missed teenaged Yankele Shvalb. He grabbed the blood-stained Torah scroll from the hands of the dying rabbi and tried to escape through the window. But outside, the murderers poured petrol over him and lit it, and as he turned into a living torch, they shot him."[29] Der Nister's transformation of the story, Kotlerman concludes, "can serve as an excellent example of the labored symbiosis between the Soviet and the Jewish ethoses forced upon Jewish literary figures in the USSR."[30]

Yet this story stands out among Soviet Yiddish writings because of its openly religious symbolism; the density of its references to the Bible, Talmud, and liturgy; and the parallelism between Judaism and communism as two equally heroic paths toward redemption through self-sacrifice. The martyrdom scene of Rabbi Aaron and his grandson is a reenactment of the story of the ten martyrs, which is part of the Yom Kippur liturgy that follows the Torah reading. While Rabbi Aaron fulfills the commandment of kiddush hashem for which he spent his entire life preparing, Itsikl dies bearing Lenin's portrait on his chest like the high priest with his breastplate in the Jerusalem temple. The characters' names underscore religious symbolism by referring to the biblical figures of Aaron, the first high priest, and the sacrifice of Isaac. The religious connotations did not escape the watchful eye of the Communist Party officials. The internal report "Concerning Nationalistic and Religious Mystical Tendencies in Soviet Yiddish Literature," signed by the head of the Personnel Department of the Central Committee of the All-Union Communist Party M. Shcherbakov but likely composed by someone with a good knowledge of Yiddish literature, criticized Der Nister's story along with several other works by Soviet Yiddish writers: "The story is abundantly garnished with the rabbi's spiritual sayings and prayerful exclamations."[31] This criticism may explain why this story was not included in the *Vidervuks* collection, although a musical montage based on this story was staged in Birobidzhan in 1943, three years before Shcherbakov's report.[32]

"Meyer Landshaft," the last story in *Korbones*, is in certain aspects similar to the first one. It is set in an anonymous location and begins with an intimate portrayal of a wealthy and cultured family. Following the traditional Jewish custom, the merchant Meyer Landshaft divides his time between business and study. His favorite authors are the nineteenth-century scholars Nakhman Krochmal and Shmuel David Luzzatto, who sought to combine enlightenment with traditional Judaism. The atmosphere in his house is patriarchal: the wife dedicates herself fully to the service of her husband, while the modest and beautiful daughter, Wanda, patiently waits for a suitable marriage to be arranged for her by her parents. She attends a gymnasium, where her pious father has arranged for a dispensation from the local priest for her not to attend school on Shabbat.

When the Germans invade the town, Meyer, like Heshl Ansheles, withdraws to his study. He is disturbed by the rumors that all young Jewish women will be taken away for the "entertainment" of the German troops. In despair, he takes to sharpening kitchen knives, preparing to slay his daughter rather than surrender her to the enemy, as his medieval Ashkenazi ancestors had done. In the end, however, Meyer is incapable of sacrificing his daughter for kiddush hashem. The knives are inadvertently discovered by the Germans, who arrest him on suspicion of planning an act of sabotage. In the Gestapo prison he tries to impress his interrogator with his knowledge of German culture, but the Nazi officer coldly and cruelly tears off his beard. Shocked and humiliated, Meyer retreats into his room and refuses to come out even to say farewell to Wanda when she is taken away with other young women to be sent to Germany. At this last moment at home, "She thought of no one but her father—who had hidden away behind the locked door."[33]

Meyer represents the middle-class Jewish type, embodying a combination of piety, learning, and wealth, but, unlike other characters in *Korbones*, he is capable of neither physical nor spiritual resistance. The prewar lifestyle of the family seems to be somewhat anachronistic, more in keeping with the Russian Empire than interwar Poland. Indeed, Nakhmen Mayzel, who published Der Nister's stories in his New York journal *Yidishe kultur*, noted in a letter to the author that Meyer Landshaft reminded him of his father, whom Der Nister knew well from his Kiev days. Der Nister agreed, explaining: "Naturally, I had in mind only the 'aura' [*oysshtralung*] of a personality, because everything else is 'poetry,' not 'truth.'"[34] Rather paradoxically, Der Nister seems to suggest here that the "truth" of the character resides in its "aura," whereas factual reality is merely "poetry," that is, fiction. This idea fits with Der Nister's belief that the writer's mission is to create national archetypes that transcend the limitations of time and space rather than reflect historical reality according to facts. Meyer's "aura" as a weak modern Jew whose identification with Judaism is purely intellectual once again brings to mind Y. L.

Peretz's "Three Gifts." One of the gifts that the poor mediocre soul brings to heaven is a bloody needle with which a Jewish girl pinned her dress to her body so as not to expose herself when she was dragged to an execution by a Christian mob in a medieval German town. A similar situation with a young Jewish woman is played out again in Nazi-occupied Poland, and the weak modern father withdraws from the horrors of reality instead of confronting it as his medieval Ashkenazi ancestors did.

The stories in *Korbones* examine intergenerational relations under the extreme conditions of the Nazi occupation. In "Heshl Ansheles" and "Meyer Landshaft" the traditional middle-class family breaks down, while in "Grandfather and Grandson" the first and the third generation are reunited in an act of sacrificial martyrdom. The fathers of Heshl Ansheles and Wanda are unable not only to defend their children but also to live up to their Jewish values, whereas Rabbi Aaron and Itsikl share a commitment to their ideals, however different they may be. Thus communism turns out to be closer to genuine Yiddishkeit than the diluted, intellectualized Judaism that seeks to combine religious observance with moderate enlightenment. In spirit, if not in letter, communism is closer than the philosophical musings of Krochmal and Luzzatto to the messianic dreams of redemption through suffering cherished by Isaak Abarbanel and the Ashkenazi rabbis. In acts of heroism and sacrifice during the Holocaust, Der Nister seeks to discover a hidden symbolic continuity between past and present, which persists in spite of the visible radical break. In the crisis of catastrophe, the mystical power of Judaism comes forcefully through by mobilizing the indestructible spiritual resources hidden in ordinary Jewish people.

## FROM VICTIMS TO VICTORS, 1944–1946

The second set of war stories was written after Der Nister's return to Moscow in 1943. As the scope of the war and the destruction of Jewish life became clearer, he was able to use a more general historical frame of reference and draw on a broader variety of sources for his fiction. But he also had to conform to the war narrative that had already taken shape in Soviet literature. These two factors explain certain differences between the new stories and *Korbones*. The emphasis shifts from martyrdom, with its openly religious connotations, to acts of heroism and resistance, in which Soviet elements become more pronounced, women assume a more active role, intergenerational dynamics become more positive, and intellectuals become essential to national survival and regeneration. At the same time, the ethical problematics become more complicated. Der Nister closely examines the potential moral conflict between personal heroism and responsibility for others, and between trust and suspicion. Explicitly Jewish religious and national symbolism gives way to a humanist, moral-psychological discourse. The narrative style becomes more varied, and in addition to the dominant omniscient chronicler, we begin to hear individual male and female voices.

Stylistically and thematically closest to *Korbones* is the story "Rive Yosl Buntses" (dated December 1945).[35] Similar to Rabbi Aaron, the protagonist, Rive, is introduced as an ancient character, "a kind of historical relic, to be displayed in a museum,"[36] and "a kind of universal grandmother from whom all were descended"[37] who serves as spiritual leader and authority for the community. Rive takes care of orphans and the poor, collects charity, and attends to the dead. Living out of touch with the modern age, she comprehends what happens when the Germans come and force the Jews into the ghetto: "She felt the evil decree more than she understood it," as one of the evils that had befallen the Jews since ancient times, about which she had read in the Yiddish adaptation of the Bible.[38] Finally, one Friday, all unemployed and "useless" women are ordered to march out of the ghetto. In the evening, as the women stand before the ditch where they will be shot, Rive takes out her family's silver candlesticks, which she has managed to keep from the Germans, and lights candles in honor of the Sabbath. After the execution, when all the bodies are covered with earth, her candles are still burning. In a final barbaric gesture, one of the policemen relieves himself on them, "Whether for the sake of his personal needs or in order to share something with others—it's all the same."[39] One can speculate on why Rive Yosl Buntses, a female counterpart to Rabbi Aaron, was deemed more acceptable for inclusion in the 1969 Soviet edition. While the Jewish religious symbolism is obvious in both stories, its significance differs. The martyrdom of Rabbi Aaron and Itsikl carries a mystical meaning as a sacrifice performed for both Judaism and communism, a parallel that was perhaps too politically dangerous even for the liberal 1960s. Rive, in her life and death, also embodies a strong attachment to the Jewish tradition, but the emphasis here is on communal solidarity. Her lighting of Sabbath candles is first and foremost a gesture of communal solidarity and defiance of imminent death. By following her in reciting the blessing over the candles, women form a community of fate. Quite strikingly, the policeman's act of defiling the candles can also be regarded, as the narrator sarcastically suggests, as a gesture of solidarity among the murderers, which, the narrator adds, has no significance.

A more complex and ambiguous female character is the heroine of "Flora" (1946).[40] The story consists of three parts written in different styles and narrated by different voices. The first and longest part is a fragment of the diary of a young woman, which, as the narrator explains later, he has edited as a "professional, who enjoys the right to straighten, edit, and pass things through a stylizing typewriter."[41] Flora addresses her diary to her father, a respectable doctor and a leader of the Jewish community in an unnamed "Polish-Jewish city." Among his achievements was the establishment of a high-quality Jewish school system that operated independently from the Polish state. Flora recalls her happy school years and her graduation dance, where she was the belle of the ball, and which marked the end of her youth and the beginning of her adult life. On that occasion, her father presented her with a family heirloom, a precious ring inherited from a distinguished ancestor, a doctor who had moved to Poland from Italy via Holland and Germany in the seventeenth century and who had published a medical manual.[42]

The happy prewar memories are interrupted by the German invasion and the establishment of a cruel new order. Flora's father is forced by the Nazis to become the head of the Judenrat, a council representing the Jewish community, but resigns when his position becomes intolerable and is put in prison. To save him, Flora appeals to the Nazi regional commander. As she confesses in the diary, for a moment she was "acting as a woman" and contemplated offering herself as a bribe; in the end, her father commits suicide in prison, and she writes in her diary the first line of the Kaddish prayer with a note of hesitation: "They say, I guess, for the dead."[43] Unlike the stories in *Korbones*, which represented Jewish martyrdom at the hands of the Nazis as a reenactment of the medieval kiddush hashem, in "Flora" and in other stories from 1945 to 1946, the national-religious message is muted. Thanks to her Jewish education, Flora is familiar with Jewish tradition and history and is inspired by their heroic examples, but she does not fully identify with these heroes' religious commitment. She thinks and acts as a modern woman, and her story does not end with the death of her father.

After her father's death she loses her privileged position and has to work in the ghetto sewing workshop, where her brave, independent attitude attracts the attention of the underground organization. In due time she is entrusted with the difficult and dangerous task of exposing a spy among the underground fighters. Using her charms, she has to keep the suspect close but not too close, until the ghetto fighters reach the partisans in the forest and the traitor can be exposed and put on trial. Her diary ends as the group leaves the ghetto, and the "professional" narrator then

takes over, "on the authority of oral reports he received after making her acquaintance."[44] Among his other sources, he names the
Jewish museum in that city (in all likelihood Vilnius), where "records of both the open war and the secret, underground one" have
been preserved, including the record of a trial, with a photograph
of an executed man and Flora next to him.[45] Cutting short the
second part that depicts Flora's life among the partisans, the narrator tells us, "It was the time before victory, when—very soon—
reality would pass over into legend, and every single participant
and contributor, more or less, would have more than enough to
add."[46] His version of the story, the narrator explains, is nothing
more than an "introduction to the essence [*iker*] of the true resistance," for which Flora had the blessing of her father and of all her
ancestors, back to the biblical "mother Deborah," "the original
singer of her people's deeds" (amol-amolike folk-zingerin).[47]

The final part, written as an eyewitness account by the narrator,
depicts the Victory Day celebration at a "Jewish social organization," evidently the Jewish Antifascist Committee, of which Der
Nister was a member. Among many decorated war heroes, Flora
attracts attention by her poise and grace. She wears a dress similar
to the one she wore to her graduation ball and betrays no traces
of the "'forest' in her eyes or connection to partisan activities."[48]
Speaking in her own language, presumably Yiddish, which she
has not used since she was in the forest, she tells the audience of
the ghetto and, touching the ring on her right hand in a symbolic
gesture of betrothal, calls upon the women in the audience, in the
name of her father, to "raise a generation that would be worthy
of upholding the thread of our national existence."[49] The festive
evening concludes with a ball, and Flora performs two dances.
First she partners with the ghetto fighter Berl to perform a Cossack dance whose movements suggest abandon and recklessness
(hefker un gots barot)[50] in a "non-Jewish fashion,"[51] which is a
reminder of the days in the forest. This is followed by a "modern"
dance with a more appropriate partner, a dashing cavalry officer,

which brings back the memory of her graduation ball, when her father withdrew into the crowd and blocked his eyes with a hand, lest he inadvertently cast upon her the "evil eye."

As Gennady Estraikh comments on this episode, the Cossack dance "became a dance of victorious Soviet Jews, whose symbiosis with hereditary Russian warriors did not denationalize them . . . but allowed them to achieve an extraordinary level of heroism."[52] Der Nister had already used dance imagery as a way of expressing the subtle and fluid nuances of female characters' feelings in *The Family Mashber*, drawing on the elaborate tradition of Hasidic dance as a mystical and ecstatic experience.[53] Jewish war heroes not only appropriate the militant Cossack tradition but also "Judaize" it, cleansing it of the historical antisemitic connotation, not unlike how the Chabad Hasidim appropriated and "purified" "La Marseillaise" and other foreign songs for their tunes (*nigunim*), as a way of transforming and defeating the forces of evil.[54] But the final, formal dance restores Flora's status according to her distinguished genealogy. Flora is associated with a wide range of illustrious Jewish women, from biblical Deborah and an anonymous young martyr in the medieval German city of Speyer (another nod to "Three Gifts") to the elegant German Jewish salon women Henriette Herz and Dorothea von Schlegel, Moses Mendelssohn's daughter, over the course of the story.[55] Unlike the tragic figures in *Korbones*, Flora embodies the hope for the future of the Jewish people, which is envisioned as a synthesis of Jewish religious and secular traditions with Soviet triumphal optimism. Rather than a historical relic, the Polish-Jewish past becomes "useful" and is integrated into the Soviet-Jewish future. Moreover, Der Nister's praise for the Jewish school system that existed independently from the state might suggest a call for the restoration of Yiddish schools in the Soviet Union.

Whereas "Grandfather and Grandson" was excluded, apparently for ideological reasons, from the Soviet edition of 1969, the novella "Meylekh Magnus" was published that year, first, in the

June issue of *Sovetish heymland,* and then as the opening story in *Vidervuks.* The publication had no introduction or commentary, leaving its interpretation to the reader. Subtitled "Pages of a Biography," it is indeed a biographical sketch of an outstanding Yiddish intellectual. It begins in the aftermath of the failed 1905 revolution, when the Jewish intelligentsia became preoccupied with developing new ideological programs for the Jewish future. Meylekh is portrayed as an introvert, equally shy and reserved with men and women. In the atmosphere of decline and disillusionment after the revolution, when many young people returned to their bourgeois occupations and lifestyle, Meylekh courts Feygele, the daughter of an affluent family. On the verge of their engagement, Feygele is shot in front of Meylekh by her previous suitor, a former revolutionary who had succumbed to alcoholism and depression. Shocked and traumatized, Meylekh withdraws to a non-Jewish part of town and neglects himself to the point that even the tsarist police dismiss him as a "demented lunatic."[56]

He slowly recovers and eventually graduates from the university in the capital city, presumably St. Petersburg. On the day of his graduation, he runs into an old acquaintance named Boris Groysbaytl (Big Purse), "a rich playboy" who dabbles in financing revolutionary activities. Boris is happy to support Meylekh's work for Jewish cultural revival and puts him in charge of his publishing projects. An extravagant character who combines the reckless lifestyle of a wealthy landowner with commitment to Jewish culture and revolutionary politics, Boris takes control of Meylekh's life and sets him up with the lively daughter of a well-off merchant. But this second marriage attempt also fails, because the frivolous girl falls for the adventurous owner of a "half-circus, half-zoo" and runs away with him, leaving behind debts, unpaid employees, and hungry animals. World War I separates the narrator from Meylekh, who finds himself in Poland, where he receives an academic position at a newly established research institute, evidently the Yiddish Scientific Institute (YIVO) in Vilnius.

Eventually he marries an older woman, but she dies in childbirth, leaving him to raise their son alone.

Bypassing the next ten to fifteen years, the narrator switches from personal memoir to epic tragedy. The shock caused by the Nazi atrocities and his inability to comprehend and explain the events render Meylekh mute, while his son joins the underground resistance in the ghetto and is killed. After the burial, the despondent Meylekh is moved, with the help of the Judenrat, to a secret underground bunker that has been built by Boris. Meeting Boris brings Meylekh back to life, and he sets about writing an account of the ghetto experience. It is not clear how he dies, but what remains of his writings is preserved by his disciple and brought to the narrator, presumably to Moscow.

These writings are described as "half-clear, half-unclear experiences," an attempt at a literary work that would be better suited to a professional writer, whose task is "always to balance his spiritual accounts and see their every part neatly arranged, fixed, and given form,"[57] which is, presumably, what the narrator did with these writings. As the narrator explains at the conclusion of his story, this kind of personal account of traumatic experience is affected by the mechanism of "sublimation," which he describes as the impulse to turn one's feelings and thoughts away from harsh reality, sometimes briefly, merely for the sake of distraction, and sometimes for a longer period, in order to "change the psychological material" in a more fundamental way, which is "one of the healthiest instincts of self-preservation."[58]

This brief digression into psychoanalysis may elucidate Der Nister's vision of his role as a writer. The writer arranges, fixes, and shapes the source material that he receives from survivors in oral or written form. These original accounts are naturally distorted by the traumatic experience of their narrators, and in particular affected by the mechanism of sublimation. The professional writer, like a trained psychoanalyst, has the necessary skills to see through these distortions and restore the "truth" (to use the term from Der Nister's letter to Mayzel) behind the "half-clear, half-unclear" accounts. Like an analyst, the writer needs the narrative to start at an early stage, which enables him to establish the character's behavioral patterns in response to critical experiences. This is why the war stories all contain a substantial and detailed account of the characters' prewar lives. Seen from this perspective, literary devices, such as symbols and metaphors, become basic tools for reconstructing the "truth" by condensing apparently chaotic original narratives into fixed and stable symbolic forms.

It is not always easy to decipher which real people and events served as source material for Der Nister's fiction. However, in the case of Meylekh Magnus, we do have reliable clues. As the Israeli scholar of Yiddish and Hebrew literature Shalom Luria reports in the afterword to his Hebrew translation of the novella, he was told by Eliezer Podriatshik that Der Nister explicitly tried to portray the personality of Luria's father, the prominent Yiddish linguist and political activist Zelig Kalmanovitch. However, the likeness between this supposed model and Der Nister's character is not clear. Luria writes that some "knowledgeable people" found many details of the story completely wrong. On the other hand, the poet Avraham Sutzkever told him that "Der Nister came to his little room in Moscow and asked for a detailed account of [Kalmanovitch], his life and fate, and when he listened, his eyes filled with tears." Evidently, it was a "deep human feeling hidden in the depths of the soul that the artist sought to express in words,"[59] rather than to accurately reproduce historical details. Luria also identifies the model for Boris Groysbaytl as Boris Kletskin, a prominent publisher of quality Yiddish literature and scholarship, who indeed employed Kalmanovitch as managing editor in 1910, after Kalmanovitch's return from Berlin and Königsberg, where he was studying at the university.[60] However, the real Kletskin died in 1937 and was therefore unable to support Kalmanovitch/Meylekh in the ghetto.

In his analysis of the story, Luria contrasts the prewar biographical sketch of Meylekh with the story of the Nazi occupation, which are separated by ten to fifteen years.[61] He describes the first part as "purely realistic" and similar in style and content to Der Nister's unfinished novel *Fun finftn yor* (From the year 1905), which has Ber Borokhov as a protagonist. It is conceivable that both texts belong to the same literary project of creating a fictionalized portrayal of the young Jewish generation after 1905 based on Der Nister's own milieu in provincial Ukraine.[62] Luria notes the ironic detachment of the narrator from his characters—with whose models Der Nister was presumably close at that time—reflected in the choice of their names (the Hebrew-Latin concoction Meylekh Magnus, meaning "Great King"). The ironic and somewhat gossipy tone disappears in the second part, which is narrated in a somber tragic mode. Whereas the first part of Meylekh's life has ups and downs, the second part is a steady descent into the abyss.[63]

"An Acquaintance of Mine" (Mayn bakanter, February 1944) is a variation on the same theme, which helps us to better understand Der Nister's narrative and stylistic strategies.[64] It is the narrator's personal memoir about an unnamed senior colleague from prerevolutionary days, a budding Hebrew writer. There is the familiar motif of a poor intellectual and his ill-fated love for a rich merchant's daughter, who inevitably prefers more dashing and flirtatious types unburdened with a "surplus of erudition and seriousness."[65] He is ridiculed for his weird manners and unkempt appearance and dismissed by her and her friends. In his frustration, he turns to drinking and chess playing, which leaves him penniless. He soon collects himself, however, and in one year completes the full course of studies for Russian gymnasium. In a few years' time, he graduates from the university, where he studies Greek and Latin classics, performing all these feats wearing the same pair of galoshes on bare feet, winter and summer.

After much suffering over his unrequited love, he finds another object for his affections, this time directing his passion "toward a region where he was free, unrestrained, and unlimited—and without the fear that he will encounter any obstacle, resistance, or opposition from the other side": "He gave himself over to the people and its awakening."[66] He immerses himself in the study of ancient and medieval sources of Jewish history and visits old Jewish settlements in Europe, which makes him look "like an ancient apostle who can change his life for what he believes in."[67] This detailed portrayal of a young Jewish intellectual who embraces the nationalist cause in reaction to failed love illustrates Der Nister's understanding of the concept of "sublimation." Moreover, the narrator confesses to his readers, "If truth be told (and to employ our crude literary jargon)—from time to time, I also thought about 'exploiting' [oysnutsn] him for certain occasions and in certain thematic contexts, adding an entirely different beginning and ending to events."[68] This brief remark elucidates Der Nister's literary technique of using real people as prototypes for his literary characters but placing them in a different framework of events, as if putting their personalities to test under imaginary, and unexpected, circumstances. Initially, the narrator relates, "I presumed to provide the portrait of my friend in full measure and in a fitting manner," but in reality the end of his friend was "unexpected and premature."[69] This admission supports Luria's hypothesis that Der Nister used literary materials that he had accumulated working on a literary project about his prerevolutionary milieu for his war stories.

In "An Acquaintance of Mine," World War I separates the narrator from his friend, who stays in Poland. The second, tragic part of the story is told to the narrator by an anonymous Polish-Jewish writer (literat) who managed to escape from occupied Poland. Having no success with his grand cultural-nationalist project, the friend withdraws from the world and dedicates himself to a love object "of a wholly exalted kind," a cosmological treatise titled in Hebrew, "Haya, Hove, veYihye" (He Was, Is, and Shall Be), a reference to God in the well-known medieval hymn "Adon Olam." This treatise is described as "a kind of encomium [*loybgezang*] of all that comes into being and goes away,"[70] from the most ancient times to the most distant future. But his work is interrupted by the war, and large parts of the manuscript are destroyed in a bombardment. Aloof to what is happening around him, he goes into the street of the ghetto and encounters a group of German soldiers who humiliate him by forcing him to perform "circus tricks." He spends the next few days in bed, refusing to take food or speak, until one morning he takes the remaining pages of his work, sets them on fire, and throws them out of the window—after which he jumps himself, while pronouncing the words, "Haya, Hove, veYihye," "like a kind of *Shma Yisroel*."[71] After the friend's suicide, the Polish-Jewish *literat* collects a few remaining half-burned pieces of the manuscript from his apartment and brings them to Moscow. "He showed them to me," says the narrator, "and I recognized my friend's handwriting. Then, I undertook the work that is hereby given to the reader. Honor his memory!"[72] Structurally and typologically, this story is similar to "Meylekh Magnus," although I have not yet been able to identify its prototype. The story is dated February 1944, which is about one month before Sutzkever arrived in Moscow by plane from the Lithuanian forest where he was fighting with the partisans after his escape from the Vilnius ghetto; therefore, there must have been another Polish-Jewish *literat* who told Der Nister about the tragic fate of an old friend.

A different variation of the two-part structure is the story "Regrowth" (Vidervuks, 1946). Its protagonists are two neighbors who live in a building in a big Soviet city, both successful middle-aged Jewish single parents: the surgeon Dr. Zemelman and the pedagogue Ms. Zayets. Over the years they have become estranged from their Jewish origins and from all that occurred in the "thickets of the masses."[73] Soon after the outbreak of the war, they lose their children, and the shared loss brings them closer to each other. News of the deaths of Dr. Zemelman's brother and his wife under the Nazi occupation reminds them of their places of origin somewhere in the Soviet-Polish borderlands. In an act of reconnection with the Jewish people, they each decide to adopt Jewish orphans who lost their parents in the occupied territories. They receive "more than they desired: not ordinary children but children of action, children who already had a story in their lives, children who had passed through the smoke and fire—in a word: partisan children."[74] At first, the adopted children do not seem able to speak as a result of their traumatic experiences. When Dr. Zemelman encourages his adopted son, Moyshke, to speak as he likes, "a stream of words rushed out" in a "strangely personal language, which had been preserved by the people from whom he had been torn."[75] To the acculturated ear of Dr. Zemelman, his words sound like "a greeting from an old, dear home that could never be forgotten."[76] Moyshke is able to recall what happened to him among the partisans in the Belarusian forest in great detail, which attracts the interest of "professional historians"[77] and gives Dr. Zemelman much to ponder. Thus, a vernacular variety of Yiddish mixed with other languages has a therapeutic effect on Jews from both Poland and the Soviet Union, estranged by the years of separation but now reunited through talking about the shared past.

Ms. Zayets's adopted daughter, Elke, survived in a ghetto in Ukraine and is somewhat mentally slow because of her traumatic experience, but "her soul had a voice," which finds its expression in the songs that she composes. Her songs draw from the ancient poetic resources of the biblical lists of curses and calamities (a klole-lid, vi fun der toykhekho),[78] giving voice to "everyone— all those who lived with her in the ghetto."[79] Like Moyshke, Elke cannot speak pure Yiddish, mixing it with Ukrainian and German, but her corrupt language is "close to her body," her most precious possession, which retains the memory of her lost family.[80]

The attraction between the young people gradually transfers to their adoptive parents. It unfolds in the subconscious of Dr. Zemelman and Ms. Zayets, finding its expression in dreams but not in words. In one of his dreams, Dr. Zemelman sees himself and Ms. Zayets in a sled, with his murdered brother and his sister-in-law sitting behind them and holding candles. With their "half-living, half-dead mouths," the brother and his wife greet Dr. Zemelman and Ms. Zayets with a mazel tov, and then a voice (perhaps from heaven) is heard, whose message is not entirely clear to Dr. Zemelman. One thing that he is "allowed to hear" is the reiteration of the biblical commandment of "growth and regeneration," "despite all that has struck everyone and, especially, us."[81] After this dream, Dr. Zemelman resolves to speak clearly to Ms. Zayets, presumably to propose marriage.

In this story, the surviving children act as therapists, and their stories reconnect their assimilated adoptive parents with the historical experience of the Jewish people. Narrated in an uncultivated raw language, the children's stories awaken the suppressed Jewish feelings in the estranged Russian-Jewish intellectuals and prompt them to restore the nearly broken chain of Jewish generations by performing the most basic commandment to "be fruitful and multiply," which Der Nister rephrases as "vaksn un vider vaksn" (grow and grow again),[82] thus providing an additional religious layer of meaning to the title of the story, "Regrowth." In this way the vernacular Yiddish serves as a key instrument in the restoration and reunification of the fragmented remnants of the Jewish people.

As we have seen, Der Nister's war stories are typically split by the sudden outbreak of the war. The first part gradually establishes the protagonist's psychological profile and highlights his or her most characteristic features. It focuses, with varying degrees of elaboration, on his or her moments of crisis, such as ill-fated love, death of loved ones, depression, and so forth, sometimes offering detailed depictions of the protagonist's appearance, lifestyle, and social behavior. This part of the story is told in a detached, somewhat ironic, and occasionally gossipy tone. Yet the tone becomes somber and tragic in the second part. The stories reach their climax in episodes of suffering and martyrdom, in which the inner spiritual strength of the character reveals itself in a heroic act of resistance. The psychological type that has been portrayed in the first part transforms into a mythological Judaic archetype.

In the foreword to *Vidervuks*, the Soviet critic Moyshe Belenki offers insights into Der Nister's literary method. He detects Der Nister's main philosophical concern in the first book, *Gedanken un motivn* (Thoughts and motifs, 1907): "How can contradictions and unity fit into one soul."[83] To convey this tension between contradiction and unity, the writer uses symbolic language, which serves as an artistic instrument for "generalizing and reflecting the contradictions and the depth of reality."[84] During the first half of Der Nister's literary career, his symbolic characters and their actions were mostly of a "fantastic" nature, Belenki argues, borrowing this concept from Fyodor Dostoevsky, but during the last two decades of Der Nister's life, symbolism became an artistic method for depicting socio-historical reality.[85] Applying Belenki's scheme to the war stories, one can see how socio-historic reality, which is represented in the first part of each story, becomes transformed into a symbolic fantasy in the second part, thus reversing the chronology of symbolism's replacement by realism in Der Nister's career.

In Der Nister's grand historical scheme, the destruction of Polish Jewry by the Nazis becomes yet another link in the long chain of the tragedy of Jewish history. This unexpected catastrophe reconnects the present generation with its ancestors through acts of heroism and martyrdom and restores the eternal unity of the Jewish people. The unity had been disrupted by modernity, which spawned separation and discord between old and young, religious and secular, assimilated and traditional, Soviet and Polish

Jews. Der Nister's narrator, like Rabbi Aaron, is eager to find out whether the present generation of Jews who are removed from their religious and communal foundation is still strong enough to withstand the ordeal of their age like previous generations of Jewish victims, heroes, and martyrs. All of the case studies, each one in its own way, give an affirmative answer. The writer plays a crucial role in this process of restorative investigation: using his professional skills, he reconnects the fragments of written and oral memories of the traumatic experience, creates archetypical characters out of real protagonists, and constructs a narrative by way of organizing reality through symbolic structures.

## IN MOSCOW

Der Nister's move to Moscow from Central Asia was marked by a literary evening in his honor that was held on October 11, 1943. In a press release that the Jewish Antifascist Committee transmitted by cable to the foreign press, the journalist Moyshe Notovitsh reported that Der Nister read one of his recent stories about the destruction of Jews in Poland. It made a "strong impression" on the audience: "As usual," Der Nister demonstrated a masterful command of literary Yiddish and psychological perceptiveness in his portrayals of characters. Other speakers noted the epic tone and the "folkish" quality of his prose. In the original draft of the report, Notovitsh also quoted the words of the writer Noyekh Lurye: "Der Nister's story overwhelms. One has to be a great writer to master this kind of material. This story impresses by its powerful depiction of the sufferings and travails of our people in this great war."[86] This part, however, was not included in the press release, in accordance with the general editorial policy of the JAC (the Jewish Antifascist Committee) not to single out the fate of the Jews in the war. Similarly, the Russian translation of Der Nister's article "Moskve salutirt" (Moscow celebrates), prepared by the JAC, omitted the most outspoken Jewish part. Starting on a festive note by describing the fireworks marking the liberation of Zhitomir, his "nearly native town," Der Nister swiftly turns to lamenting the total destruction of Ukrainian Jewry. He recalls the memorial grave of ten martyrs at the old Jewish cemetery in Zhitomir who were murdered as a result of blood libels: "I used to visit that cemetery frequently, and the grave of the ten innocent victims evoked sad thoughts and memories about the sufferings that my people had to endure in the old hard times." But those old sorrows, he continues, pale in comparison with the present full-scale destruction of Jews, which can drive one to total despair. But the Moscow fireworks and the advance of the Red Army bring some glimmer of hope, to which his heart responds with an "almost mystical feeling of witnessing the resurrection of the whole country."[87] Nevertheless, this article, like a few other pieces whose edited versions have been preserved in the archives of JAC, was not published in *Eynikayt* (Unity), the official organ of JAC. Altogether Der Nister published only four articles in *Eynikayt*, by contrast with other Yiddish writers, especially his former Kiev colleagues Peretz Markish, David Bergelson, Itsik Fefer, and Leyb Kvitko, whose publications appeared in *Eynikayt* on a regular basis. Der Nister's contribution is absent among the series of articles marking the thirtieth anniversary of Y. L. Peretz's death in March 1945, even though he was one of the few Soviet Yiddish writers who knew Peretz personally. Nor is Der Nister mentioned among the speakers at the commemorative event that took place in GOSET on August 6, 1945.[88]

Der Nister settled in a small back room at the Moscow State Yiddish Theater (GOSET) with his wife Elena Sigalovskaia, an actress at the theater. His association with GOSET goes back to the 1930s, when the theater considered staging Nikolai Gogol's *Wedding* in his translation.[89] In Tashkent, Der Nister translated, in collaboration with one of the authors, the play *Khamza*, by the Uzbek authors Amin Umari and Kamil Iashen, which was performed in 1942.[90] After more than two years of disruption caused by the evacuation, the first Moscow season opened on December 25, 1943. Der Nister reported about this event with joy and enthusiasm: "The audience consisted of all kinds of representatives of the masses [*folks-mentshn*], from simple menial workers to high-ranking commanders and generals, from clerks to officials of the People's Commissariats. They came to demonstrate that, despite the hard time of the war, there is a growing longing for art and culture, both general and Jewish. The sense of connection with Jewish culture gives strength and courage to perform heroic deeds to everyone, [whether] on the front lines or in the rearguard."[91] The audience enthusiastically received the theater director and leading actor, Solomon Mikhoels, who outdid himself in the role of Sholem Aleichem's Tevye the Dairyman. Even the hardened soldiers could not contain tears of joy watching the great actor, being among so many Jews, and hearing Yiddish.

Yuri Smolych, who visited Der Nister at that time, found him in a "very depressed state." He recalls Der Nister's words: "Smolych, tell me that I am asleep, tell me that this is merely a nightmare, and wake me up, wake me up! But this is impossible, people are not capable of doing this." Der Nister complained that he had no strength to carry on: "Where can we, Jews, derive strength? We are scattered, and they get us together only to drive us to Babi Yar with machine guns or to make us rot in the ghetto."[92] On May 31, 1944, Der Nister had another visitor, the young Jewish partisan Shloymke Perlmuter, and they had a long conversation about the sufferings of Jewish children, which became the basis of Der Nister's essay "Has" (Hate; the original title was "On the Third Anniversary of the War"[93]), published in *Eynikayt* on June 29.[94] Telling the story of a Jewish boy's escape from the massacre of his shtetl in Volhynia and his difficult journey to the Soviet partisans, Der Nister invokes biblical and Talmudic metaphorical images that can be understood as veiled references to the Land of Israel. Analyzing the "semantic field" of this essay, Kotlerman suggests that Der Nister's later Birobidzhan writings "inherited" this sense of tragedy and hope for the restoration of the "national building" from the Jewish religious tradition.[95]

Even in his publications on the most official Soviet occasions, Der Nister expressed his hope for Jewish revival in the Soviet Union. On February 9, 1947, the day of the elections to the Supreme Council of the Russian Soviet Federative Socialist Republic, *Eynikayt* published his article "Tsu di valn!" (Toward the elections). While the results of the Soviet elections were fully predetermined, this event had a certain political significance and was accompanied by a propaganda campaign to drum up public support for Stalin and the Communist Party. Der Nister's article stands out among the flood of obligatory celebratory publications in more than one respect. First, and perhaps most remarkably, it does not mention Stalin's name. Second, it draws risky parallels between the Soviet present and the tsarist past and makes daring statements, which a year later would undoubtedly be qualified as provocative and nationalistic. Der Nister begins by comparing the Soviet elections with the elections to the Fourth State Duma of the Russian Empire in 1912. Back then, he recalls, "It was not possible for Jews to put forward a Jewish candidate," even though in Zhitomir, where he was living, Jews constituted a significant portion of the population. And although a tiny number of Jews had been elected, they happened to be the "most incompetent" ones (same shlimazolim) and needed to be closely supervised by the St. Petersburg Jewish "plutocrats," the prominent lawyers Genrikh Sliozberg and Maksim Vinaver. In the Duma, they were constantly harassed by right-wing nationalists. Der Nister does not draw an explicit comparison between the two assemblies, but he implies that the Jewish deputies in the Supreme Council of the Russian Federation are treated with more respect than their predecessors in the imperial Duma. To illustrate the progress of the Jews in the Soviet Union, he turns to statistics: "Out of eight thousand students who study in all the faculties of the Moscow State University, more than 1300 are Jewish. And there are other educational institutions in Moscow, and Moscow is not the only city in the country." This remarkable statistic was provided by Evgenii Sergeev, the secretary of the Communist Party Committee. Sergeev's article celebrating the high number of Jews among university students and faculty appeared in *Eynikayt* a few days earlier.[96] But given Sergeev's involvement in the campaign against "cosmopolites," a term used as a code word for Jewish intellectuals, just two months later, one can assume that these data had been actually collected in order to justify restrictions on the number of Jews in higher education.[97] But Der Nister, as well as the editors of *Eynikayt*, were probably not aware of those plans. Der Nister concludes with his favorite metaphorical image, a building representing Soviet society: a "tall multistoried building whose foundation was laid with so much hardship."[98]

## IN SEARCH OF A NEW HOMELAND IN BIROBIDZHAN

On June 10, 1947, Der Nister boarded a train carrying about a thousand Jewish survivors from southern Ukraine to Birobidzhan.[99] He described this nineteen-day journey in ten episodes, which were published in two parts, the first of which was subtitled "Bildlekh un ayndrukn" (Images and impressions) in an obvious nod to Y. L. Peretz's *Bilder fun a provints-rayze* (Impressions of a journey to the provinces).[100] As Kotlerman remarks in his comprehensive reconstruction of Der Nister's Birobidzhan adventure, "In these notes one feels the almost ecstatic exuberance over the renewal of resettlement in Birobidzhan after the Holocaust."[101] Der Nister was not the only Yiddish writer who reported about the resettlement movement in the summer of 1947. *Eynikayt* published dozens of enthusiastic reports by several authors, some of them with nearly identical titles like "On a train to Birobidzhan." The most detailed series of reportages was written by Ilya Lyumkis, the staff writer of *Eynikayt*, who later collected them in a book.[102]

The series opens with the narrator's encounter with a Jew who represents the archetypical Jewish wanderer and sets the ideological tone with his programmatic statement: "The present wandering is not at all like all those previous ones. . . . A deep break is occurring in the psychology of the Jewish masses, for the sake of reconstruction, in order to repair the broken wholeness. . . . After the recent Catastrophe came the fundamental reexamination. In the Middle Ages, such events, which occurred far and wide in the Diaspora, would awaken hopes in false messiahs. Now—we see a striving for a real action."[103] The Jew reminds the narrator that the Birobidzhan project was officially sanctioned by the Soviet authorities for the sake of the "consolidation of the Jewish people," quoting, as Kotlerman points out, the 1934 statement of Mikhail Kalinin, at that time chairman of the Central Executive Committee, de jure president of the Soviet Union.[104] Now, after "the Jewish masses have received an historical lesson and SOS signal," the time is ripe to bring this project to completion, concludes the Jew.[105] The following episodes record the narrator's impression of his fellow travelers, stressing their resilience and optimism. The echelon becomes the Jewish people in miniature, moving to the destination where it would rebuild itself. Hope and communal spirit heal the wounds of the war, helping orphaned children and adults who have lost their loved ones to recover from their traumas.

The second part, "Mit ibervanderer keyn Biro-Bidzhan" (With the new settlers to Birobidzhan, 1947), opens with a long and detailed list enumerating the people who travel to settle in Birobidzhan, from a post office manager to a group of *gerim* (converts to Judaism): "Typical Russians, with their evil desires somewhat suppressed in a sectarian way and with pious quotations from Scripture [*psukim*] on their lips."[106] "In short," Der Nister concludes his two-page inventory, "you have here a kind of Noah's Ark, modern style, that is, not on water but on the train, and not in a flood, but after a horrific world war."[107] He envisions the motley mixture of Jewish survivors from the ghettos and camps of Transnistria, evacuees from Central Asia, and demobilized Red Army soldiers as a Jewish microcosm, a kernel from which the regeneration of the Jewish people will grow in the Soviet Far East. Each episode in the narrative is presented in a dynamic cinematic style, framed by the moving natural landscapes of Siberia and written as if captured on film by an accompanying cameraman.

The climax of the journey is the wedding of two survivors, which is performed on the train according to the Jewish custom, with chuppah and kiddushin (officiated under a wedding canopy and with a betrothal contract) and klezmer music and dancing. The celebration, a "symbol of the revival of the entire community,"[108] is admired by an assortment of people who happen to be nearby, including Japanese prisoners of war traveling in a prison train in the opposite direction and healthy Siberian peasants waving from the station platform. Before the wedding the bride feels compelled to tell the bridegroom the story of her painful and miraculous survival in the shtetl of Khmelnik, where the entire Jewish population was murdered: "The bride talks fast, the hasty stream of memories overflows her, and she rushes to pour as much as possible into the stranger's ear."[109] The bridegroom, still in his Red Army uniform, listens but is unable to talk, overwhelmed by the sudden flood of words. The Yiddish writer Yosef Kerler, who traveled on the same train, remembers how Der Nister was always looking for people with great stories to tell, to collect material that he would later transform into his fiction.[110] Sharing the experience of death and survival with fellow passengers during the journey was the key mechanism for rebuilding a community through therapeutic storytelling. Der Nister's role on the train is similar to the anonymous narrator in Sholem Aleichem's classic series *Railroad Stories* (1903–11). For both writers, storytelling on a train serves as, to use David Roskies's words, "the last frontier of hope."[111]

The Jew from the opening chapter reappears at the end of the story, and now we learn that he is the author's "alter ego." He asserts that "that place" (meaning Birobidzhan) will become the site for a "creative assembly of the people" (folks-sheferisher onzamlung), in which their "new birth and reeducation" (nay-geburt un iberdertsiung) will take place.[112] As Kotlerman notes, the dialogue between the pessimistic narrator and his optimistic "alter ego," which frames the entire text, revolves around the fundamental question of the Jewish condition as a permanent wandering in galuth (exile).[113] In *The Family Mashber* this condition was personified by Luzi, and it seemed that this state of permanent wandering preserved the Jews through history by allowing them to escape the imminent danger of destruction. Now, after the catastrophe of the war, Jews were no longer able to sustain this mode of existence and needed a place of their own. Birobidzhan presumably offered them security and stability, a "new birth," but the price for it was "reeducation." As Kotlerman further suggests, the narrator's optimistic doppelgänger, "a shadowy double who induced the writer to behave in an uncharacteristic manner, introduces a certain ambiguity, not only in the text but also in his real attitude toward his extraordinary journey."[114] Indeed, a narrator with a split personality or alter ego has been a feature of Der Nister's prose since 1929. The two voices engage in an intense debate, rife with political accusations and ideological conflicts that will never be resolved satisfactorily. Seen from the perspective of Der Nister's entire Soviet oeuvre, the Birobidzhan solution to the "Jewish problem" would also appear unsatisfactory.

The train was welcomed in Birobidzhan with great fanfare, and at every station in the territory of the Jewish Autonomous Region, it was greeted by speeches in Yiddish and orchestras playing Jewish tunes. In Birobidzhan, Der Nister was received as a guest of honor, put up in the only hotel in town and assigned a special cook to prepare meals that would fit his diet. No one was allowed to disturb him during his writing hours, but the rest of the time, he met with the local intelligentsia and simple folk. He tried to convince the local authorities that developing Yiddish culture and turning the region into a "Jewish home" would attract more Jewish migrants and bring international fame. It was apparently under his influence that Yiddish was introduced briefly in all schools in the region. According to the memoirs of the Polish Yiddish writer Yisroel Emiot, Der Nister was "intoxicated" by the reception, for never, in his entire lifetime in Russia, had he enjoyed such "worship" (farherlekhung) as in Birobidzhan.[115] At the same time his mind was constantly preoccupied with the destruction and the future of the Jewish people. In the old days, he told Emiot, "Jews did not play with Yiddishkeit; every moment they were prepared to sacrifice their life." (Zeyer yeder rege iz geven a geyn tsu der akeyde.) By contrast, "we"—the modern Jews—practice a "stylized Yiddishkeit," which costs little. Emiot believed that Der Nister was especially interested in Polish refugees because of their authentic, "not distorted Yiddishkeit."[116]

Remarkably, Der Nister undertook this long and arduous trip to Birobidzhan on his own initiative. As Kotlerman notes, "This trip does not easily fit into Der Nister's way of life," because he tended to stay away from official Soviet social life and showed no interest in the Birobidzhan project.[117] Moreover, in contrast to the usual Soviet practice, this trip was not initiated by the authorities; Der Nister merely arranged a recommendation letter from the JAC. Kotlerman suggests that Der Nister, in a Hasidic mystical fashion, regarded his journey as a travel into "exile" that would be transformed into redemption: "A voyage made out of personal distress became a public mission."[118] But even though Der Nister certainly was knowledgeable about Hasidism and Kabbalah and used its metaphorical language, his worldview was secular; Emiot describes him as a "modern" and "national" Jew, who admired Hasidism but had no connection to the Hasidim.[119] Der Nister portrays Birobidzhan as a place where a new Soviet-Jewish synthesis would be forged, far away from the "Golgotha landscape" of Europe where "the last stretch of our history has been crucified martyrdom [*martirerish gekreytst*]."[120]

In the final episode of his travelogue, he describes a friendly wrestling match between two young Jewish men. The winner, who is younger and smaller than his adversary, brings to mind the battle between David and Goliath. It turns out that just before boarding the train in Ukraine, this "David" was attacked and stabbed by a band of "hooligans." This somewhat veiled reference to the outbreak of antisemitism in the liberated Soviet territories brings Der Nister to the concluding vision of Birobidzhan as a gathering place for those "little brave Dovidlekh" who will be ready to defend their tribe (*shtam*) and their Soviet homeland from any "Goliath."[121] In a rough draft of notes titled "Birobidzhan," Der Nister outlined a grand vision for the new Jewish homeland in the Soviet Far East. He emphasized the primary significance of a territory for the preservation of the Jewish nation, specifically pointing out: "It is necessary to say here that we are talking about the Jewish Autonomous Region, which could, today or tomorrow, with our good will, turn into a republic, the seventeenth, in addition to the sixteen that already exist." As Kotlerman notes, "Surprisingly, Der Nister devotes no attention whatsoever to the issues of language and culture in these lines."[122] Indeed, this shift from culture to territory seems to reflect a dramatic change from Der Nister's attitude of the 1930s, as it was remembered by Smolych. Most likely, the change in Der Nister's thinking was caused by the experience of the war and the Holocaust, which may have convinced him that wandering offered no escape from total destruction.

## CONCLUSION

Upon his return from Birobidzhan in the fall of 1947, Der Nister reconnected with his brother Motl via the JAC. He wrote to him: "During the past three years I had an opportunity to enquire about you, but I feared the answer I would receive. I was almost certain that you and your entire family had perished at Hitler's murderous hand like many thousand, many millions of our brethren." He reported sad family news: the death of their mother before the war in her own bed at the age of eighty-four, the tragic circumstances of the deaths of their aunts, uncles, and cousins, and the death of his daughter in Leningrad. He concluded:

> As you see, my dear Motl, our family tree is left without leaves, it's naked and hollow. How I live after what happened to me, I don't know.... Only one thing is left: to curse fascism, which has brought such bitter misfortunes to us, as well as to our entire people and to the whole of humankind.

> (Vi du zest, tayerer Motl, iz undzer mishpokhe-boym geblibn on bleter, a naketer, a hoyler. Vi azoy ikh leb nokh dem, vos s'hot mikh getrofn, veys ikh nit.... S'iz geblibn nor eyns: tsu sheltn dem fashizm, vos hot undz gebrakht azoyne bitere umglikn. Undz, vi dem gantsn folk undzern, azoy vi der gorer mentshheyt.)

Der Nister also mentioned his novel and its success in the Soviet Union and the United States, asking his brother to enquire about it among Yiddish writers in Paris. He sounded somewhat doubtful, however, that his brother would remember enough Yiddish to read the novel (despite the fact that the letter was written in Yiddish!)[123]

Solomon Mikhoels, the director of the Moscow State Yiddish Theater (GOSET) and the head of the JAC, was brutally murdered in Minsk by the secret police, who camouflaged his murder as a car accident, on January 12, 1948. In a cynical gesture, Mikhoels's death was mourned at the official level, and he was given a grand funeral that was attended by Soviet dignitaries and large crowds of ordinary people. A Yiddish collection of twelve eulogies was published in March in an impressive print run of fifteen thousand copies. The opening chapter was appropriately written by the head of the Union of the Soviet Writers, Aleksandr

Fadeev, who a year later would become one of the instigators of the antisemitic campaign. Der Nister's piece was the second one, indicating—given the specific attention to the order of appearance of names in official Soviet documents—his prestigious rank in the Soviet Yiddish cultural hierarchy. Ilya Ehrenburg's eulogy was in the third position. Der Nister begins with the description of a kilometers-long line of people waiting in the cold outside the GOSET building in central Moscow to pay their last respects to the great man. Like his report on the opening of the 1943 season, Der Nister highlights the diversity of the crowd, which included old and young, government officials, professors, military commanders, and simple workers, representing the entire Jewish people, "all of the same pedigree" (ale in eyn yikhes).[124]

Der Nister describes Mikhoels as *khad bedoro* (exceptional in his generation), using the Talmudic Aramaic expression traditionally reserved for outstanding rabbis and sages. Using an even more remarkable allusion, Der Nister proclaims that by his death Mikhoels had overcome death (durkhn toyt vi goyver geven dem toyt), creatively appropriating the wording from the Orthodox Easter liturgy, "Christ is risen from the dead, trampling down death by death." Looking at Mikhoels's magnificent face (which had been horribly disfigured by his murderers and was expertly made up by his friend Professor Boris Zbarski, who was in charge of preserving Lenin's body in the mausoleum), Der Nister imagines that the great actor is not dead but rather playing the last and greatest role of his life, ready to wake up from death. "A King Lear, a King Man, a king in a mask who plays high values, high pride, and high mastery all at once" (i hoykhe yesoydes, i hoykhe shtolts, i hoykhe maystershaft) before an audience made up of the entirety of the Jewish people.[125] Der Nister notes that many people mourn Mikhoels's death as they would mourn a member of their own family, observing the traditional custom of covering mirrors in their homes.[126] The Jewish people have lost their favorite son, but: "The people did have him; and will have again.

A son is born to us." (Dos folk hot gehat im; un vet oykh vayter hobn. Ben yulad lonu.)[127] The Hebrew words are a paraphrase of Isaiah 9:5 (9:6 in the Christian Bible): "For to us a child is born, to us a son is given," a verse that carries strong messianic connotations in both Judaism and Christianity. Elaborating on the messianic theme of resurrection, Der Nister prophesizes: "A son, and not just one son, will be born to us, to spite our enemies and to console our own people and all the best children of other peoples who love us." (A zun, un nit eyn zun, vet undz geboyrn vern, af lehakhis sonim un tsum treyst far undzer eygn folk un far ale undz libhobndike beste kinder fun felker.)[128] Thus Mikhoels emerges as a messianic figure whose artistic genius is a kind of holy spirit that will continue to live and sustain the Jewish people after his death.

Mikhoels, Der Nister argues, occupies a special place in Jewish history. Previously, Jewish creativity was directed primarily at preserving the people, but Mikhoels's art enables the Jewish people to live out their lives naturally through artistic expression. He is a new, modern type of national leader who possesses a unique combination of artistic talent, wisdom, and public temperament, all of which he put to the service of the Jewish people. "He served us not only as a professional artistic personality but much more as a symbol and an inspiring emblem of the awakening and revival of the creative powers of the people" (Er hot undz gedint nit nor mit zayn perzenlekher, baruflekher kunst, nor nokh mer als symbol un als derfreyendiker simen fun der oyfderfakhung un vider-oyflebung fun di sheferishe folks-koykhes), powers that had been suppressed in previous generations. In conclusion, Der Nister humbly admits:

> I did not stand in his guard of honor. It was beyond my power: neither my heart nor my nerves could bear it. And more: it is as if the utmost degree of my admiration for him did not allow me to see him dead. I looked at him from afar and had a complete illusion that I saw him alive, but acting dead . . . and so he has remained with me.

(Kh'bin in zayn ern-vakh nit geshtanen. S'iz geven hekher fun mayne koykhes: nit dos harts hot mir fartrogn, nit di nervn. Un nokh iber a tam: di greste mos mayn farerung tsu im hot mir vi nit derloybt im tsu zen a toytn. Kh'hob gekukt af im fun vayt un hot gehat di fulshtendike iliuzye, az kh'ze im lebedik, nor in der rol fun a toytn . . . un azoy iz er mir farblibn.)[129]

This was one of Der Nister's very last texts published in the Soviet Union. Der Nister tries to inscribe Mikhoels and his tragic death into the grand narrative of Jewish history that he has been creatively constructing in his writing since the mid-1930s. This narrative, which was expanded and modified in response to the unfolding tragedy, incorporated elements of Hasidic and kabbalistic mysticism, Christianity, European Romanticism, and symbolism. It centered on the role and responsibility of the individual in a critical moment in history. Der Nister readily utilized traditional Jewish tropes such as kiddush hashem, *goles* (galuth), and wandering, as well as messianic motifs, but he was equally open to the influences of modern European, Russian, and Soviet culture. Kotlerman describes Der Nister's late work in terms of "hybridization," a "labored symbiosis between the Soviet and the Jewish ethoses forced upon Jewish literary figures in the USSR." He also notes, "Der Nister never expressed opposition to the Soviet regime, even though it was undoubtedly alien to him."[130] It should be noted, however, that any political regime would have been alien to Der Nister's carefully cultivated persona of the reclusive artist. Indeed, given his public attitude, it is remarkable how closely he was actually engaged with the Soviet regime, and how successful—until the last fatal blow, of course—his strategy was. He commanded respect among some of the regime's leading cultural figures, such as Yuri Smolych, who occupied a high position in the Ukrainian literary hierarchy. Der Nister's works were published both in the USSR and the United States and were greeted with almost universal critical acclaim on both sides of the ideological divide. His texts were censored and quite a few were not published for ideological reasons, but this was by no means exceptional. What seems exceptional, however, is the degree of artistic and intellectual freedom that Der Nister was able to maintain in the face of totalitarianism. His main achievement was the ability to speak as an engaged witness to his people, using a narrative voice that combined features of Soviet reporter, modernist artist, medieval community chronicler, mystical visionary, Hasidic tzaddik (spiritual leader), and biblical prophet.

## NOTES

1. For a more detailed analysis of that episode, see Krutikov, *From Kabbalah to Class Struggle*, 242–46.
2. Krutikov, "'Turning My Soul Inside Out,'" 116.
3. Der Nister, "Perets hot geredt," 279.
4. Ibid., 283.
5. Ibid., 283–84.
6. Ibid., 289.
7. Der Nister, "A briv tsu Dovid Bergelson," 290.
8. Ibid.
9. Krutikov, "'Turning My Soul Inside Out,'" 130.
10. USHM Archives, RG-22.028, Reel 174 (GARF, f. P-8114, op. 1, d. 486 [Der Nister, "Shloyme fun tschekhoslovakey"], l. 62).
11. Ibid., l. 65.
12. Ibid., l. 67.
13. Ibid.
14. Ibid., l. 66.
15. Der Nister, *Regrowth*, 190.
16. Ibid., 191.
17. Der Nister, *Regrowth*, 196. The English translation has been corrected according to the Yiddish original.
18. Der Nister, *Dertseylungen un eseyen*, 47.
19. Der Nister, *Regrowth*, 196.
20. Murav, *Music from a Speeding Train*, 141.
21. Ibid., 142.
22. For a summary of the debates and their contemporary relevance, see Abelson and Weiss, "Burial of Non Jewish Spouse and Children."

23. Peretz, "Three Gifts," 230. Wisse, *The I. L. Peretz Reader*, tr. Hillel Halkin, 230.

24. Der Nister, *Korbones*, 22. English translation by Joseph Sherman, in Sherman, *From Revolution to Repression*, 203.

25. Ibid., 209.

26. Ibid., 209.

27. Ibid., 226.

28. Ibid., 227.

29. Kotlerman, *Broken Heart/Broken Wholeness*, 79-80.

30. Ibid., 80.

31. "A Report by M. Scherbakov to A. A. Kuznetsov on Soviet Yiddish Literature (October 7, 1946)," in Redlich, *War, Holocaust and Stalinism*, 420.

32. Ibid., 78.

33. Der Nister, *Regrowth*, 217.

34. Published by Shmeruk, "Arba igrot shel Der Nister," 238.

35. In the 1957 New York edition, this story is subtitled "About a Fourth Case in Formerly Occupied Poland," but in the Moscow edition of 1969 the subtitle is changed to "Third Case in the Provisionally Occupied Poland of the Past," apparently reflecting the editorial decision to remove "Grandfather and Grandson."

36. Der Nister, *Regrowth*, 219.

37. Ibid., 221.

38. Ibid., 233.

39. Ibid., 241.

40. "Flora" is analyzed in detail by Erik Butler in his afterword to *Regrowth*, 279-85.

41. Der Nister, *Regrowth*, 134.

42. Like some other pseudo-historical characters in Der Nister's fiction, this one is an amalgam of several real figures who lived at different times. One is the famous Jewish scholar Joseph Solomon Delmedigo (1591–1665), who studied medicine in Padua but never set foot in Poland or wrote a medical treatise; the other is Moyshe Markuze (1743–?), from Poland, the author of the first popular medical handbook in colloquial Yiddish, *Sefer refues* (1790). Apparently, some of Delmedigo's descendants lived in Belarus (http://ha-historion.blogspot.com/2007/09/colorful-jewish-historical-figure.html).

43. Der Nister, *Regrowth*, 109.

44. Ibid., 134–35.

45. Ibid., 145.

46. Ibid., 148.

47. Ibid., 148, translation slightly modified.

48. Ibid., 150.

49. Ibid., 157.

50. Der Nister, *Vidervuks,* 159.

51. Der Nister, *Regrowth,* 153.

52. Estraikh, "Jews as Cossacks," 100.

53. On Der Nister's varied use of dance motifs in different contexts, see Estraikh, Hoge, and Krutikov, *Uncovering the Hidden,* 40, 41, 83, 85, 135–36, 140, 170.

54. Koskoff, *Music in Lubavitsher Life,* 99–100.

55. Née Brendel, she married the famous German Romantic writer Friedrich von Schlegel (second marriage) and changed her name to Dorothea, after their joint conversion to Catholicism.

56. Der Nister, *Regrowth,* 16.

57. Ibid., 90.

58. Ibid.

59. Der Nister, *Meotsar sipurey hanistar,* afterword by Luria, 277.

60. Karlip, *Tragedy of a Generation,* 78–79.

61. Interestingly, Karlip's study of Kalmanovitch's political activity similarly skips the period between the early 1920s and 1939.

62. Der Nister, *Meotsar sipurey hanistar,* 282.

63. Ibid., 281.

64. Butler's identification of the protagonist with Der Nister (*Regrowth,* 298) does not seem to be justified by the text.

65. Der Nister, *Regrowth,* 247.

66. Ibid., 256–57.

67. Ibid., 257.

68. Ibid., 258.

69. Ibid.

70. Ibid., 260.

71. Ibid., 272.

72. Ibid., 273.

73. Ibid., 155.

74. Ibid., 165.

75. Ibid., 167.

76. Ibid., 167.

77. Ibid., 171.

78. Der Nister, *Vidervuks,* 171.

79. Der Nister, *Regrowth,* 168.

80. Ibid., 169.

81. Ibid., 179.

82. Der Nister, *Vidervuks*, 181.

83. Ibid., 10.

84. Ibid., 11.

85. Ibid., 11.

86. USHM Archives, RG-22.028, Reel 106 (GARF, f. 8114, op. 1, d. 262 [Notovitsh, "Der Nister-ovnt in Moskve,"] l. 12.)

87. USHM Archives, RG-22.028, Reel 174 (GARF, f. 8114, op. 1, d. 486 [Der Nister, "Moskve salutirt"], ll. 11–12.)

88. "Peretz ovnt," 3.

89. Veidlinger, *Moscow State Yiddish Theater*, 197.

90. Ibid., 236.

91. USHM Archives, RG-22.028, Reel 174 (GARF, f. 8114, op. 1, d. 486 [Der Nister, "Mit glik"], ll. 8–9.)

92. Smolych, "Z 'zapysiv na skhyli viku,'" 172–73.

93. USHM Archives, RG-22.028, Reel 174 (GARF, f. 8114, op. 1, d. 486, l. 116.)

94. This episode is analyzed in Kotlerman, *Broken Heart/Broken Wholeness*, 87–101.

95. Ibid., 91.

96. Sergeev, "Yidishe yugnt in moskver melukhisher universitet," 3.

97. Mlechin, *Kreml'-1953: Bor'ba za vlast' so smertel'nym iskhodom*, 207.

98. Der Nister, "Tsu di valn," 4.

99. For a detailed reconstruction of this trip, see Ber (Boris) Kotlerman, "We Are Lacking 'A Man Dieth in a Tent'" and *Broken Heart/Broken Wholeness*.

100. Der Nister, "Mitn tsveytn echelon (bildlekh un ayndrukn)," 2.

101. Kotlerman, "We Are Lacking 'A Man Dieth in a Tent,'" 176.

102. Lyumkis, *Eshelonen geyen keyn Birobidzhan*.

103. Der Nister, "With the Second Echelon," 24.

104. Kotlerman, *Broken Heart/Broken Wholeness*, 25.

105. Ibid.

106. Der Nister, "Mit ibervanderer keyn Biro-Bidzhan," 257.

107. Ibid., 258.

108. Ibid., 270.

109. Ibid., 271.

110. Kerler, *Geklibene proze*, 111–12.

111. Roskies, *Bridge of Longing*, 178.

112. Der Nister, "Mit ibervanderer keyn Biro-Bidzhan," 278.

113. Kotlerman, *Broken Heart/Broken Wholeness*, 68.

114. Ibid., 71.

115. Emiot, *In mitele yorn*, 12.
116. Ibid., 10.
117. Kotlerman, *Broken Heart/Broken Promise*, 8–9.
118. Kotlerman, "We Are Lacking 'A Man Dieth in a Tent,'" 179.
119. Emiot, *In mitele yorn*, 11.
120. Der Nister, "Mit ibervanderer keyn Biro-Bidzhan," 267.
121. Ibid., 278.
122. Quoted in Kotlerman, *Broken Heart/Broken Wholeness*, 112.
123. RGALI, f. 3121, op. 1, d. 37 (Letter to Max Kaganovitch, no date), l. 25.
124. Der Nister, "Di umfargeslekhe aveyre," 7.
125. Ibid., 7–8.
126. Ibid., 9.
127. Ibid., 10.
128. Ibid.
129. Ibid., 13.
130. Kotlerman, *Broken Heart/Broken Promise*, 80.

# DEATH OF THE AUTHOR AND HIS AFTERLIFE IN LITERARY CRITICISM, MEMOIRS, AND FICTION

DER NISTER WAS ARRESTED ON the night of February 20, 1949, and delivered to the Lefortovo prison in Moscow. On September 21 he was sentenced to ten years of hard labor "for criminal ties with nationalists and anti-Soviet agitation."[1] His activity in Birobidzhan constituted an important part of the evidence against him. He was "chosen to play the fabricated role of organizer and catalyst sent by the JAC (Jewish Antifascist Committee) to set up what the MGB (Ministry of State Security) called the 'anti-Soviet nationalist grouping in Birobidzhan.'"[2] The "evidence" collected during the investigation was used against a group of Birobidzhan writers, journalists, and cultural activists. At the time, Der Nister's health was deteriorating rapidly. While he was still in Moscow, the prison doctor examined him and recommended hospitalization, but he was sent to the Abez mineral camp in the Komi area of northern Russia. This was a special camp for political prisoners, in which many prominent figures of the Russian and Jewish intelligentsia were imprisoned, including the prominent art historian Nikolai Punin, the philosopher Lev Karsavin, and the Yiddish poet Shmuel Halkin. Der Nister died, of "growing inadequacy of heart activity," on July 4, 1950.[3]

Coincidentally, the same month that Der Nister was arrested in Moscow, the second issue of the literary journal *Di goldene keyt* was published in Tel Aviv, which contained a short essay about Der Nister by Gitl Mayzel, Nakhmen Mayzel's sister. She recalls an episode from soon after the October Revolution, when a group of young admirers of Der Nister decided to visit the writer in his forest abode near Kiev. They wanted to "experience the place and the atmosphere where Der Nister's peculiar tales are conjured" with their own eyes and ears. But after reaching the fence of the small, snow-covered house, they turned around and silently went back to town: "We will wait. The secret of Nister's creativity will eventually reveal itself to us." And she continues, even after the publication of *The Family Mashber*, readers were still eagerly awaiting Der Nister's new works. Gitl Mayzel, like her brother Nakhmen but unlike some American and Israeli critics of that time, evaluates Der Nister's entire oeuvre positively, including his most Soviet works. She also notes, unaware of what was going on in the Soviet Union, that Soviet critics had been highly appreciative of the ideological and artistic value of Der Nister's recent work.[4]

The sudden silence of Yiddish voices coming from the Soviet Union was noticed almost immediately, but details surrounding the persecution of Soviet Yiddish culture were slow to emerge. The last issue of the New York literary almanac *Zamlbikher*, published in 1952, was almost entirely dedicated to Soviet Yiddish writers who had disappeared. It contained critical appreciations by leading American writers, poets, and critics, as well as publications of their literary works. The Der Nister chapter was written by Shmuel Niger, and his evaluation was somewhat ambiguous. He praises Der Nister's early symbolist work as a daring attempt to merge the kabbalistic tradition with modernist fiction, which made Der Nister unique among Yiddish writers: "His goal was not to take Kabbalah and make literature out of it, but the other way around, to take literature and strike sparks of kabbalist fantasy out of it."[5] As Niger puts it, Der Nister's literary ambition was to become "our generation's Rabbi Nahman."[6] But life under the

Soviet regime presented Der Nister with a difficult test. Initially he had been able to fit in by adapting his mystical imagination to the romantic symbolism of the revolution, but as proletarian realism tightened its control over Soviet culture, Der Nister's way of thinking became alien, and he fell silent for several years. His last attempt to fit in without changing his style was the collection *Fun mayne giter* (From my estates), which Niger interprets as an attempt to put mystical allusions and images to the service of "kosher" ideas learned at the "revolutionary heder."[7] But even this deliberate denigration of his creative self did not help Der Nister. It seemed that he would remain silent forever, incapable of adjusting to the stylistic requirements of socialist realism. In a factual misrepresentation common among foreign critics, Niger describes the ten-year period between 1929 and 1939 as a time of total silence for Der Nister, broken by the publication of *The Family Mashber*.

Niger's initial impression is rather negative, from his depiction of the city of N. and its inhabitants in the first chapters of the novel. He dislikes the way in which the narrator established a distance between his own time and the time of narration in order to emphasize his critical attitude toward the past, which Niger interprets as a compromise with socialist realism. Niger is able to recognize Der Nister's style but not his spirit and taste. He no longer recognizes the Der Nister whom he had known, "who was simply unable to look at the world through someone else's eyes and to speak in words that were not his own."[8] Yet gradually, as the novel continues, Niger begins to realize that even though Der Nister "had learned a lot during the quarter of a century of Bolshevism, he also had forgotten little, and the 'socialist realism' of his prose is not fully drained of his previous Hasidic and folkloric romanticism."[9] Most of all, Niger appreciates Der Nister's sympathetic portrayal of Bratslav Hasidism, even though it had to be camouflaged as a primitive proto-proletarian class protest movement. He also likes Luzi Mashber: "Perhaps the only bright

character from the previous Jewish world in Soviet Yiddish literature."[10] In the end, Niger concludes, Der Nister looks even more
original in the context of "monotonous" Soviet Yiddish literature
than he had in Yiddish literature before the revolution.[11]

The most detailed and scholarly evaluation of Der Nister's life
and work belongs to the Israeli historian of Yiddish literature
Chone Shmeruk, who drew from an extensive array of sources.[12]
Der Nister's creative imagination received an initial impulse from
his elder brother Aaron, a devout Hasid who tried his own hand
at creative writing. After his initial experiments with a psychological realist style, Der Nister, probably as a consequence of his
meeting with Y. L. Peretz, turned to a neo-Romantic symbolist
style, drawing upon mystical sources and appropriating the genre
of the Hasidic tale, which remained the hallmark of his writing
style from 1913 to 1929.[13] During that period, his creative imagination took shape by merging elements of Jewish and non-Jewish
cultural traditions. His early enthusiasm for the revolution as
a new beginning, which is felt in "Naygayst," gradually wanes
and is replaced by grotesque satire in the tales written after his
return to Soviet Ukraine.[14] As a fellow traveler, he found himself increasingly alienated from the Soviet literary mainstream,
which by the late 1920s became dominated by the doctrine of
proletarian realism. His despair and anxiety over his perceived
inability to continue as a symbolist artist reached a climax in his
last symbolist story, "Under a Fence," which triggered an aggressive campaign against him, discussed by Shmeruk in great detail
as the watershed between the two periods.

According to Shmeruk's periodization, the years 1906–29 were
a time of free and original creativity, whereas after 1929 Der Nister had to adjust to external political and ideological pressure.
The early 1930s were the most difficult years, when Der Nister
tried to support himself through reportages, translations, and
editorial work. Shmeruk suggests that Der Nister was initially
not opposed to general Soviet social policy and regarded many

changes that took place in the country positively, "But his eyes were open to everything that was happening around him."[15] His critical attitude of some aspects of Soviet reality is discernible in his depiction of Jewish provincial life, as opposed to his upbeat reportages about life in the three capital cities. Shmeruk notes that the elements of fantasy in Der Nister's reportages on the Soviet capitals do not fit the Soviet concept of *ocherk* as a strictly realist genre. Shmeruk quotes extensively from Der Nister's first letter to his brother but does not specify the source, stating somewhat enigmatically, "The time to publish it in full has not come yet."[16] "There is no doubt," Shmeruk concludes, that Der Nister regarded *The Family Mashber* as his only shot at cementing his literary reputation.[17] Shmeruk places *The Family Mashber* in the genre of family saga, noting that, like Thomas Mann's *Buddenbrooks*, Der Nister's novel follows the general pattern of charting a family's decline, even though, in Shmeruk's opinion, Der Nister's novel remained unfinished and so his full plan remains unclear. Shmeruk cautions against a simplistic reading of the novel as purely realistic: "In *The Family Mashber* Der Nister revisited the issues that concerned him in the early years, using the same artistic means that he developed before 1929." He finds prototypes of Luzi Mashber in some of the characters from Der Nister's tales, but he also points out the important difference between the novel's historical setting and the imaginary time and space of Der Nister's symbolist tales.[18]

Der Nister returns to the depiction of Soviet life in his postwar story "Flora," which, uniquely in Soviet Yiddish literature, celebrates the spirit of unity among the Jewish people using traditional religious language.[19] In Der Nister's Birobidzhan reportages, Shmeruk hears an echo of early debates around Zionism and territorialism.[20] Concluding his survey, Shmeruk relates the episode of Der Nister's arrest according to the memoirs of Sheyne Miram Broderzon, the wife of Polish Yiddish writer Moyshe Broderzon, who, in turn, had heard it from Elena Sigalovskaia. Der Nister greeted the secret police officers with a "contemptuous smile" and said, "Don't get angry, I am very glad that you have finally come"—apparently, because the arrest released him from the anxiety and insomnia he had been experiencing since the arrest of his colleagues. Shmeruk concludes his biographical sketch with a reference to an anonymous witness who claimed that Der Nister refused to hand over his manuscripts to the secret police and succeeded in hiding them. This unverified story gave rise to a hypothesis about a "hidden" part 3 of *The Family Mashber*.[21]

Shmeruk's brief but insightful analysis of Der Nister's Soviet writings had little impact on Der Nister scholarship. Until the late twentieth century, it was Niger's conceptualization of Der Nister's literary trajectory that remained prevalent among Western and Israeli scholars. Der Nister was valued first and foremost as an author of enigmatic symbolist tales, which were read as a modernist appropriation of traditional Jewish mystical exegesis. His "Soviet" works between 1929 and 1939, as well as his stories about the war and the Holocaust, were largely ignored, while *The Family Mashber* was celebrated as a bold attempt to smuggle a positive representation of Hasidism into Soviet literature under the assumed mask of socialist realism, to which Der Nister had to pay lip service. On the Soviet side of the Iron Curtain, Der Nister's symbolist period was not discussed and his tales were not reprinted, while *The Family Mashber* was praised for its critical portrayal of the prerevolutionary Jewish past, and his war writings were celebrated as an expression of his Soviet patriotism. A number of valuable publications, including *Fun finftn yor* (From the year 1905), appeared in *Sovetish heymland* during the 1960s and early 1970s, and a collection *Vidervuks* (Regrowth) and two Yiddish editions of *The Family Mashber* were published by major Moscow presses. In the Soviet canon, Der Nister and David Bergelson were recognized as the two best Yiddish prose writers.

Yet, unlike Bergelson's works, those by Der Nister did not appear in Russian translations. The story of the failed attempt to publish a Russian translation of *The Family Mashber* is indicative of the particular niche position that Yiddish came to occupy in Soviet literature after Stalin. According to the common practice, the Union of Soviet Writers created a "Commission on Der Nister's Literary Legacy" after Der Nister's official rehabilitation in 1956, headed by the prominent Soviet Russian writer Emmanuil Kazakevich, who began his literary career as a Yiddish author. On November 27, 1956, Kazakevich wrote a letter to Goslitizdat (the State Publishing House for Literature), requesting the inclusion of a Russian translation of *The Family Mashber* in the publication plan for 1957 and recommending the publishing of Der Nister's *Mayselekh in ferzn* (Tales in verse) with Detgiz (the State Publishing House for Children). Obviously, this request was difficult to honor because there was no Russian translation of *The Family Mashber* yet. In 1958, Goslitizdat signed a translation contract with Solomon Apt, a prominent Russian translator from German, and Tevye Gen, a Yiddish writer. Apt eventually withdrew from the project, citing his poor health and his commitment to the translation of Thomas Mann, but Gen delivered his draft, which was given to professional Yiddish translator Mikhail Shambadal for editing.

Between 1962 and 1965, the translation went through three internal reviews, with each reviewer being more critical than the previous one. The first review recommended publication in a shortened and improved form with a "serious analytical introduction." The second reviewer suggested substantial revisions to remove "all kinds of goodie-goodie talk [*siusiukanie*] about Judaism" and insisted on adding critical commentaries. The third reviewer flatly rejected the publication, arguing that the novel was unfinished, "compositionally unkempt," and that the translators' knowledge of Russian was poor. Its publication would only cause "annoying misunderstandings" (dosadnye nedorazumeniia).[22] The language of these internal reviews suggests that their authors, Soviet Marxist academics, were apprehensive of the potential subversive effect of the publication of a novel with outspoken Jewish content on the broader Russian-language audience and tried to mitigate it. Eventually, as the liberal "thaw" was coming to an end, it was decided to make the novel available in new editions to the shrinking and aging community of Yiddish readers but to keep it away from a wider and younger Russian readership. Shambadal's translation was preserved by his family and was eventually published in 2010.

## MEMOIRS AND LEGENDS

A number of memoirs about Der Nister were written by Polish Jewish refugees who met him during and after World War II in the Soviet Union. These memoirs began to appear in the 1950s and contributed to the mythologization of Der Nister as a hidden tzaddik, portraying him as the only Soviet Yiddish writer who was able to preserve his human and artistic integrity under the harsh conditions of the Soviet regime. An example of this type of characterization, somewhat affected by backshadowing, are the memoirs of Yitskhok Yanasovitsh, who got to know Der Nister in Moscow during 1944 to 1947. Yanasovitsh identified two particular qualities that made Der Nister different from other Soviet writers: his rejection of everyday Soviet reality (*oylem-haze*) and lack of interest in literary success coupled with his intense, "twenty-four-hour" sense of grief for the "tragedy of Jewish life in the Soviet Union."[23] For Der Nister, Yanasovitsh explained, the mission of Soviet Yiddish literature was to preserve the language through the dark times, and this led him to change his attitude toward Birobidzhan: in the 1930s, Jews went to Birobidzhan to "build socialism," but after the war its function was to "save the national soul."[24]

Yanasovitsh remembers Der Nister as an archetypal "eternal wanderer" who, like Luzi Mashber, can never find a place in the world.[25] But Yanasovitsh's memoirs have few concrete details about the time, place, and circumstances of particular episodes. Der Nister emerges as an idealized loner detached from Soviet reality, and his words are mediated by the memoirist's somber, eulogistic tone. Like Niger, Yanasovitsh claims, without providing a timeframe, that Der Nister "did not take a pen in his hand" for many years.[26] At the same time, Der Nister was not afraid to criticize his fellow Soviet writers for their compliance with the regime and lack of commitment to Jewish culture. He passed allegorical judgments on Soviet Yiddish writers, for example, comparing Peretz Markish with Samson, who, instead of fighting the Philistines, kept turning the wheels of their mills. But the main object of Der Nister's critical anger was, according to Yanasovitsh, Bergelson, whom he could not forgive for wasting his talent on the negative depiction of the Jewish past.[27] And yet, all bitterness and sorrow notwithstanding, Der Nister remained an optimist and believed in a better future for the Jewish people and the imminent end of the Stalinist regime.

An interesting early example of the formation of what can be described as the "Der Nister legend" is a story about the publication of *The Family Mashber*, which Yanasovitsh heard from a female Soviet writer whose name he chooses to keep secret. One cold winter day in the mid-1930s, the story goes, Der Nister was sent with a truck from Kiev to another town to deliver a load of paper. On his way he encountered a broken-down car with a driver freezing outside. He gave the driver a lift, and a few weeks later the grateful driver visited him in his home in Kiev. Surprised by Der Nister's modest dwelling, the guest enquired why he could not make a better living by his writing. Der Nister complained that nobody wanted to publish his novel because of its positive depiction of prerevolutionary religious life, to which the mysterious visitor replied that Soviet literature was no longer afraid of historical themes. A few weeks later, Der Nister was invited to the Der Emes press in Moscow and informed that a decision had been made to publish his novel. It turns out that the person whom he had rescued from the cold was none other than the personal secretary of Mikhail Kalinin, at that time the nominal president of the Soviet Union (in another version of the story, it was a high Soviet official who took the manuscript of the novel and delivered it to the press with his recommendation). Der Nister himself never told this story, presumably because the official in question later perished in the purges.[28]

Interestingly, this legendary story includes some details that resemble Der Nister's earlier works, such as a freezing man lost on his way, his miraculous rescue, and his transformation into a powerful figure; what makes it markedly different from Der Nister's tales is the happy ending. Kalinin was known as the highest-ranking supporter of the Jewish colonization projects in the Soviet government, and he had a reputation as a supporter of Jews, so his apparent intervention on Der Nister's behalf fits his profile. It is interesting that the novel was published through the intercession of non-Jewish officials, presumably against the will of the Yiddish establishment. And of course, it does not matter for the legend that Der Nister lived in Kharkiv and that the novel was being published in installments in the most prestigious Moscow annual, *Sovetish,* beginning in 1935. What is important for this legend and for the later fictional portrayals of Der Nister is the identification of the writer and his life with characters and situations from his works.

### DER NISTER AS A FICTIONAL CHARACTER

Der Nister's enigmatic figure attracted creative writers who attempted to reconstruct the dark atmosphere of Jewish life under Stalin. Der Nister is mentioned in Elie Wiesel's French novel *The Testament,* written in the form of a confession left by an imaginary Soviet Yiddish writer named Paltiel Kossover. Kossover admires Der Nister even though he has never met him: "I would have liked to become better acquainted with that austere, reserved, almost ascetic man who radiated the knowledge and fervor of Rabbi Nahman."[29] For Kossover, Der Nister embodies the high moral standard that eludes opportunistic Soviet Yiddish writers like himself: "Der Nister had some reservations about me. I think he considered me something of an opportunist. I was hurt and sought a way of explaining my attitude to him, but the opportunity never arose."[30] A similar figure appears in *Yizker* (Memorial prayer), the last novel of the Soviet Yiddish author Shmuel Gordon. Written during the 1980s, it was published in installments in *Sovetish heymland* and its successor, *Di yidishe gas*, from 1989 to 1996, and issued as a book in Israel in 2003. It is a fictional reconstruction of the tragic events following the murder of Solomon Mikhoels, with a cast of characters based on actual Soviet Yiddish writers and actors. One of the secondary characters, a writer named Pinkhes Mashberg, is a transparent double of Der Nister. For the autobiographical protagonist of the novel,

> Pinkhes Mashberg was a model of how to behave in life and how to depict life. If Pinkhes had been just a tiny bit compliant and closed his eyes to what was going on around him like many other people did—some of them of their own will, others following the will of various powerful figures—he could have been the wealthiest among the writers. But he was one of the poorest among them. Even when he was in danger of remaining without a piece of bread, he would not give in and did not agree to delete or insert a line if it was against his wish. Besides himself, he recognized no other master over his work. As a result, not everything that he created in his life was published. And maybe this was a reason why, instead of people, he dealt in his works mostly with devils, spirits, imps, witches.[31]

The most elaborate fictionalization of Der Nister was created by the contemporary American author Dara Horn in the novel *The World to Come*. The action moves between the Soviet Union of the 1920s and the 1940s, and the United States at the time of the Vietnam War and in the late 1990s. Der Nister's character makes his first appearance as a literature teacher at the Jewish orphanage in Malakhovka near Moscow, where his prototype worked in 1920–21. He is introduced as a "strange little man" sitting hidden among a pile of books and paintings. Appropriately for his penname, he speaks in an enigmatic fashion, seeking to reveal a hidden Jewish essence behind gentile appearance. When a new student is introduced to him by his fellow art teacher who is modeled on Marc Chagall, Der Nister asks him about his and his father's Jewish names and then links them in a quote from the Bible: "Benjamin and Jacob. *Nafsho keshure be nafsho.* You know what that means?"[32] (The Bible quote means "His soul was bound to his," but Der Nister would not have spoken Hebrew with a normative Israeli pronunciation.) Der Nister proceeds to read one of his mystical symbolist stories, evoking in the student's mind the distant memory of studying some kabbalistic concepts from long ago, presumably, as a young boy in heder. (Kabbalah was, of course, far beyond the heder curriculum.) Der Nister composes and recites his stories in a kind of trance, oblivious to his environment but in touch with a higher, transtemporal reality: "By nature he was timid, a quiet believer that the happiness from the world before birth was still waiting for him."[33]

Der Nister has a dual function in Horn's novel: he is a mystical visionary capable of seeing through the surface of things and a mediator between secular modernity and the Jewish tradition. By creatively reconstructing his visit to Peretz in Warsaw and his friendship with Chagall in Malakhovka, Horn introduces her reader to ideas, concepts, and figures of modern Yiddish culture. Der Nister follows Chagall from Moscow to Berlin, but there their paths part. While Chagall makes steady progress to financial success and world fame, Der Nister remains stuck in poverty and obscurity, preoccupied with rendering the ugly, everyday reality of Weimar Berlin into the dark fantasy of his tales. Chagall and Der Nister come to personify the two opposite directions of Jewish culture: success and recognition in the West, and suppression and decline in the Soviet East, where Der Nister eventually moves:

> Once Der Nister moved his family back to Russia [actually, Ukraine], he had no chance at all of publishing his stories. . . . His previously published work was panned, denounced in all the journals as decadent and absurd. Even the children's books he had written with Chagall were gathered up and destroyed.
>
> For ten long years he wrote almost nothing, struggled to find odd jobs, nearly starved. And then he began writing something realistic, a novel that the censors would approve. While Chagall ensconced himself in France, befriending Picasso and Matisse and painting pictures of bright green Jews, crucified Jesuses, flowers, and fruit, the Hidden One started writing the only story in the world.
>
> It was called *The Family Crisis*.[34]

Here again we encounter the familiar trope of Der Nister's forced silence, and Horn goes even further than Niger in denying, erroneously, any possibility of the publication of Der Nister's symbolist work in the Soviet Union (whereas in fact he published two collections, in 1928 and 1929, not counting publications in periodicals).

The reader reconnects again with Der Nister when he is in Tashkent, having left his first wife and published the first part of his novel, whose title Horn translates as *The Family Crisis*. The novel was received favorably thanks to his clever manipulations with the text by inserting "little pieties" "every forty pages or so to placate the censors." But in Tashkent, Der Nister forgets about the censors and begins to write freely, "slowly releasing his mind from his head and emptying its contents onto scraps of paper," which eventually grow into a "paper forest" and take up his whole room. "His unfinished book had become his obsession," taking him back from the Tashkent present to mid-nineteenth-century Berdichev.[35] The writer withdraws from the world to become a medium through whom his characters speak: "He tied himself up in long ropes of memory, caged himself in with iron bars of memory, drew the curtains and hid himself in a dark tomb which he filled with an entire world of memory." [36]

Der Nister spends his last years after the return from the evacuation frantically working on the third part of his novel, which, Horn assumes, would be centered on Moyshe's son Mayerl. The censors, sensing the direction the novel is going, prohibit its publication in installments. Aware of his imminent arrest, Der Nister tries to hide pages of his manuscript. At first he stuffs them behind the walls and beneath the floorboards of his tiny apartment, inscribing his name on each page in a different cipher in a kabbalistic style. But realizing that his apartment is not safe, he decides to relocate the precious manuscript of part 3 to the Moscow State Yiddish Theater (GOSET) building, secretly depositing it, page by page, underneath the frame of the large murals that decorated the walls of the auditorium. The murals were painted by Marc Chagall for the opening of the theater in 1920, before his departure from Russia (in reality, the set of murals was removed from display in 1923 and held behind the stage; the murals were transferred to the State Tretyakov Gallery after GOSET was closed down in 1950). Thus, symbolically, the two great works of Yiddish culture become secretly reunited and preserved for posterity. Many years later, the manuscript makes its way to New York, where the murals are exhibited, only to mysteriously disappear again.

Horn, like many memoirists, critics, and scholars, portrays Der Nister as an introverted artist fully devoted to his calling and largely disconnected from the world around him. His imagination has more power over him than reality does, and it also has a visionary quality about it, enabling him to see through the surface of things, both in space and time. While this image has a great attraction for creative writers and fits well the general dichotomous paradigm of the irresolvable conflict between Yiddishkeit and the Soviet regime, the available materials seem to suggest Der Nister as a more complex, contradictory, and humane character.

He was torn by internal conflicts that were often caused by external circumstances but were also a product of his own making. He had great artistic intuition but sometimes lacked a sense of reality. He was never detached from the world and was always curious about life around him. It was his engagement with the issues of the day that fed his writing, and the strength of his imagination transformed reality into fantasy. He experimented with different styles and genres: some attempts were more successful than others, but it was his failures that paved the way to his greatest achievements.

## NOTES

1. Maggs, *Mandelstam and "Der Nister" Files*, 30.
2. Kotlerman, *Broken Heart/Broken Wholeness*, 133.
3. Maggs, *Mandelstam and "Der Nister" Files*, K–29.
4. Mayzel, G., "Der Nister," 189.
5. Niger, "Der Nister," 64.
6. Ibid., 65.
7. Ibid., 67.
8. Ibid., 71.
9. Ibid.
10. Ibid., 73.
11. Ibid., 75.
12. Shmeruk, "Der Nister, khayav veyetsirato."
13. Ibid., 23–24.
14. Ibid., 28.
15. Ibid., 31.
16. Ibid., 48, n. 13.
17. Ibid., 15.
18. Ibid., 36.
19. Ibid., 42.
20. Ibid., 46.
21. Ibid., 17. Broderzon, "Mayn laydns-veg," 89.
22. RGALI, f. 613, op. 10, d. 3569.
23. Yanasovitsh, *Mit yidishe shrayber in Rusland*, 217.
24. Ibid., 236–38.

25. Ibid., 220–21.
26. Ibid., 226.
27. Ibid., 235–36.
28. Ibid., 242.
29. Wiesel, *Testament*, 258–59.
30. Ibid., 324.
31. Gordon, *Yizker*, 137.
32. Horn, *World to Come*, 32.
33. Ibid., 82.
34. Ibid., 138.
35. Ibid., 195–96.
36. Ibid., 200.

# BIBLIOGRAPHY

## ARCHIVAL DOCUMENTS

### Russian State Archive of Literature and Art (RGALI), Moscow

f. 613 (Publishing House "Khudozhestvennaia literatura")
f. 2270 (Aron Gurshteyn Collection)
f. 3121 (Der Nister Collection)

### United States Holocaust Museum (USHM), Washington DC

RG-22.028M (Records of the Jewish Antifascist Committee [State Archives of the Russian Federation (GARF), Moscow, f. 8114])

### YIVO Institute for Jewish Research

RG 1226 (Records of the Yidisher Kultur Farband)

## DER NISTER'S WORKS

"A briv tsu Dovid Bergelson." In Mayzel, *Dertseylungen un eseyen*, 290–96.
*Dertseylungen un eseyen*. Edited by Nakhmen Mayzel. New York: Yiddish Cultural Association Press (YKUF), 1957.
*Dray mayselekh*. Odessa: Kinder-farlag, 1934.
*Fun finftn yor. Sovetish heymland*, no. 1 (January 1964): 3–73.
*Fun mayne giter*. Kharkiv: Melukhe farlag fun Ukraine, 1928.
*Gedakht*. Kiev: Kultur-Lige, 1929.
*Hoyptshtet*. Kharkiv: Literatur un kunst, 1934
*Korbones*. Moscow: Emes, 1943.
"Luzis tsoymen oyfgebrokhn." *Sovetishe literatur*, no. 5 (May 1941): 8–29.

"A mayse mit a grinem man." Parts 1 and 2. *Di royte velt,* nos. 7–8 (1926): 10–21; 9 (1926): 6–19.

*Mayselekh.* Odessa: Kinder-farlag, 1936.

*Mayselekh in ferzn.* Warsaw: Kultur-Lige, 1921.

*Di mishpokhe Mashber.* Moscow: Der emes, 1941.

*Di mishpokhe Mashber.* Part One. New York: Yiddish Cultural Association Press (YKUF), 1943.

*Di mishpokhe Mashber.* Part Two. New York: Yiddish Cultural Union Press (YKUF), 1948.

"Mit ibervanderer keyn Biro-Bidzhan." In Mayzel, *Dertseylungen un eseyen,* 257–78.

"Mitn tsveytn echelon (bildlekh un ayndrukn)." *Eynikayt,* 103 (30 August 1947):2-4

"Moskve." *Di royte velt,* nos. 7–8 (July–August 1932): 125–40; no. 9 (September 1932): 125–61.

"Nokhvort un forvort." *Sovetish heymland,* no. 2 (February 1967): 97–123.

"Perets hot geredt un ikh hob gehert." *Yidishe kultur* 13 (July 1951): 30–32; (August–September 1951): 31–33. Reprinted in Mayzel, *Dertseylungen un eseyen,* 279–89.

"Pupe: A mayse fun tsurik mit yorn." *Parizer tsaytshrift* 17 (1957): 3–52.

"Tsigayner." *Di royte velt,* nos. 8–9 (August–September 1927): 74–87.

"Tsu di valn!" *Eynikayt* 17 (February 9, 1947): 4.

"Di umfargeslekhe aveyre." In Falkovitsh, *Mikhoels,* 6–13.

"Unter a ployt (Reviu)." *Di royte velt,* no. 7 (July 1929): 8–34. Also published in *Gedakht,* 272–312.

*Vidervuks. Dertseylungen, Noveln.* Moscow: Sovetskii pisatel', 1969.

*Zeks mayselekh.* Kiev: Ukrmelukhenatsmindfarlag, 1939.

### English Translations

*The Family Mashber.* Translated by Leonard Wolf. New York: Summit Books, 1987.

*Regrowth: Seven Tales of Jewish Life before, during, and after Occupation.* Translation of *Vidervuks* by Erik Butler. Evanston, IL: Northwestern University Press, 2011.

"Under a Fence: A Review." Translated by Seymour Levitan. In *Ashes out of Hope: Fiction by Soviet Yiddish Writers,* edited by Eliezer Greenberg and Irving Howe, 193–218. New York: Schocken, 1977.

"With the Second Echelon." Translated by Sara Davolt. In Kotlerman, *Broken Heart/Broken Wholeness,* 23–34.

## Hebrew Translations

Bet Mashber: roman histori. Translated by Haim Rabinzon and Shimshon Nahmani. Merhavya: Sifryat po'alim. 1963.

Hanazir vehagdiya: Sippurim, shirim, maamarim. Translated by Dov Sadan. Jerusalem: Mosad Bialik, 1963.

Meotsar sipurey hanistar. Translated by Shalom Luria. Jerusalem: Carmel, 2006.

## Ukrainian Translation

"Sp'ianilo." Translation of "Shiker" by E. Raytsin. Literaturnyi iarmarok (February 1929): 157–94.

## SECONDARY SOURCES

1905 yor in Barditshev; notitsn un zikhroynes. Berdichev, 1927. Russian translation: 1905 god v Berdicheve. Zametki I vospominaniia. Accessed February 21, 2018. http://berdicheva.net/index.php?categoryid=8&p600 _bookid=75&p600_page=ALL

Abelson, Kassel, and Loel M. Weiss. "Burial of a Non Jewish Spouse and Children." Paper of the Committee on Jewish Law and Standards of the Rabbinical Assembly, February 2, 2010.

Annenkov, Iurii. Dnevnik moikh vstrech. Moscow: Direct-Media, 2016.

Barthes, Roland. "Semiology and Urbanism." Translated by Richard Howard. In Architecture Culture 1943–1968: A Documentary Anthology, edited by Joan Ockman, 412–18. New York: Rizzoli, 1993.

Bechtel, Delphine. Der Nister's Work, 1907–1929: A Study of a Yiddish Symbolist. Berne: Peter Lang, 1990.

Belaia, Galina. Don Kikhoty 20kh godov: "Pereval" i sud'ba ego idei. Moscow: Sovetskii pusatel', 1989.

Bely, Andrei. "Krizis kul'tury." In Symvolizm kak miroponimanie, 260–96. Moscow: Respublika, 1994.

———. Petersburg: A Novel in Eight Chapters with a Prologue and an Epilogue. Translated by David McDuff. London: Penguin Books, 1995.

———. "Revolutisa i kultura." In Symvolizm kak miroponimanie, 296–308. Moscow: Respublika, 1994.

———. "Simvolism." In Symvolizm kak miroponimanie, 255–59; 334–38. Moscow: Respublika, 1994.

———. Symvolizm kak miroponimanie. Moscow: Respublika, 1994.

Bemporad, Elissa. "'What Should We Collect?': Ethnography, Local Studies, and the Formation of a Belorussian Jewish Identity." In *Going to the People: Jews and the Ethnographic Impulse*, edited by Jeffrey Veidlinger, 85–99. Bloomington: Indiana University Press, 2016.

Benjamin, Walter. *The Arcades Project*. Translated by Howard Eiland and Kevin McLaughlin. Cambridge, MA: Harvard University Press, 2002.

———. "Moscow." In *Selected Writings*, vol. 2, translated by Rodney Livingstone et al., edited by Michael W. Jennings, Howard Eiland, and Gary Smith, 22–47. Cambridge, MA: Belknap Press, 1999.

Bergelson, David. "Moskve." *Frayhayt*, September 5, 1926, 5.

Bertelsen, Olga. "The House of Writers in Ukraine, the 1930s: Conceived, Lived, Perceived." *The Carl Beck Papers in Russian and East European Studies* 2302 (August 2013): 1–72.

Boehlich, Sabine. *"Nay-gayst": Mystische Traditionen in einer symbolistischen Erzählung des jiddischen Autors "Der Nister"(Pinkhas Kahanovitsh)*. Wiesbaden: Harrassowitz, 2008.

Bracka, Mariya, and Artur Bracki. *Ukraïnśka humanistyka i słowiańskie paralele*. Gransk: Athenae Gedanenses, 2014.

Broderzon, Sheyne Miryem. *Mayn laydns-veg mit Moyshe Broderzon*. Buenos Aires: Tsentral-farband fun poylishe yidn in Argentine, 1960.

Buckler, Julie A. *Mapping St. Petersburg: Imperial Text and Cityshape*. Princeton, NJ: Princeton University Press, 2005.

Caplan, Marc. "The Hermit and the Circus: Der Nister, Yiddish Literature and German Culture in the Weimar Period." *Studia Rosentaliana* 41 (2009): 173–96.

Chudakova, Marietta. *Izbrannye raboty. Literatura sovetskogo proshlogo*. Moscow: Iazyki russkoi kul'tury, 2001.

Clark, Katerina. *Moscow, the Fourth Rome: Stalinism, Cosmopolitanism, and the Evolution of Soviet Culture, 1931–1941*. Cambridge, MA: Harvard University Press, 2011.

Clark, Katerina, and Galin Tikhanov. "Soviet Literary Theory in the 1930s: Battles over Genre and the Boundaries of Modernity." In Dobrenko and Tikhanov, *History of Russian Literary Theory and Criticism*, 109–43.

Dekel-Chen, Jonathan L. *Farming the Red Land: Jewish Agricultural Colonization and Local Soviet Power, 1924–1941*. New Haven, CT: Yale University Press, 2005.

Diner, Hasia, and Gennady Estraikh eds. *1929: A Year in Jewish History*. New York: New York University Press, 2013.

Dobrenko, Evgenii. "'Zanimatel'naia istoriia': Istoricheskii roman i sotsialisticheskii relizm." In *Sotsrealisticheskii kanon*, edited by

Günther, Hans and Evgenii Dobrenko, 274–95. St. Petersburg: Akademicheskii proekt, 2000.

Dobrenko, Evgeny, and Galin Tikhanov, eds. *A History of Russian Literary Theory and Criticism: The Soviet Age and Beyond*. Pittsburgh: University of Pittsburgh Press, 2011.

Dolgopolov, Leonid K. "Tvorcheskaia istoriia i istoriko-literaturnoe znachenie romana A. Belogo 'Peterburg.'" In Bely, *Petersburg*, 525–623. Moscow: Nauka, 1981.

Dunets, Khatskl. "Oyfn literarishn front. Notitsn tsum yorikn literatur-balans." *Shtern* 10 (1929): 70–72.

———. "Vegn opgebliakevetn mundir on a general: Notitsn vegn Dem Nisters *Fun mayne giter*." In *In shlakhtn*, 127–41. Minsk: Tsentrfarlag, 1931. First published in *Shtern* 6, no. 1 (January 1930): 61–74.

Emiot, Yisroel. *In mitele yorn (eseyen, dertseylungen, lider)*. Rochester, NY: Jewish Community Council, 1963.

Estraikh, Gennady. "Der Nister's 'Hamburg Score.'" In Estraikh, Hoge, and Krutikov, *Uncovering the Hidden*, 7–26.

———. *Evreiskaia Literaturnaia zhizn' Moskvy, 1917–1991*. St. Petersburg: Evropeiskii Universitet, 2015.

———. *In Harness: Yiddish Writers' Romance with Communism*. Syracuse, NY: Syracuse University Press, 2005.

———. "Jews as Cossacks: A Symbiosis in Literature and Life." In *Soviet Jews in World War II: Fighting, Witnessing, Remembering*, edited by Harriet Murav and Gennady Estraikh, 85–103. Boston: Academic Studies Press, 2014.

———. "The Yiddish Kultur-Lige." In Makaryk and Tkacz, *Modernism in Kyiv*, 197–217. Toronto: University of Toronto Press, 2010.

Estraikh, Gennady, Kerstin Hoge, and Mikhail Krutikov, eds. *Children and Yiddish Literature: From Early Modernity to Post-Modernity*. Oxford: Legenda, 2015.

———, eds. *Uncovering the Hidden: The Works and Life of Der Nister*. Oxford: Legenda, 2014.

Estraikh, Gennady and Mikhail Krutikov, eds. *Three Cities of Yiddish: St. Petersburg, Warsaw and Moscow*. Oxford: Legenda, 2016.

Falkovitsh, Eli, ed. *Mikhoels: 1890–1948*. Moscow: Der Emes, 1948.

Fateev, Andrei. *Stalinizm i detskaia literatura v politike nomenklatury SSSR (1930e–1950e gody)*. Moscow: MAKS, 2007.

Fefer, Itsik. *Mayselekh in ferzn*. Minsk: Vaysruslendisher melukhe farlag, 1929.

Finkin, Jordan. "Der Nister's Hebrew Nosegay." Estraikh, Hoge, and Krutikov, *Uncovering the Hidden*, 27–40.

Fowler, Mayhill C. *Beau Monde on Empire's Edge: State and Stage in Soviet Ukraine*. Toronto: Toronto University Press, 2017.

Frankel, Jonathan. *Prophecy and Politics: Socialism, Nationalism, and the Russian Jews, 1862–1917*. Cambridge: Cambridge University Press, 1981.

Getty, J. Arch. "*Samokritika* Rituals in the Stalinist Central Committee, 1933–38." *Russian Review* 58 (January 1999): 49–70.

Godiner, Shmuel. *Figurn afn rand*. Kiev: Kultur-Lige, 1929.

Gordon, Shmuel. *Yizker. Di farmishpete shrayber*. Jerusalem: Veltrat far yidisher kultur, 2003.

Grekov, Boris, et al., eds. *Protiv istoricheskoi kontseptsii M. N. Pokrovskogo*. Moscow: Academy of Sciences of USSR, part 1, 1939; part 2, 1940.

Gruschka, Roland. "Symbolist Quest and Grotesque Masks: *The Family Mashber* as Parable and Confession." In Estraikh, Hoge, and Krutikov, *Uncovering the Hidden*, 145–60.

Gurshteyn, Aron. *Izbrannye stat'i*. Moscow: Sovetskii pisatel', 1959.

———. "Kvitko." In *Literaturnaia entsiklopediia*, 5:169. Moscow: Kommunisticheskaia akademiia, 1931.

Hellman, Ben. *Fairy Tales and True Stories: The History of Russian Literature for Children and Young People (1574–2010)*. Leiden: Brill, 2013.

Hoge, Kerstin. "Andersen's *Mayselekh* and Der Nister's Symbolist Agenda." In Estraikh, Hoge, and Krutikov, *Uncovering the Hidden*, 41–54.

———. "The Design of Books and Lives: Yiddish Children's Book Art by Artists from the Kiev Kultur-Lige." In Estraikh, Hoge, and Krutikov, *Children and Yiddish Literature*, 52.

Horbachov, Dmitro. "In the Epicentre of Abstraction: Kyiv during the Time of Kurbas." In Makaryk and Tkacz, *Modernism in Kyiv*, 170–95.

Horn, Dara. *The World to Come*. New York: W. W. Norton, 2006.

Ivanov, Vladislav. "'Milyi lektor,' on zhe—'sovremennyi markiz de Sad': Nikolai Evreinov, 'Teatr i eshafot: k voprosu o proiskhozhdenii teatra kak publichnogo instituta." In *Mnemozina* 1 (1996): 14–44.

Karlip, Joshua. *The Tragedy of a Generation: The Rise and Fall of Jewish Nationalism in Eastern Europe*. Cambridge, MA: Harvard University Press, 2013..

Kerler, Yoysef. *Geklibene proze (eseyen, zikhroynes, dertseylungen)*. Jerusalem: Yerusholaymer almanakh, 1991.

Kochan, Lionel, ed. *The Jews in Soviet Russia since 1917*. Oxford: Oxford University Press, 1978.

Koller, Sabine. "*A mayse mit a hon. Dos tsigele.* Marc Chagall illustrating Der Nister." In Estraikh, Hoge, and Krutikov, *Uncovering the Hidden*, 55–72.

———. "Der Nister's 'Leningrad': A Phantom *fartseykhenung.*" In Estraikh and Krutikov, *Three Cities of Yiddish*, 73–89. Oxford: Legenda, 2016.

Koskoff, Ellen. *Music in Lubavitsher Life.* Urbana: University of Illinois Press, 2001.

Kotlerman, Ber. *Broken Heart/Broken Wholeness: The Post-Holocaust Plea for Jewish Reconstruction of the Soviet Yiddish Writer Der Nister.* Boston: Academic Studies Press, 2017.

———. "We Are Lacking 'A Man Dieth in a Tent': Der Nister's Search for Redemption in the Summer of 1947." In Estraikh, Hoge, and Krutikov, *Uncovering the Hidden*, 174–84.

Kotliar, Elena. "Obrazy shtetla v grafike Moiseia Fradkina." *Visnyk KhDADM* 9 (2008): 168–77.

Koznarsky, Taras. "Three Novels, Three Cities." In Makaryk and Tkacz, *Modernism in Kyiv*, 98–137.

Krutikov, Mikhail. "Berdichev in Russian-Jewish Literary Imagination: From Israel Aksenfeld to Friedrich Gorenshteyn." In *The Shtetl: Image and Reality*, edited by Gennady Estraikh and Mikhail Krutikov, 91–114. Oxford: Legenda, 2000.

———. "An End to Fairy Tales: The 1930s in the *Mayselekh* of Der Nister and Leyb Kvitko." In Estraikh, Hoge, and Krutikov, *Children and Yiddish Literature*, 111–22.

———. *From Kabbalah to Class Struggle: Expressionism, Marxism and Yiddish Literature in the Life and Work of Meir Wiener.* Stanford, CA: Stanford University Press, 2011.

———. "Learning Stalin's Yiddish: Two Debates on Literary Theory at the Kiev Institute for Jewish Proletarian Culture in the Spring of 1932." In *The Politics of Yiddish*, edited by Shlomo Berger, 7–30. Amsterdam: Menasseh ben Israel Institute, 2010.

———. "Soviet Yiddish Scholarship in the 1930s: From Class to *Folk.*" *Slavic Alamanch: The South African Year Book for Slavic, Central, and East European Studies* 7 (2001): 223–51.

———. "'Turning My Soul Inside Out': Text and Context of *The Family Mashber.*" In Estraikh, Hoge, and Krutikov, *Uncovering the Hidden*, 111–44.

———. "Writing between the Lines: 1905 in the Soviet Yiddish Novel of the Stalinist Period." In *The Revolution of 1905 and Russia's Jews*, edited by Stefani Hoffman and Ezra Mendelsohn, 212–226. Philadelphia: University of Pennsylvania Press, 2008.

———. *Yiddish Fiction and the Crisis of Modernity, 1905–1914*. Stanford, CA: Stanford University Press, 2001.

Krutikov, Mikhail, and Viacheslav Selemenev. "Yasha Bronshteyn and His Struggle for Control over Soviet Yiddish Literature." *Jews in Russia and Eastern Europe* 1, no. 50: 175–90.

"Kultur-khronik." *Eynikayt* 36 (September 7, 1944): 4.

Kvitko, Betty, and Miron Petrovskii, eds. *Zhizn' i tvorchestvo L'va Kvitko*. Moscow: Detskaia literatura, 1976.

Kvitko, Leyb. "Derklerung," *Di royte velt*, no. 9 (1929): 195.

Litvakov, Moyshe. *Af tsvey frontn*. Moscow: Tsentrfarlag, 1931.

———. *In umru*. Part 1. Kiev: Kiever farlag, 1918.

———. *In umru*. Part 2. Moscow: Shul un bukh, 1926.

Lunts, Lev. *Literaturnoe nasledie*. Moscow: Nauchnyi mir, 2007.

Lyumkis, Ilya. *Eshelonen geyen keyn Birobidzhan*. Moscow: Der Emes, 1948.

Magentsa-Shaked, Malka. "Singer and the Family Saga Novel in Jewish Literature." *Prooftexts* 9 (1989): 27–42.

Maggs, Peter B. *The Mandelstam and "Der Nister" Files: An Introduction to Stalin-era Prison and Labor Camp Records*. Armonk, NY: M. E. Sharpe, 1996.

Makaryk, Irena R., and Virlana Tkacz, eds. *Modernism in Kyiv: Jubilant Experimentation*. Toronto: University of Toronto Press, 2010.

Mantovan, Daniela. "The 'Political' Writings of an 'Unpolitical' Yiddish Symbolist." In Estraikh, Hoge, and Krutikov, *Uncovering the Hidden*, 73–89.

———. "Reading Soviet-Yiddish Poetry for Children: Der Nister's *Mayselekh in ferzn* 1917–39." In Estraikh, Hoge, and Krutikov, *Children and Yiddish Literature*, 93–110.

———. "Transgressing the Boundaries of Genre: The Children's Stories of the Soviet Yiddish Writer Der Nister (1884–1950)." In *Report of the Oxford Centre for Hebrew and Jewish Studies (2006–2007)*, 25–48.

Markovs'ki, Yevhen. *Ukrayins'ky vertep: rozvidky y teksty*. Kiev: Akademiia nauk, 1929.

Mayzel, Gitl. "Der Nister." *Di goldene keyt* 2 (February 1949): 188–95.

Mayzel, Nakhmen. "Der Nister—mentsh un kinstler." In Der Nister, *Dertseylungen un eseyen*, 9–29.

———. *Forgeyer un mitsaytler*. New York: Yiddish Cultural Union Press, 1946.

———. "Tsum leyener." In Der Nister, *Di mishpokhe Mashber*, part. 2, 7–8.

Miron, Dan. *The Image of the Shtetl and Other Studies of Modern Jewish Literary Imagination*. Syracuse, NY: Syracuse University Press, 2000.

———. Introduction to *Tales of Mendele the Book Peddler*, vii–lxx. New York: Schocken, 1996.

Mlechin, Leonid. *Kreml'—1953: Bor'ba za vlast' so smertel'nym iskhodom*. Moscow: Tsentrpoligraph, 2016.

Morgulis, Mikhail. "Iz moikh vospominanii." *Voskhod*, no. 2 (February 1895): 108–28.

Morse, Ainsley. "Detki v Kletke: The Childlike Aesthetic in Soviet Children's Literature and Unofficial Poetry." PhD diss., Harvard University, 2016.

Moss, Kenneth B. "Jewish Culture between Renaissance and Decadence: *Di Literarishe Monatshriftn* and Its Critical Reception." *Jewish Social Studies* 8, no. 1 (August 2001): 153–98.

———. *Jewish Renaissance in the Russian Revolution*. Cambridge, MA: Harvard University Press, 2009.

Moykher Sforim, Mendele. *Dos vintshfingerl*. In *Geglibene verk*, vol. 4. New York: Yiddish Cultural Union Press, 1946.

Murav, Harriet. "'The Feast Has Ended': Time in *The Family Mashber*." In Estraikh, Hoge, and Krutikov, *Uncovering the Hidden*, 161–73.

———. "Moscow Threefold: Olgin, Bergelson, Benjamin." In Estraikh and Krutikov, *Three Cities of Yiddish*, 45–55.

———. *Music from a Speeding Train: Jewish Literature in Post-Revolution Russia*. Stanford, CA: Stanford University Press, 2011.

Niger, Shmuel. "Der Nister." *Zamlbikher* 8 (1952): 62–75.

Novershtern, Avraham. "Igrotav shel Der Nister el Shmuel Niger." *Khuliyot* 1 (1993): 159–244.

Oushakine, Sergei, ed. *Formal'nyi metod: Antologiia russkogo modernizma*. Vol. 2. Moscow: Kabinentnyi uchenyi, 2016.

Oyslender, Nokhum. *Veg-ayn-veg-oys*. Kiev: Kultur-Lige, 1924.

"Partey-baratung baym kiever kreyz-partkom." *Prolit* 5 (1929): 87.

Peretz, Isaac Leib. "Three Gifts." Translated by Hillel Halkin. In Wisse, *The I. L. Peretz Reader*, 222–30. New Haven, CT: Yale University Press, 2002.

"Peretz ovnt." *Eynikayt* 80 (August 11, 1945): 3.

Pike, David. *German Writers in Soviet Exile, 1933–1945*. Chapel Hill: University of North Carolina Press, 1982.

Pisarev, Dmitrii. *Sochineniia*. Vol. 2. Moscow: Khudizhestvennaia literatura, 1955.

Piskunov, Vladimir. "'Vtoroe prostranstvo' romana A. Belogo 'Peterburg.'"
    In *Andrei Belyi: Problemy tvorchestva*, edited by Stanislav Lesnevskii
    and Aleksandr Mikhailov, 193–214. Moscow: Sovetskii pisatel', 1988.
Podriatshik, Leyzer. "Arum dem roman 'Fun finftn yor,'" *Sovetish
    heymland*, no. 1 (January 1964): 74–76.
———. "Genize-shafungen in der yidish-sovetisher literatur." In *In profil
    fun tsaytn*, 103–6. Tel-Aviv: I. L. Peretz Publishing House, 1978.
Pokrovskii, Mikhail N. *Russkaia istoriia v samom szhatom ocherke*. 4th ed.
    Moscow: Partizdat, 1933.
Rapoport, Yehoshua. "Notitsn vegn Dem Nisters 'Di mishpokhe
    Mashber'." *Di goldene keyt* 43 (1962): 68–73.
Ravitsh, Melekh. "A khronik fun a mishpokhe—an epos fun a dor." *Di
    tsukunft* 49 (July 1944): 457–58.
Redlich, Shimon. *War, Holocaust and Stalinism: A Documented History of
    the Jewish Anti-Fascist Committee in the USSR*. Luxembourg: Harwood
    Academic Publishers, 1995.
Reyzen, Zalmen. *Leksikon fun der yidisher literatur, prese un filologye*. Vol. 2.
    Vilna: B. Kletskin, 1927.
Roskies, David G. *A Bridge of Longing: The Lost Art of Jewish Storytelling*.
    Cambridge, MA: Harvard University Press, 1995.
Sadan, Dov. "Vegn Dem Nister." In *Toyern un tirn: Eseyen un etyudn*,
    43–68. Tel Aviv: Yisroel-bukh, 1979.
Senderovich, Sasha, and Harriet Murav. "David Bergelson's *Judgment*:
    A Critical Introduction." In David Bergelson, *Judgment: A Novel*,
    translated by Harriet Murav and Sasha Senderovich, ix–xxxvii.
    Evanston, IL: Northwestern University Press, 2017.
Serebriani, Yisroel. "Tsu der problem fun azoygerufenem 'kiever period'
    in der yidisher nokh-oktoberdiker poezie (materialn)." In *Literarisher
    zamlbukh*, 153–70. Minsk: Vaysrusishe visnshaft-akademie, 1934.
Serebrianskii, Mark. *Sovetskii istoricheskii roman*. Moscow:
    Khudozhestvennaia literatura, 1936.
Sergeev, Evgenii. "Yidishe yugnt in moskver melukhisher universitet."
    *Eynikayt* 14 (February 1, 1947): 3.
Shapiro, Lamed. *The Cross and Other Jewish Stories*. Edited and with
    an introduction by Leah Garrett. New Haven, CT: Yale University
    Press, 2007.
Sherman, Joseph, ed. *From Revolution to Repression: Soviet Yiddish Writing,
    1917–1952*. Nottingham, UK: Five Leaves, 2012.
Sherman, Joseph, and Gennady Estraikh, eds. *David Bergelson: From
    Modernism to Socialist Realism*. Oxford: Legenda, 2007.

Shkandrij, Myroslav. "Politics and the Ukrainian Avant-garde." In Makaryk and Tkacz, *Modernism in Kyiv*, 219–41.

Shmeruk, Chone. "Arba igrot shel Der Nister: Letoldot sifro 'Di mishpokhe mashber' vedfusotav." *Bekhinot* 8–9 (1977–78): 223–45.

———. "Der Nister, khayav veyetsirato." In Der Nister, *Hanazir vehagdiya*, 9–52.

———. "Der Nister's 'Under a Fence': Tribulations of a Soviet Yiddish Symbolist." In *The Field of Yiddish: Studies in Language, Folklore, and Literature; Second Collection*, edited by Uriel Weinreich, 263–87. London: Mouton, 1965.

———. "Yiddish Literature in the USSR." In Kochan, *Jews in Soviet Russia since 1917*, 242–80.

Shneer, David. *Yiddish and the Creation of Soviet Yiddish Culture, 1918–1930*. Cambridge: Cambridge University Press, 2004.

Shulman, Eiyohu. *Di sovetish-yidishe literatur*. New York: Tsiko, 1971.

Smolych, Yuri. "Z 'zapysiv na skhyli viku.'" *Prapor* 1, no. 9 (September 1990): 160–75.

Staliunas, Darius. *Making Russians: Meaning and Practice of Russification in Lithuania and Belarus after 1863*. Amsterdam: Rodopi, 2007.

Strongin, Lev. "Dos yidishe bukh in 1947 yor." *Eynikayt* 14 (February 1, 1947): 3.

Tretyakov, Sergei. "Dramaturgovy zametki." In Oushakine, *Formal'nyi metodii*, 238–41.

———. "Evoliutsiia zhanra." In Oushakine, *Formal'nyi metod*, 406–12.

———. "Iskusstvo v revolutsii i revolutiia v iskusstve." In Oushakine, *Formal'nyi metod*, 209–16.

[Untitled]. *Di royte velt*, nos. 5–6 (1927), 139–42.

Veidlinger, Jeffrey. *The Moscow State Yiddish Theater: Jewish Culture on the Soviet Stage*. Bloomington: Indiana University Press, 2000.

Von Geldern, James. *Bolshevik Festivals, 1917–1920*. Berkeley: University of California Press, 1993.

Waskiw, Mykola. "Mandrivnyi narys iak sposib piznannia inshoho i samoho sebe." *Ukraińska humanistyka i słowiańskie paralele*, 135–55.

Wiesel, Elie. *The Testament*. Translated from the French by Marion Wiesel. New York: Schocken Books, 1981.

Wisse, Ruth, ed. *The I. L. Peretz Reader*. New Haven, CT: Yale University Press, 2002.

Wolf, Leonard. Translator's introduction to Der Nister, *The Family Mashber*, 7–26. New York: Summit Books, 1987.

Yanait (Ben Zvi), Rahel. *Anu olim: Pirke hayim.* Tel Aviv: Am oved, 1960.

Yanasovitsh, Yitskhok. *Mit yidishe shrayber in Rusland.* Buenos Aires: Kiyem, 1959.

Zeitlin, Hillel. *R. Nakhman Braslaver: Der zeer fun Podolye.* New York: Matones, 1952.

Zerubavel, "Di grindungs-peryod fun der YSDAP-poyle tsien." *Royter pinkes,* no. 1 (1925): 121–51.

# INDEX

Rabbi Aaron (fictional character), 225–28

Abramovitsh, Sholem Yankev. *See* Mendele Moykher Sforim (Sholem Yankev Abramovitsh)

actors/puppeteers, 72–73, 133–34. *See also* art/artists/writers

agricultural colonization. *See* collectivity/collectivization

Akakii Akakievich (fictional character), 92

*Alexander III* (statue), 88, 114n60

allegorical symbolism: collapse of, 32, 37; historical, 3; Der Nister's use of, 31, 110; political, 128

American writers/critics, 42, 44, 80, 265, 274

anarchists, 141–42. *See also* revolutionaries

Andersen, Hans Christian, 10–11

animal motifs, 127–28

animal tales, 125–29

Annenkov, Iurii, 109

Ansheles, Heshl (fictional character), 222–24

An-sky, S., 6, 10, 199

Apt, Solomon, 270

*Arcades Project*, 100–101

architecture/architectural symbols, 110–12; as bridge between past and future, 92, 97 (*see also* historiography, Soviet: cities and; history); Kharkiv, 79, 87; Kiev, 81, 87; Leningrad, 91–92; Der Nister's view, 111–12, 174, 207; as reconciling art and ideology, 97. *See also* urban spaces

art/artists/writers, 257; failure of, 96; function/mission/role of, 61–62, 96, 187–88, 218–19, 237–38; ideology and, 96–97; survival/value of, 94–95, 97–100; transcend sociopolitical constraints of time and place, 112–13, 218, 229. *See also* literary development; literature

"Art as Technique," 72–73

artistic devices. *See* literary devices

artistic imagination. *See* art/artists /writers; imagination/fantasy and reality

assimilation theme, 38, 243–45

autotelic view of literature, 61

Babel, Isaac, 181

Balzac, Honoré de, 176

Barthes, Roland, 111

Bechtel, Delphine, 6–7, 10, 19n14; on alcohol and intoxication, 81; on *Gedakht* and *Fun mayne giter*, 16; on Der Nister's symbolist tales and use of box structure, 31–32; on symbolism/symbolist city/realism, 37, 87, 211

Belaia, Galina, 42

BelAPP. *See* Belorussian Association of Proletarian Writers (BelAPP)

Belarus, 48, 67. *See also* Yiddish culture, language, and literature

Belenki, Moyshe, 244

Belorussian Association of Proletarian Writers (BelAPP), 22, 48

Bely, Andrei, 13, 17, 90; on artistic creativity and revolutionary reality, 23; influences on, 96; *Petersburg*, 88, 90–93, 96; on spiral scheme, 31

Bemporad, Elissa, 42, 48

Ben Gavriel, Moshe Yaakov. *See* Hoeflich, Eugen (Moshe Yaakov Ben-Gavriel)

Benjamin, Walter, 100–102; on history, 111; on Moscow, 104–5, 107; on Paris, 100

Berdichev, 176–78, 184–85, 206; birthplace of Der Nister, 5; Bratslav synagogue, 208; economic, political, and social aspects, 145, 148, 150–51, 183–84; in *The Family Mashber*, 18, 183 (*see also* N. (city in *The Family Mashber*))

Berdichev Conference of December 1905, 152–53

Bergelson, David, 8–9, 269; on artistic portrayal of political upheaval, 23–24; on Moscow, 102; Der Nister and, 166. *See also* "Letter to David Bergelson"; *Midas-hadin* (Measure of judgment)

Bertelsen, Olga, 78

*Besy* (Demons), 95–97

biblical and rabbinic imagery, 247; Aaron and Isaac, 228; Deborah, 234–35; growth and regeneration, 243; Hagar and Ishmael, 71–72; Jacob, 76; Job, 203–4

*Bilder fun der provintsrayze* (Impressions from a journey to the provinces), 65–66

"Bildlekh un ayndrukn" (Images and impressions), 250

Birobidzhan/Birobidzhan visit and writings, 247, 249–54, 264, 271

Blakitny Literary Club, 59n96

Blank, Ber, 123

Blinov, Nikolai, 147, 157n17

Boehlich, Sabine, 12–13, 15

Bohomazov, Oleksander, 99

Bolshevik leadership/party, 148, 149–50, 155–56, 180. *See also* communism/Communist Party

Bolshevik Storming of the Winter Palace [reenactment], 108–9

Borokhov, Ber, 152–54

"A Bove mayse" (A tale of kings), 206

box structure, 31, 38

Boy (Construction) literary association, 21–22. *See also* Kiev Kultur-Lige

"A briv tsu Dovid Bergelson." *See* "Letter to David Bergelson"

Brodsky family, 52

Bronshteyn, Yashe, 22, 48, 54, 159

*Bronze Horseman. See* Peter the Great (person; statue)

builders and building. *See* architecture /architectural symbols; construction sites/constructivism

Bukharin, Nikolai, 106

Bukyer, Mikhl (fictional character), 186, 202–6

Bund (The General Union of Jewish
    Workers in Lithuania, Poland, and
    Russia), 148, 150
business and religion, 175–76, 180,
    228–29

capital cities of Soviet Union, 60,
    77, 101–2, 111. See also *Hoyptshtet*
    (Capitals); Kharkiv; Kiev;
    Leningrad; Moscow
capitalism (commercial), 89, 175–79,
    184. *See also* business and religion
Caplan, Marc, 35–36
catastrophe, sense of, 191–92, 194.
    *See also* Nazism/Nazi occupation;
    war stories
central squares of cities, 111. *See also*
    Red Square
Chagall, Marc, 11–12, 85, 274–76;
    illustrator of Der Nister children's
    book, 123; portrayal in Horn's book,
    275–77
Chen, Jonathan Dekel. *See* Dekel-
    Chen, Jonathan
child psychology, 35
children, cruelty of, 35
children's literature, 11–12, 118–36,
    136n2. *See also* fairy tales; Kvitko,
    Leyb; Der Nister (Pinhas
    Kaganovich/Kahanovitsh):
    translations; poetry, children's
Chudakova, Marietta, 121–22
churches. *See* Kiev; Moscow
church trope, 114n49
cities: fictional, 174–79, 181; flying,
    81–83. *See also* capital cities of Soviet
    Union
Clark, Katerina, 103
class struggle, 73, 150, 187. *See also*
    revolution of 1905
collective commitment. *See* creative
    freedom vs. collective commitment

collectivist art, 42–43
collectivity/collectivization, 13, 70–75,
    84–86
communism/Communist Party,
    155–56; buildings/construction and,
    80, 98; Judaism and, 199, 227–28,
    230, 232, 249; Kvitko and, 47–48, 121;
    literature and, 21–22, 47–50, 54–55,
    162, 228; Der Nister and, 14–15,
    25–26, 70, 86, 112, 123–24, 248–49;
    RAPP and, 43, 53–54; reconstruction
    projects, 79–81, 103; theater and,
    73–74, 133–34. *See also* Moscow;
    purges
community: Jewish (*see* Jewish
    community/communities); role
    of women (*see* women, role in the
    community and family)
construction sites/constructivism,
    79–81, 111. *See also* architecture
    /architectural symbols;
    communism/Communist Party
Cossacks, 132, 234–35. *See also*
    "Kozekl-royt" (A little red Cossack)
creative freedom vs. collective
    commitment, 42–43, 60–61, 119.
    *See also* communism/Communist
    Party
Crimea, 53, 70–73

dance imagery/dancing, 83–85;
    Hasidic, 209, 235 (see also *The Family
    Mashber* [*Di mishpokhe Mashber*]);
    as literary device, 210, 234–35
*Dead Souls* (prose "poema"), 176
defamiliarization (*ostranenie*), 72–73
Dekel-Chen, Jonathan, 71–72
Delmedigo, Joseph Solomon, 260n42
*Dem shturem antkegn* (Toward the
    storm), 155
despitists (*voprekisty*), 94
"dialectical images," 100

Diaspora. *See* exile

*Dictatorship* (play), 74

*din* (judgment, justice), 39–40

Dobrenko, Evgeny, 43, 186–87

Dobrushin, Yekhezkl, 42

Dolgopolov, Leonid, 90

Dostoevsky, Fyodor, 90, 93–97, 106

*Dray mayselekh* (Three fairy tales), 123–24

Dreyer, Heinrich (fictional character), 226

drinking/intoxication motif, 38, 81–82, 87, 91, 93, 101, 132

drives. *See* inclinations, good/evil

Dunayevtsy, 67–70

Dunets, Khatskl, 22, 44, 47–49; on *Fun mayne giter*, 45; on Kvitko, Pilniak, and Zamiatin, 47; on Der Nister, 48–49

*The Dybbuk*, 199

economics. *See* capitalism (commercial)

editors, 159–60. *See also individual names*

elections, Soviet, 248

Elke (fictional character), 242–43

*Der emes* (The truth) periodical, 25, 46

Der Emes press, 163, 166, 170–72, 213nn31–32, 222, 272

Emiot, Yisroel, 253

Epshteyn, Shakhne, 25, 169

Erik, Max, 54, 186

eroticism, 201–2, 204

Estraikh, Gennady, 21–22; on "Flora," 235; on Litvakov and Kharkiv writers, 47

eulogies, 255–58

Evreinov, Nikolai: on origin of public theater, 34–35, 86, 134; reenactment of storming of Winter Palace, 108–9

executions, 34–35, 86. *See also* purges; Red Square

exile, 175, 206–7, 252. *See also* Birobidzhan/Birobidzhan visit and writings; wanderer figure or legend /wandering motif

experimentation, stylistic, 5–9, 22–23, 63, 278; children's literature and, 119, 122–23; as progression, 31, 43; Soviet literature and, 17

*Eynikayt* (Unity), 246–49

"Eyns a shtetl" (One of the shtetls), 67–69, 134

"factual literature" (*literatura fakta*), 61

Fadeev, Aleksandr, 40, 255–56

fairs, 50, 178

fairy tales, 11–12, 122–27. See also *Mayselekh* (Fairy tales); *Zeks mayselekh* (Six fairy tales)

family decline theme, 139–43

*The Family Mashber* (*Di mishpokhe Mashber*), 2, 18, 73, 112, 159–212; American edition, 173, 194, 197; anti-Polish imagery, 181; break with abstract symbolism, 62–63; ideological aspects, 180, 183–88; possible sequel to, 173–74, 179, 269; publication of, 167–74, 213n31, 213nn36–37, 219, 272–73; role of history, 191–92; Shmeruk's view, 268; trial motif, 134

family saga novels, 191–93. See also *The Family Mashber* (*Di mishpokhe Mashber*)

farmers/farms, 70–73, 76

*fartseykhenung* (hybrid of essay and reportage), 65

Fefer, Itsik, 137n23, 167–68

fiddler figure/image, 84–85

*Figurn afn rand*, 39

fire motif, 205–6

the flaneur, 100–101

"Flora," 232–35, 260n42, 268

folkishness/"national folksiness"
(*folkstimlekhkeyt*), 27, 122

folk theater. *See* puppet theater, Ukrainian

Fowler, Mayhill, 50, 74

Fradkin, Moisei, 123

Frankel, Jonathan, 153

free will. *See* inclinations, good/evil

"Der fuks un der ber" (The fox and the bear), 127

*Fun finftn yor* (From the year 1905), 17–18, 143–56

*Fun mayne giter* (From my estates), 16, 45, 266

*galut. See* exile

*Gedakht* (Imagined), 16, 28–32

*Gedanken un motivn* (Thoughts and motifs), 244

Geldern, James von, 109

Gen, Tevye, 270

*Gerangl* (Struggle), 47

Gevirts, Yakov, 78

Glupsk (fictional city), 177

Gnyessia, 150

Godiner, Shmuel, 39–40, 49

Gogol, Nikolai, 90, 92, 176, 246

Gol, Sruli (fictional character), 194, 202, 204–5

Gordon, Shmuel, 44, 174, 274

GOSET. *See* Moscow State Yiddish Theater (GOSET)

Gosprom complex, 79, 81–82, 87, 110

Gromeka, Stepan, 184

Groysbaytl, Boris (fictional character), 236–37

Gruschka, Roland, 214n63; on Mikhl Bukyer, 203; on Der Nister, 176, 183, 196; on Sruli Gol, 202

Gurshteyn, Aron: death, 168, 219; editing of/on *The Family Mashber*, 159, 166, 192–93; on Kvitko, 136n5;

letter from Wiener, 161; letters from Der Nister, 163–68, 193, 212n14, 219

Halpern, Yankev Yoysef, 183–85

"Has" (Hate; originally "On the Third Anniversary of the War"), 247

Hasidim/Hasidism, 183–86. *See also* *The Family Mashber* (*Di mishpokhe Mashber*); Bratslav, 190, 201, 207–9, 266; Chabad, 235; folklore, 26–27; inspiration for Der Nister, 207, 253

Haskalah/maskilim, 183–86

Hebrew literature, 118, 155, 191, 202

Heine, Heinrich, 105–6

*Hello from Radiowave 477!*, 50

heroism and resistance. *See* war stories

"Heshl Ansheles," 222–25

the "Hidden One." *See* Der Nister (Pinhas Kaganovich/Kahanovitsh): reclusiveness

historical fiction, 18, 138, 214n72; caricature and, 181; Gurshteyn's view of *The Family Mashber*, 192–93; socialist realism and, 159, 186–89. *See also* narrative devices, style, and technique

historical time. *See* urban spaces

historiography, Soviet, 148–49, 153, 156, 186–88; architecture and, 111 (*see also* architecture/architectural symbols); cities and, 102, 106

history, 93, 99, 111, 211–12; family saga novels and, 175–76, 191–94; Jewish, 3, 191–92, 207, 244, 258 (*see also* Mikhoels, Solomon; wanderer figure or legend/wandering motif); literature and, 10, 18, 24–27, 88–90, 191–94, 218

Hodl (Olga; Der Nister's daughter), 162, 197, 219

Hoeflich, Eugen (Moshe Yaakov Ben-Gavriel), 13

Hoffmann, E. T. A., 37

Hofshteyn, Dovid, 44, 119

Hoge, Kerstin, 11, 119

Holocaust. *See* Nazism/Nazi occupation; war stories

Holodomor. *See* Ukraine: famine

Horn, Dara, 274–77

*Hoyptshtet* (Capitals), 60, 62, 67–68, 71, 112, 118. *See also* "Kharkiv" [chapter]; "Leningrad" [chapter]; "Moscow" [chapter]

identity, 38–39, 53, 119

ideology: art/artists/literature/writers and, 96–97, 122–26; communist /Soviet, 15, 41–42, 112, 123, 174, 186–87 (*see also* communism/Communist Party); national-democratic, 55–56; Der Nister and, 27–28, 49, 52, 63, 112, 124–25, 154–56, 164, 258–59 (*see also The Family Mashber* [*Di mishpokhe Mashber*]); Peretz and (*see* Peretz, Y. L.). *See also* Borokhov, Ber; historiography, Soviet; Zionism

imagery: anti-Polish, 181; dance (*see* dance imagery/dancing); dialectical, 100; ghost, 89–91; symbolic, 3, 13, 22, 27–28, 200, 222 (*see also* "Der zeyde mitn eynikl" [Grandfather and grandson]). *See also* themes and motifs

imaginary stranger device. *See* the stranger device/strangers

imagination/fantasy and reality, 3, 15–16, 25, 41; in "A mayse mit a noged un mit a tsigele," 30–31; Der Nister's approach/method, 60–61, 65

inclinations, good/evil, 93–94; in a divided self, 134; influence of imagination on reality, 41

individuality vs. collectivity, 42–43, 84–85. *See also* collectivity /collectivization

Institute for Noble Maidens. *See* Smolny Institute

intelligentsia: attacks on, 43, 62; imprisonment of, 264; populist, 10; Russian/revolutionary, 51, 88, 179. *See also* Jewish/Yiddish intelligentsia

intelligentsia, Ukrainian: Jewish intelligentsia and, 51–52; show trials, 62

"In tsekh," 120–21

Itsikl (fictional character), 225–28

JAC. *See* Jewish Antifascist Committee (JAC)

Jewish Antifascist Committee (JAC), 168–69, 213n26, 234, 245–46

Jewish Autonomous Region. *See* Birobidzhan/Birobidzhan visit and writings

Jewish community/communities, 180, 183, 190, 201, 232, 251

Jewish culture, 7, 13, 118–19. *See also* Hebrew literature; Jewish community/communities; Yiddish culture, language, and literature

Jewish Enlightenment. *See* Haskalah /maskilim

Jewish history. *See* history

Jewish-Polish relations, 182–84

Jewish revival/unity, 244–45, 250–51, 268

Jewish socialist groups meeting (fictional), 151–52

Jewish/Yiddish intelligentsia, 13, 62, 67, 185, 236; imprisonment of, 264; Ukraine intelligentsia and, 51–52; Yiddish literature and, 55 (*see also* Yiddish culture, language, and literature)

Judaism: communism and (*see* communism/Communist Party); intellectualized, 230; normative, 179, 202, 207, 224, 227–28

justice, revolutionary, 39–40

Kabbalah/kabbalistic concepts, 15–16, 79–80, 253, 265

Kaganovich, Aaron, 267

Kaganovich, Max (Motl), 63–65, 160–62, 254–55

Kaganovich/Kahanovitsh, Pinhas. *See* Der Nister (Pinhas Kaganovich /Kahanovitsh)

Kalinin, Mikhail, 273

Kalmanovitch, Zelig, 238

Karakozov, Dmitry, 93–94

Kaverin, Veniamin/Benyomin, 37–38

Kazakevich, Emmanuil, 270

Kazakevich, Henekh, 48

Kerler, Yosef, 251

*Khamza* (drama), 246

Kharkiv, 17, 21, 63, 77–80: architecture, 79; literature and, 50, 52; Der Nister's view, 78–79; purges/show trials, 62, 79–80. *See also* Tractor Factory

"Kharkiv" [chapter], 81–82, 86, 133–34

Khreshchatyk thoroughfare. *See* Vorovsky Street (Kiev)

Khvyl'ovyi, Mykola, 50

kiddush hashem theme, 224–25, 228–29, 233. *See also Korbones* (3 novellas)

Kiev, 83–85, 150; as capital of Ukraine, 63, 83, 87; Christian pilgrimage ritual, 81–83; literary circles /literary-political aspects, 42, 44, 54–55, 164–65, 167; Der Nister and, 64, 76; publishers/writers, 9–10, 64, 132, 162, 246; rivalry with Minsk, 56

Kiev Institute for Jewish Proletarian Culture, 54

Kiev Kultur-Lige, 11, 123: Bolshevization of, 55, 119; production and distribution of Yiddish literature, 119, 123. *See also* Boy (Construction) literary association; *Kievskaia mysl'* (Kiev thought) periodical, 23

Kipnis, Itsik, 170–71, 213n32

Kletskin, Boris/Kletskin press, 10, 238

Koller, Sabine, 11–12, 61, 63, 100

*Korbones* (3 novellas), 222–30

Kossover, Paltiel (fictional character), 273–74

Kotlerman, Ber, 227, 247, 249–50, 252–54, 258

"Kozekl-royt" (A little red Cossack), 130–34

Koznarsky, Taras, 82–83

Kremlin, 103

Kremlin wall, 107–8

Krutikov, Georgii, 83

kulaks/dekulakization, 72, 74

Kulyk, Ivan (Izrail), 50

Kurbas, Les, 50–51, 74

Kvitko, Betty, 120

Kvitko, Leyb, 14, 17, 120; attack on /campaign against, 44, 46–48; children's literature and, 119–22, 135; on Litvakov, 46–47; poetry and translations, 50, 119–20, 128

Landshaft, Meyer (fictional character), 228–30

Leningrad, 88–92, 98

"Leningrad" [chapter], 88–90, 93, 100–102, 211

Lenin's Mausoleum, 107–8

"Letter to David Bergelson," 187, 218

Levin, Lipman, 155

Leybl (fictional character), 145–49

Leybl's mother (Malke Mints; fictional character), 145–49, 156–57

Lifshits, Moyshe, 13, 15, 20n30

Lisitsin-Sventislavski (fictional character), 181–82

*Di literarishe monatshriftn* periodical, 9–10, 22, 55

literary development, 21–22, 27–28, 31; historical novel and, 188; Ukrainian, 66; the writer as the people's voice, 219. *See also* art/artists/writers literary devices, 41, 69–70, 238, 240. *See also* narrative devices, style, and technique; themes and motifs

literary politics, 54. *See also* literary development; Soviet literary politics

literature, 10, 61–62; autotelic view, 61 (*see also* imagination/fantasy and reality; socialist realism); as bridge between past and future, 92; deriving meaning (Der Nister's view), 36–37; history and (*see* history). *See also* art/artists /writers; children's literature; Hebrew literature; Soviet literature; Yiddish culture, language, and literature

*Literaturnaia gazeta* (literary newspaper), 166, 188, 192

*Literaturnyi iarmarok* (literary fair) periodical, 50

Litvakov, Moshe (Moyshe), 46–49, 56; on Jewish social protest, 190; on the maskilim, 186; Der Nister and, 22, 28, 159; on Der Nister/symbolism, 25–26, 49

Loyter, Efraim, 74

Lukács, Georg, 94, 188

Lukashevich, 151

Lunts, Lev/Yehudah, 37–38

Luria, Shalom, 238–40

Lurye, Note, 181

Lurye, Noyekh, 245

Luzi. *See* Mashber, Luzi (fictional character)

Lyumkis, Ilya, 250

Magentsa-Shaked, Malka, 191–92

magic fish motif, 81, 83

Magnus, Meylekh (fictional character), 236–37

Malakhovka orphanage, 12

Malke-Rive (fictional character), 204

Mantovan, Daniela, 123–24, 133, 156

Markish, Peretz, 44, 119; *Eynikayt* and, 246; Der Nister and, 163, 166; Poland and, 192

Markovs'ky, Yevhen, 132

Markuze, Moyshe, 260n42

martyrdom/sacrifice themes, 225–28, 230–31. *See also* kiddush hashem theme; war stories

Marxism-Leninism: *The Family Mashber* and, 175; on Jews and the revolution, 190, 203; Leningrad architecture and, 91–92; Der Nister and, 15, 101, 156; on prerevolutionary cultural legacy, 94–95; Yiddish literature and, 54–56. *See also* Borokhov, Ber; Erik, Max; Gurshteyn, Aron; Nusinov, Isaac; Pokrovskii, Mikhail; Wiener, Meir

Mashber, Alter (fictional character), 198, 201–2

Mashber, Gitl (fictional character), 198, 203–4

Mashber, Luzi (fictional character), 194–95, 200–201; Niger's view, 266–67; vision and exile, 206; as a wanderer, 252

Mashber, Moshe (fictional character), 188, 200–201, 204–5; financial situation, 175–76, 178, 181–82; illness, 183; imprisonment, repentance, and death, 194, 198

Mashberg, Pinkhes (fictional character), 274

maskilim. *See* Haskalah/maskilim

the masses, 188; Haskalah/maskilim and, 185–86; Jewish, 189, 203–4, 247, 250; the modern city and, 87; totalitarian regimes and, 74

Mayerl (fictional character), 194–95, 197–98

*Mayn bakanter* ("An Acquaintance of Mine"), 239–41

*mayselekh. See* fairy tales

*Mayselekh* (Fairy tales), 128

*Mayselekh in ferzn* (Fairy tales in verse), 123

"A mayse mit a ber" (A tale about a bear), 125–27

"A mayse mit a fuks" (A tale about a fox), 128–29

"A mayse mit a noged un mit a tsigele" ("A Tale of a Hermit and a Kid"), 29–31

Mayzel, Gitl, 265

Mayzel, Nakhmen, 4, 44; on *The Family Mashber*, 173, 185; letter from Itsik Fefer, 168, 213n26; letters from Der Nister, 168–70, 213n28; Der Nister and, 229, 265

memoirs: fictional, 236–37, 239, 277–78; of/about Der Nister, 212n14, 217–18, 271–72, 277–78; Smolych, 51. *See also 1905 yor in Barditshev* (The year 1905 in Berdichev)

Mendele Moykher Sforim (Sholem Yankev Abramovitsh), 51, 177

Mercury (god), 177

messianic figures/themes, 199, 206–7, 230, 257–58

"Me tantst oyf di gasn" (Dancing in the streets), 83–85

"Meyer Landshaft," 228–30

"Meylekh Magnus," 235–39

*Midas-hadin* (Measure of judgment), 40, 181

migration of Jews, 70–71. *See also individual names*

Mikhoels, Solomon, 247, 255–58

Milye (fictional character), 145–49

Milye's mother (fictional character), 148–50

Minsk: intelligentsia/working class, 42, 47–48, 67; proletarian writers, 22, 159, 164; rivalry with Kiev, 56

Mints, Malke. *See* Leybl's mother (Malke Mints; fictional character)

Miron, Dan, 199; on fire motif, 206; on Glupsk, 177

*Di Mishpokhe Mashber.* See *The Family Mashber* (*Di mishpokhe Mashber*)

"Mit ibervanderer keyn Biro-Bidzhan" (With the new settlers to Birobidzhan), 250

modernism/modernists, 12–13, 30, 36, 54–55; children's literature and, 118–23; elitist, 55; journals, 5, 50; Der Nister and, 8, 10, 268–69; Russian, 69–70, 207; Ukrainian, 61–62, 69–70. *See also* narrative devices, style, and technique; wanderer figure or legend/wandering motif; Yiddish culture, language, and literature;

Morgulis, Menashe (Mikhail), 184–85

Morse, Ainsley, 122

Moscow, 102–3; Bergelson's view, 102; as center of Yiddish literature, 56; churches, 103–5, 107; Der Nister's view, 102–10; transformation of, 103

"Moscow" [chapter], 102–4, 211

Moscow State Yiddish Theater (GOSET), 74, 246–47; location of hidden Der Nister manuscript, 277; murder of director, 255–56

Moscow Yiddish Theater Company, 72–73

"Moskve salutirt" (Moscow celebrates), 245–46

Moss, Kenneth, 10, 118

*The Mother*, 150

motifs. *See* themes and motifs

Moyshke (fictional character), 242–43

Muni (fictional character), 139–43

Murav, Harriet, 40; on Alter Mashber, 201; on *The Family Mashber*, 188, 210–12; on story in *Korbones*, 223

Murav'ev, Mikhail, 182

Mykytenko, Ivan, 74

mysticism, 230, 266–67; influence on
Der Nister, 5, 7, 9, 22; Der Nister and,
15–16, 26–28, 275. *See also* Hasidim
/Hasidism; inclinations, good/evil;
Kabbalah/kabbalistic concepts

N. (city in *The Family Mashber*),
174–79, 181
Rabbi Nahman of Bratslav, 27, 206, 274
"A nakht mit a tog" (A night with a
day), 75–77
narrative devices, style, and technique,
112, 154, 196, 240; duplications
and repetitions, 204–5; epic, 2;
*The Family Mashber* and, 193–95;
the stranger/imaginary stranger,
72–73, 199. *See also* literary
devices; narrators; realism/reality;
symbolism/symbolist poetics
/symbolists
narrators, 194–97; as accuser and
accused, 133, 136; adult in children's
literature, 128; as communist
prophet, 110; eye witness, 234;
intoxicated, 81; omniscient,
195–96, 220–31; pessimistic, 190,
252; professional, 233–34; "we"
/manipulative, 194–96. *See also*
"Meylekh Magnus"
"Naygayst" (New spirit), 12–15, 55
Nazism/Nazi occupation, 191–92, 222,
226–27, 230, 233, 244
neorealism, 43
neo-Romanticism, 187–88; depiction of
Hasidim, 208; versus realism, 208–9
Niger, Shmuel: editorial work, 10;
letters to, 6, 8–9, 13–14; on Der
Nister, 265–67, 269
1905 revolution. *See* revolution of 1905
*1905 yor in Barditshev* (The year 1905 in
Berdichev), 150–51
Der Nister (Pinhas Kaganovich
/Kahanovitsh): anxiety and fear, 62,

70, 163–64, 269; arrest, imprisonment,
and death, 2, 264, 269; birth and
education, 5; career, 1–2, 12, 46, 122–25,
135, 274, 277–78; fictionalizations
of, 274–77; influence on younger
writers, 39, 49–50; influences and
inspirations, 6–9, 27–28, 37, 66–67,
113n12, 175–77, 207 (*see also* symbolism
/symbolist poetics/symbolists);
journeys/travelogues, 18, 67–71
(*see also* Birobidzhan/Birobidzhan
visit and writings); on literature
/writers, 36–37, 188, 229, 272; poverty,
161, 163, 167, 275–76; publication of
works (*see also under various works*);
reclusiveness, 1, 3–4, 26–27, 217,
258, 271, 275–76; rehabilitation, 270;
relocations, 4, 15–17, 21, 219–20;
works (*see* symbolism/symbolist
poetics/symbolists; under individual
titles); worldview, 86, 253. *See also*
Kaganovich, Max (Motl); Peretz,
Y. L.; Smolych, Yuri; *under various
entries*
Nisterism/"The Nister Problem,"
45–46, 49
Notovitsh, Moyshe, 245
Nusinov, Isaac: on "A Tale of a Hermit
and a Kid," 30; on depiction of
reality, 95; editorial work on *The
Family Mashber*, 159; as Marxist
authority on literature, 56; on
modernism/Yiddish literature,
54–55; on Der Nister, 26–28; on
symbolism, 27

*ocherk* (hybrid) genre, 65–66, 118, 268.
*See also* reportage
October 11, 1943, literary meeting,
245–46
October Manifesto, 150
"On a Worn-Out 'Uniform' without a
'General,'" 48

"On the Jewish Question," 190
"On the Literary Front: Notes to the Annual Literary Balance Sheet," 44–45
"On the Third Anniversary of the War." See "Has" (Hate; originally "On the Third Anniversary of the War")
Orshanski, Ber, 48, 164, 166–67
"The Overcoat," 92
Oyslender, Nokhem, 22–26, 144; letter from Der Nister, 4; on Der Nister, 23–25; Der Nister and, 28

Passover, 221
"Perets hot geredt un ikh hob gehert," (Peretz spoke and I listened), 212n14, 217–18
Peretz, Y. L., 19n14, 217–18, 246; on artistic inspiration, 188; commemoration of death, 246; critique of glorifying suffering, 224–25; dancing as link between material and spiritual, 210; fartseykhenung and, 65–66; influence on Der Nister, 8–9, 67–69; Der Nister and, 27, 165–66, 212n14, 217–18; rehabilitation of, 165–66, 217; travelogue, 69
Pereval (Pass) group, 42–43
performance. See public theater
Perlmuter, Shloymke, 247
persona, hidden. See Der Nister (Pinhas Kaganovich/Kahanovitsh): reclusiveness
Petersburg (novel), 88, 90–93, 96
Peter the Great (person; statue), 88
Petrograd, 37–38. See also Leningrad; St. Petersburg
Pilniak, Boris, 47
Pisarev, Dmitry, 109–10
Piskunov, Vladimir, 88
Poale Zion (Labor Zionist) party, 152–53

Pobedonostsev, Konstantin, 95–96
Podriatshik, Eliezer (Leyzer), 143–45, 152, 179–80, 238
poetry, children's, 17, 118–19, 122–35. See also individual titles
poetry/poets, 120–21, 137n23. See also Yiddish culture, language, and literature; individual names
Pokrovskii, Mikhail, 88–89, 99, 175, 186
Poland/Polish-Russian relations, 180–83
Polish Jewry/Polish-Jewish relations, 182–84, 244
Prechistaya Fair, 178
Pritsker, Rabbi Osher, 183
"Problem of the So-Called Kiev Period in Yiddish Poetry after the October Revolution," 54–55
proletarian writers and organizations, 43. See also Russian Association of Proletarian Writers (RAPP); individual names
protest. See social protest
public theater, 34–35, 72–74. See also puppet theater, Ukrainian
"Pupe: A mayse fun tsurik mit yorn" (Pupe: A tale from years ago) [novella], 138–43
"Pupe's guy" (fictional character), 140–41
puppet theater, Ukrainian, 131–34, 136
purges, 67, 73, 114n56, 134, 159; as celebration, 79–80; Der Nister's view, 86, 125. See also executions
Purishkevich, Vladimir, 93
Pushkin, Alexander, 103–4

Rabinovich, Solomon (Sholem) Naumovich. See Sholem Aleichem
Rapoport, Yehoshua, 174, 197
RAPP. See Russian Association of Proletarian Writers (RAPP)
Ravitsh, Melekh, 193–94

*Rayzes un poemes* (Travels and poems), 121

*Razgrom* (The rout), 40

readership, 188; American, 168; elitist, 28; for Der Nister's fairy tales, 135; Russian, 166, 271

realism/reality, 31, 204–5; versus neo-Romanticism, 208–9; proletarian, 120; socialist (*see* socialist realism); sociohistoric, 244 (*see also* war stories); symbolism and, 99–100, 200, 204–5, 211, 244. *See also* imagination/fantasy and reality; urban spaces

redemption theme, 207, 211. See also "*Der zeyde mitn eynikl*" (Grandfather and grandson)

Redlich, Shimon, 165

Red Square, 106–8, 110

"Regrowth" ("*Vidervuks*"). *See* "*Vidervuks*" ("Regrowth"; short story)

Regrowth (*Vidervuks*). *See Vidervuks* (Regrowth; story collection)

religion and business, 175–76, 180, 228–29

reportage, 60–61, 249, 268; Jewish collective farms, 71–77; travel, 66–70. *See also* Birobidzhan /Birobidzhan visit and writings; *fartseykhenung* (hybrid of essay and reportage); *Hoyptshtet* (Capitals); *ocherk* (hybrid) genre

resistance and heroism. *See* war stories

resurrection theme, 246, 257. *See also* messianic figures/themes

revolutionaries, 92–93, 95–96, 142–54, 179

revolutionary struggle/theme, 13, 18, 22–25, 27–28, 39–40, 42–44. *See also* class struggle

revolution of 1905, 143–47, 150–55

Reyzen, Zalman, 5

*Rimon/Milgroym* (periodical), 14–15

"Rive Yosl Buntses," 231–32, 260n35

"Rodina" (The homeland), 37–38

Romanticism/Romantic nationalism, 7, 187, 266–67. *See also* neo-Romanticism

Roskies, David: on "A mayse mit a noged un mit a tsigele," 30–31; on "Naygayst," 13; on Der Nister, 14–16; on "Unter a ployt (reviu)" (Under a fence: A review), 33–34

*Di royte velt* (The red world) periodical, 21–22, 32; defense of prerevolutionary writers, 45–47; Der Nister and, 45–46, 60

Russian Association of Proletarian Writers (RAPP), 42–44; dissolution of, 53–54; on fairy tales, 123. *See also* Belorussian Association of Proletarian Writers (BelAPP)

*Russian History in a Brief Survey*, 89

Russian-Polish relations, 180–83

Ryabushinsky family, 52–53

sacrifice. *See* martyrdom/sacrifice themes

Sadan, Dov, 183, 198

scaffold. *See* executions

Schulman, Elias, 156

self, divided, 134

Senderovich, Sasha, 40

Serapion Brethren, 37

Serebriani, Israel, 54–56

Serebrianskii, Mark, 189, 193, 214n72

Sergeev, Evgenii, 249

Shaked, Malka Magentsa. *See* Magentsa-Shaked, Malka

Shambadal, Mikhail, 270–71

Shapiro, Lamed, 80

Shcherbakov, M., 228

Shestov, Lev, 207–8

*shevirah*/disintegration. *See tikkun* (improvement)/*shevira* (disintegration)

Sheynfeld, Azriel (fictional character), 139, 141
Sheynfeld, Pupe (fictional character), 139–43
Sheynfeld, Shloyme (fictional character), 139, 141
Sheynfeld family, 139–43
"Shiker" (The drunk), 81–82
Shkandrij, Myroslav, 61–62, 70
Shklovsky, Viktor, 72–73
Shloyme, the contrabandist, 220–22
Shmeruk, Khone: on *The Family Mashber*, 173, 196, 268; on *Fun finftn yor*, 156; on *Hoyptshtet* (Capitals), 60; on Der Nister, 187, 189, 267–69; on "Unter a ployt (reviu)" (Under a fence: A review), 34
Shneyer (fictional character), 76–77
"Shnit" (Harvest), 71
Sholem Aleichem, 51
show trials: as motif, 133–34, 136; of Ukrainian intelligentsia, 62
*Shtern* periodical, 44, 48, 60, 83
"Shtet un derfer" (Cities and villages), 54
Sigalovskaia, Elena [Der Nister's wife], 138–39, 144, 246, 268
Singer, Israel Joshua, 42
Slezkine, Yuri, 177
Smolny Institute, 93, 97–98, 110
Smolych, Yuri, 258; Der Nister and, 51–53, 63, 247; on Der Nister's turn to reportage, 61
socialism, 186. *See also* communism /Communist Party
socialist realism, 17, 53, 121; formative period, 103–5; historical novel and, 187; Der Nister and, 60–61, 86, 112, 189 (see also *Fun finftn yor* [From the year 1905]); Romantic nationalism and, 187; triumph of, 87. *See also* Levin, Lipman

social protest, 189–90, 204
socioeconomics, 179; in *The Family Mashber*, 175–76, 191, 194, 200; history and, 99
*Sovetishe literatur* periodical, 173
*Sovetish heymland* periodical, 143–44, 174
Soviet literary politics, 41–45, 162, 188–89
Soviet literature, 55, 66. *See also* Soviet Yiddish culture and literature
Soviet Union/Soviet policies: centralization/Russian cultural hegemony, 62; cryptic criticism of, 133; forced migration of Jews, 70–71; on literature, 48, 162 (*see also* communism/Communist Party; Soviet literary politics; Soviet literature); progress of Jews, 248–49; on Zionism, 53
Soviet Yiddish culture and literature, 4, 22, 47; control /destruction/persecution of, 48–49, 162, 174, 265; Der Nister's place, 2, 13, 16–17, 216–17, 270–71; revitalization of, 216. See also *Di royte velt* (The red world) periodical; Yiddish culture, language, and literature
spaces, open and enclosed, 149
spaces, urban. *See* urban spaces
Stalin/Stalinist policies, 17–19, 103, 149, 174; anti-Ukrainian, 62; historiographical concepts, 186–87; military-political, 180; terror, use of, 33, 87, 124, 132–34, 159, 182 (*see also* "Kozekl-royt" [A little red Cossack])
St. Basil's Church, 107
"Der step brent" (The steppe is on fire), 74
*Der step ruft* (The steppe calls), 181
the steppe, 70–72

storytelling, 36; collapse of, 32, 87;
  on a train/therapeutic, 251. *See also*
  Rabbi Nahman of Bratslav; war
  stories
St. Petersburg, 37–38, 88, 92, 96.
  *See also* Leningrad; Petrograd
the stranger device/strangers, 72–73,
  128, 135, 195, 199, 206
Strongin, Lev, 166, 171
St. Sophia's Cathedral, 81–82, 87
sublimation (concept), 237, 240
Sutzkever, Avraham, 238, 241
"Symbolism," 23
symbolism/symbolist poetics
  /symbolists, 1–3, 6, 8, 13, 28,
  135; allegorical (*see* allegorical
  symbolism); avoiding, 81;
  nationalist, 234–35; realism/reality
  and, 99–100, 200, 204–5, 211, 244;
  religious, 3, 27–28, 80–81, 175, 207,
  222–32; translations of Andersen
  and, 11. *See also* Bely, Andrei;
  imagination/fantasy and reality;
  "Naygayst"
synagogues, 77–78, 175, 208

Tauride Palace, 93, 97–99, 110
"The Teaching of Hasidim," 210
terror, use of, 74, 182; anarchists
  and, 141–42; Der Nister's
  view, 124–25, 132–34. *See also*
  revolutionaries; revolutionary
  struggle/theme; Stalin/Stalinist
  policies
"thankists" (blagodaristy), 94–95
theater. *See* public theater
themes and motifs, 6; animal, 127–28;
  assimilation, 37–39; dance (*see*
  dance imagery/dancing); drinking
  /intoxication, 81; family decline,
  139–43; fiddler, 84–85; fire, 205–6;
  kiddush hashem (*see* kiddush
  hashem theme); magic fish

(*see* magic fish motif); martyrdom
  /sacrifice (*see* martyrdom/sacrifice
  themes); messianic (*see* messianic
  figures/themes); redemption,
  207; resurrection (*see* resurrection
  theme); revolutionary struggle
  (*see* revolutionary struggle/theme);
  the stranger (*see* the stranger device
  /strangers); trial and execution
  (*see* trial and execution motif);
  wanderer (*see* wanderer figure or
  legend/wandering motif). *See also*
  imagery
"Three Gifts," 224–25, 230
*tikkun* (improvement)/*shevira*
  (disintegration), 15–16, 32, 72–73
"A tog-bikhl fun a farfirer," 9
"Der toyt fun a khinezer" (The death of
  a Chinese man), 123–25
"Toyt-urteyl" (Death sentence), 39
Tractor Factory, 120
translations, 50; children's literature
  and, 11–12, 118–20; Kvitko, 50,
  119–20; Der Nister and, 10–11, 36, 46,
  246, 270–71; symbolist works and,
  59n90
travelogue genre/travel writing,
  66, 254. *See also* Birobidzhan
  /Birobidzhan visit and writings;
  *Hoyptshtet* (Capitals)
trends: anti-Polish, 181; cultural,
  10, 47, 55, 106, 127–28; literary,
  15–17, 32; modernist, 207. *See also*
  Nisterism/"The Nister Problem"
Tretyakov, Sergei, 66, 73–74
trial and execution motif, 34–35. *See
  also* show trials
Trotsky, Leon/Trotskyism, 132, 180
Tsadek (Der Nister's uncle), 198
"Der tseylem" (The cross), 80
"Tsu di valn!" (Toward the elections),
  248
Tychyna, Pavlo, 50

Ukraine: antisemitism and, 52, 80, 246; cultural revival/destruction, 50–52, 86, 99; famine, 70; Jewish intelligentsia and, 50–52, 67; modernists, 47, 61 (*see also* Kiev); persecution of intelligentsia, 62–63, 67; travel writing, 66; Yiddish culture and literature, 5, 8, 21–22, 119 (*see also* Yiddish culture, language, and literature). *See also* Kharkiv; Kiev; puppet theater, Ukrainian
Union of Soviet Writers, 270; consolidation/control of literature, 56, 121, 162; establishment of, 53–54, 60
unity. *See* Jewish revival/unity
"Unter a ployt (reviu)" (Under a fence: A review), 17, 32–38, 41, 46, 267; Dustman figure, 75; mutation of trial into a performance, 86, 133
urban spaces, 110–11. *See also* Hoyptshtet (Capitals)

*vertep* performance. *See* puppet theater, Ukrainian
Vevyorke, Avrom, 45, 74
"Vidervuks" ("Regrowth"; short story), 241–43
*Vidervuks* (Regrowth; story collection), 222, 244
"Vint" (Wind), 137n23
"A volf in a shofener fel" (A wolf in a sheepskin), 128–29
Voronskii, Aleksandr, 43
Vorovsky Street (Kiev), 84

Wanda (fictional character), 228–30
wanderer figure or legend/wandering motif, 24, 26, 29–30, 206, 220–22, 250, 252. *See also* exile
war stories, 220–45
*What Had Happened to Vasyl Rolenko*, 50

Wiener, Meir, 49–50, 100
Wolf, Leonard, 199, 205
women, role in the community and family, 203, 232
*The World to Come*, 274–76
writers. *See* art/artists/writers; *individual names*; Yiddish writers
writers' groups, 21–22. *See also* Belorussian Association of Proletarian Writers (BelAPP); Russian Association of Proletarian Writers (RAPP); Union of Soviet Writers

Yanasovitsh, Yitskhok, 271–72
Yiddish Bureau of VUSPP (All-Ukrainian Association of Proletarian Writers), 22
Yiddish Cultural Association (YKUF), 168, 173
Yiddish culture, language, and literature, 6, 228, 247; deparochialization of, 10; effect of RAPP campaigns, 44; founding writers, 1–2; modernism and, 45–47, 55; Soviet perspective and, 54, 165 (*see also* communism/Communist Party); travelogue genre and, 66. *See also* children's literature; family saga novels; themes and motifs; Union of Soviet Writers; Yiddish writers
Yiddish intelligentsia. *See* Jewish /Yiddish intelligentsia
Yiddishkeit. *See* Judaism, normative; Yiddish culture, language, and literature
Yiddish writers, 1–2, 44, 269. *See also individual names*
*Yizker* (Memorial prayer), 274
YKUF. *See* Yiddish Cultural Association (YKUF)
Yosele "the Plague" (fictional character), 185

Zamiatin, Evgenii, 47
*Zamlbikher* (literary almanac), 265
Ms. Zayets (fictional character),
    241–43
Zeitlin, Hillel, 207–8
*Zeks mayselekh* (Six fairy tales), 128

Dr. Zemelman (fictional character),
    241–43
"Der zeyde mitn eynikl" (Grandfather
    and grandson), 225–28
Zhitomir, 157n17, 246, 248
Zionism, 52–53

MIKHAIL KRUTIKOV is Professor of Slavic Languages
and Literatures and Preston R. Tisch Professor of Judaic
Studies at the University of Michigan, Ann Arbor. He
is author of *Yiddish Fiction and the Crisis of Modernity,
1905–1914*; *From Kabbalah to Class Struggle: Expressionism,
Marxism, and Yiddish Literature in the Life and Work of
Meir Wiener*; and *Tsvisn shures: Notitsn vegn yidisher kultur*.